A
FEAST
OF
FESTIVALS

A FEAST OF FESTIVALS

INTERNATIONAL FESTIVALS ASSOCIATION

CELESTIALARTS

Berkeley, California

CELESTIAL ARTS
P.O. Box 7327
Berkeley, California 94707

Cover and text design by Bob Rauchman
Composition by Wilsted & Taylor

Library of Congress Catalog Card Number 89–60906
ISBN 0–89087–563–4

First Printing, 1989
0 9 8 7 6 5 4 3 2 1

Manufactured in the United States of America

ACKNOWLEDGMENTS

I n the years when my mother, Maysie Yates Beller, was building the Coconut Grove Arts Festival from a small sidewalk show (1964) to one of the top arts festivals in the country, I worked for her in all sorts of volunteer jobs. As my children grew up, they did, too. We teased her about calling all the people "my artists." And then, in 1979, I became Executive Director, and I found myself doing the same thing. I became involved with the artists and craftspeople and vendors and volunteers, and they became "my" to me, as I understood more and more about the time, effort, and devotion that went into what they were doing. I loved being a show director, in spite of some of the difficulties, but it was lonely being the "Truman." I yearned for contact with others who were in the business. Then I went to my first IFA convention, and met the marvelous people who were my fellows. I'm proud to have been involved with them, and with IFA, during this decade when civic celebrations, and the people who put them on, have come into their own.

This book is dedicated to my mother, Maysie Yates Beller, who is still remembered by hundreds of people as a great lady, and a great show director. It is also dedicated to all the artists, craftspeople, volunteers, vendors, entertainers, and events professionals who make this world a joyful place to be, and, most of the time, do it with such style and grace.

Many people have meant a great deal to me in terms of friendship, assistance, and fun. Under the IFA designation, I especially want to thank the following: Pip Martin, my first and best buddy; Don Whiteley, a generous and delightful compatriot; Elma Broadfoot, who introduced me to IFA; Jim Walls, "Little Jimmy Wonderful"; Fran and George Pitzke, for "Rondy," and other good times; JoAnn Ward, my "name"; Barbara Claybaugh; Lesa Ukman; Janice Meyer and Jo Hauck, for their efforts and success in bringing about the Certified Festival Executive program with Purdue University; and to Ian and Margaret Ferguson, for giving us London, and Hampton Court Palace.

Everyone needs a best friend; I'm blessed with Eloise Keene, who is always there, in festivals, music, traveling, and trouble. And for filling out part of my life, Ann-Marie Adker, the "Mayor of Overtown."

Thanks for all sorts of wonderfulness to my sons, Drew Holshouser and Nicholas Holshouser.

Thanks to Bob Rauchman, for making me look so good.

Thanks to Phil Wood, for taking me seriously, and David Hinds for being patient.

And thanks to Catherine for helping it come true.

IN MEMORY

KEN WALSTAD
MINNEAPOLIS AQUATENNIAL ASSOCIATION
MINNEAPOLIS, MINNESOTA

As a founding member of International Festivals Association, and its Managing Director, Ken helped build the IFA into the successful organization it is today, and was loved and respected for the dedication and patience he gave the organization and its members. With a grin, and a twinkle in his eye, he used to say, "Festivals are a business, and fun is our product." In his last speech to us, Ken said, "Civic celebrations are very much a part of the quality of universal life."

IN MEMORY

BOB MOORS
THE MELBOURNE MOOMBA FESTIVAL, LTD.
MELBOURNE, AUSTRALIA

A talented gentleman, wise in the ways of entertainment, festivals, and good food, and a courageous man, Bob was a consummate professional. His interest and encouragement when I first spoke of this book was most appreciated.

TABLE OF CONTENTS

The story of the International Festivals Association (IFA) spans twenty-six years so far. It begins with a handful of people meeting in a New York hotel room to discuss their involvement with civic festivals and progresses to an association of hundreds of members from the United States, Canada, and other countries worldwide.

The special events that delight people everywhere don't just happen. They are produced by a special group of people who work long hours on a variety of jobs to create celebrations of all sorts of things: a town, a city, an anniversary, an event, a sport, a season. There's no end to the reasons people get together, and no end to the events they dream up for those occasions.

As the world becomes more complex, so does the production of special events. That's why IFA is so important to so many people. A new breed of leaders is evolving in the world of festivals and special events. No matter what the title— executive director, chairperson, coordinator—no matter whether the position is paid or volunteer, the people involved in the world of nonprofit civic events give their all to the community and the audience.

INTERNATIONAL FESTIVALS ASSOCIATION

Everyone in this exciting field shares enthusiasm for the work of creating celebrations and, through the years, participants have shared information, labor, contacts, and advice. Once a year IFA members gather at an annual convention for several days of seminars, lectures, workshops, and displays by members who supply the widely varied resources needed for event production. From float builders to fireworks, from giant balloons to banners and buttons, there's a big industry involved in furnishing the raw materials for festival producers.

Several years ago IFA joined with Purdue University to offer an advanced course of study recognizing those who have attained the highest level of expertise through education and on-the-job experience. Those festival workers who have completed this program are now qualified as certified festival executives, and can add C.F.E. after their names.

IFA is now holding one- and two-day seminars in various cities, both to introduce IFA to interested people and to allow members to gain knowledge and experience in new areas. These seminars involve a growing number of certified festival executives, other experienced IFA members, and specialists from various fields, such as marketing, sponsorship, public relations, finance, and law.

Sharing information and experiences, exchanging ideas, and getting better at the art and work of festival organizing is rewarding. But the fellowship that exists in the festival world is a reward in itself. Strong friendships have developed through the years of working together, and there is a growing realization of the world as a village as we come to know more about the events we are celebrating. For what we are all celebrating is our shared humanity, and by celebrating together we are making the world a better place for all.

INTRODUCTION

FESTIVALS AND FOOD

The fifty-five festivals and festival organizations described in this book are truly a mixed bag. Whether big or small, sponsored by communities or corporations, organized around a sport, harvest, season, region, or historical event, the festivals serve to bring people together for culture, education, fun, and, of course, *food!*

There can be great significance in sharing food and experiencing the cuisines of other cultures. In 1951 the National Citizens' Committee for United Nations Day published *The World's Favorite Recipes*. Eleanor Roosevelt wrote an introduction to the booklet, which contained more than one hundred recipes from different countries. She offered these thoughts:

> To take dishes from every country in the world into our kitchens is, in itself, one of the ways to bring about better international understanding. . . . This really brings us close to the daily life of the families of other nations. I hope that in many countries people will try our American dishes while we try the dishes of foreign lands.

It is interesting to read the list of recipes from this booklet. Many termed "exotic" in 1951 are now widely incorporated into the daily lives and eating habits of Americans. Alas for Eleanor Roosevelt's hopes about American food being tried in other lands; our biggest contribution to international cuisine seems to be fast food!

But even a burger and shake can lead to better relations, and Eleanor Roosevelt's observations are especially interesting in the context of festivals (and festival feasts). People seem more open to new foods *and* new cultures when in a festive mood.

From the earliest days of recorded history, people have celebrated for many reasons: to commemorate important events; to mark seasonal changes or the stages of human life; to honor endings; and to rejoice in beginnings.

Preparing and sharing food has always been an important part of celebrating. Each society, each race, each religion has unique elements in its celebrations. The food (and its preparation) is one of these unique elements— and probably the easiest for outsiders to understand and appreciate.

A description of a festival is one thing; the "taste" of it is something else. Each festival described here is followed by recipes that will help create the flavors of that festival. These recipes were submitted by the festivals in the spirit of sharing a taste of what makes each one special.

As people share celebrations and food, so do we share feelings of joy, pride, and hope for the future. While celebrating in the spirit of friendship and fellowship, we may learn about each other, coming to understand and accept our shared humanity.

We present the festivals in chronological order, giving information about the activities and experiences offered at each. For further information, most festivals have brochures, programs, and other materials available upon request from the festival offices. (See the names and addresses of all IFA member organizations in the appendix.)

If you are planning to attend a festival, remember to check which activities require reservations or advance tickets. Also, keep in mind that even small-town festivals are often cause for full-house conditions at local hotels and campgrounds.

Your safest bet is always to call the festival office—it will advise you on the need for reservations—and plan ahead accordingly. In addition, festival offices frequently can give you information about other contacts you may need, such as chambers of commerce, visitors bureaus, and so on.

The recipes in *A Feast of Festivals* were submitted by the festivals described. Some are excerpted from cookbooks published by the festivals themselves. Others are taken (with permission) from cookbooks published by organizations that have some relationship to festivals or the communities that host them. We have included any information available to us about ordering these source cookbooks, in case you would like to have more recipes in that style.

You will find that the recipes run the gamut from gourmet to Grandma's favorite. Some recipes were created specifically for this book by professional chefs; others are being printed for the first time, having been passed down verbally through generations. We have kept the editing of recipes to a minimum to preserve the spirit of direct communication from those who wrote the recipes. **Therefore, you will be wise to read any recipe through and picture the process step by step, before you begin preparations.**

People come to festivals to mingle with other people; to revel in their own culture and to experience others. Festivals are for "feasting" on the better things in life: music, dance, art, drama, fun, spectacle, and, always, food!

You may be reading *A Feast of Festivals* to imagine various feasts and festivals, in anticipation of actually attending one of the festivals, or to recreate a memorable meal you've already had at one. Whatever your motives, may you have many good tastes.

I t has become an American tradition to usher in the New Year with pigskin and parade floats. Nowhere is this tradition older or more festive than in Pasadena, California. There the Pasadena Tournament of Roses—the Granddaddy of Them All—has been heralding and celebrating the New Year for a century.

The parade, now seen by one million curbside spectators, had humble beginnings. Back in 1890 Pasadena was a small town of whitewashed houses and dirt roads in a forest of citrus groves. The Valley Hunt Club sponsored the first parade at the suggestion of Professor Charles Frederick Holder, a zoologist, drawing "inspiration from the petals of thousands of roses in bloom while our former eastern homes are buried in the snow."

In the early years floats were horse-and-buggy units, with thousands of individual flowers tied with string to carriages. After the modest parade young men would compete in footraces, chariot races, ostrich-riding duels, and jousting exhibitions. This medieval atmosphere and the floral extravaganza of the parade inspired the title Tournament of Roses.

PASADENA TOURNAMENT OF ROSES

PASADENA, CALIFORNIA WEEK OF NEW YEAR'S DAY

Football joined the lineup in 1902. The Tournament of Roses invited Michigan, undefeated champion of the East, to meet Stanford University, the West's great hope. The idea was to add a national sports event and capitalize on America's growing football craze. Unfortunately Michigan trounced Stanford, 49–0, and the unruly crowds created chaos. The New Year's East-meets-West football match was not a part of the tournament again until 1916, but a new chapter had been opened in the history of both the Tournament of Roses and Pasadena.

Currently the Tournament of Roses is organized and carried out by the 1400-member Pasadena Tournament of Roses Association, with activities scheduled throughout the year, culminating in the parade and the Rose Bowl game.

The first big event of the year happens July 4, with the annual Fourth of July fireworks extravaganza at the Rose Bowl Stadium. Later in the summer comes the Rose Bowl golf tournament and dinner, where celebrity Rose Bowl game players and coaches are reunited in this seventy-five-year-old tradition.

In late September the first round of tryouts for the Rose queen and court gets underway. For the next two months, the court hopefuls pass through round after round of tryouts, until the final selections are made in November.

In October the grand marshal of the parade is announced. Also, months before the parade, several dozen marching bands must be carefully chosen from the more than two hundred bands that apply. Another difficult selection is that of the equestrian units, small and large, which will provide showmanship, creative attire, and gallant horses for a worldwide audience. In December, as the parade and bowl game approach and the holiday pace becomes hectic, the association members and other volunteers work feverishly toward the big day.

The last days of December bring fun and excitement. Eager fans can appreciate the Bandfest—a special performance by six of the marching bands who will appear in the Rose Parade. An equestrian festival offers a chance to see equestrians from the parade perform challenging maneuvers impossible to execute on the parade route. Former Rose queens reunite at an annual brunch, and the Rose Bowl coaches field questions from reporters at the official Rose Bowl press conference.

Finally the big day arrives. Dawn reveals that the best spots along the parade route have already been claimed by people who arrived the night before. At 8:20 A.M. "America's New Year's Celebration" officially begins. The modern Rose Parade is a far cry from that first one in 1890, but every exposed inch of a float must still be covered with natural materials (on the average, floats require 100,000 flowers). Dozens of floats, more than twenty musical units, and nearly three hundred equestrians parade 5½ miles for a worldwide audience of millions.

By afternoon yet another Rose Parade is history, and attention is turned toward the final big event: the Rose Bowl game. These days it is the champions of the Pac-10 and the Big Ten that face each other before a national audience. Since that first chaotic game in 1902, the Rose Bowl game has become one of the most prestigious of all bowl games.

The Tournament of Roses is a magnificent display of beauty, grandeur, and sportsmanship. After a century, not only is it a holiday tradition, it has become a part of America's heritage as well.

ELEGANT AND EASY
LOBSTER PÂTÉ

Soften cream cheese; beat in white wine until mixture is smooth and creamy. Blend in onion and seasoned salts and dill; stir in lobster meat. Cover and refrigerate several hours or overnight to mellow flavors. Serve with cocktail bread or crackers. To use as a dip, beat in additional white wine and some sour cream or yogurt.

This is another great recipe from Grand Rapids, Michigan.

by Margaret Bertilson Kroblack
1960 Rose Queen

1 (8-oz.) pkg. cream cheese

¼ cup Chablis or other white wine

¼ tspn. onion salt

½ tspn. seasoned salt

⅛ tspn. dried dill

1 cup finely chopped lobster meat

GRAHAM CRACKER
MUFFINS

These flavorful party muffins are ideal for a brunch. Serve with assorted salads.

If using conventional oven, preheat to 375° F. Combine graham cracker crumbs and baking powder in a bowl. Combine melted butter or margarine, dark corn syrup, egg, and milk. Add to graham cracker mixture, stirring just enough to moisten. Stir in combined pecans and flour. Spoon batter into greased pans with 3-inch muffin wells, filling wells ⅔ full. If using conventional oven, bake for 20 minutes. Makes 12 muffins. (In a microwave bake 6 muffins at a time 2–3 minutes, turning once.)

by Marilyn Martell
1955 Rose Queen

1½ cups graham cracker crumbs

2 tspn. baking powder

⅓ cup melted butter or margarine

⅓ cup dark corn syrup

1 egg, beaten

½ cup milk

½ cup chopped pecans

1 Tbspn. flour

JALAPEÑO JELLY

¾ cup ground bell pepper (2–4 bell peppers)

½ cup ground jalapeño pepper (remove all seeds, wearing plastic gloves)

5¾ cups sugar

1½ cups cider vinegar

1 (6-oz.) bottle pectin

Green food coloring

Paraffin wax

Remove pepper seeds before grinding (use fine blade). Mix peppers, sugar, and vinegar, and bring to a rolling boil in pot. Boil *1 minute*. Remove from heat and cool slightly. Add pectin and a couple drops of green food coloring. Mix well, strain, pour into sterilized jars, and then seal with paraffin.

Excellent on crackers or toast with cream cheese. Delightful for entertaining. Makes one dozen jars.

by Robin Carr Christensen
1975 Rose Queen

NATURAL CRUNCH MARVELS

½ cup chopped cashews or other nuts

1 Tbspn. whole wheat flour

2 Tbspn. bran

½ cup honey

½ cup chunky peanut butter

¼ cup raisins

¼ cup rolled oats

1 Tbspn. sesame oil

1 tspn. vanilla

Combine all ingredients, mixing well. Roll into balls, using approximately 2 Tbspn. of dough for each ball. If desired, sprinkle with cinnamon. Makes approximately 24 balls.

by Carole Gelfuso
1966 Rose Queen

ZUCCHINI QUICHE

4 cups thinly sliced raw zucchini

1 cup chopped onion

½ cup butter

½ cup chopped fresh parsley or 2 Tbspn. parsley flakes

Preheat oven to 375° F. Sauté zucchini and onion together in butter until tender (about 10 minutes). Stir in parsley and seasonings. Blend eggs and cheese in large bowl. Stir in zucchini and onion. Separate crescent dinner roll dough into 8 triangles. Place in ungreased

11-inch quiche pan and mold together to form crust. Spread the crust with a coat of Dijon mustard. Pour in vegetable mixture and bake 18–20 minutes.

by Virginia Goodhue Hese
1948 Rose Queen

½ tspn. salt

½ tspn. pepper

¼ tspn. garlic powder

¼ tspn. oregano

2 eggs

8 oz. mozzarella cheese

1 can refrigerator quick crescent dinner rolls

2 Tbspn. Dijon mustard

What to do when you're tired of winter? When you're wishing for the spring thaws? Why not have one more fling with a festival full of fun in the snow?

That's what the Lakeside Winter Celebration is all about: a celebration of all things wintery. If it can be done in, with, or to snow or ice, you'll find it being done here!

Snowmobile fans enjoy a whole host of events, starting with a full program of racing for young and old alike. Top racers from throughout the Midwest compete in oval, drag, and snowcross snowmobile events. There are demo rides and there are competitions, such as stock, powder puff, modified, and iron dog.

Meanwhile, broom-wielding skating teams from all over Wisconsin meet at Fond du Lac to compete in a unique tournament. Those people sweeping the ice are not tidying up; they are playing broomball, a mix of hockey and soccer. In fact, the broomball tournament is one of the more popular events of the festival.

Another event that attracts much interest in

LAKESIDE WINTER CELEBRATION

FOND DU LAC, WISCONSIN, LATE JANUARY

a winterbound world is the sled dog weight pull, in which dogs fitted with special harnesses compete by pulling dead weights from a standstill.

Other Lakeside Winter Celebration activities include snow sculpting, sno-volleyball, and the Wisconsin Ice Bowl Challenge. New events are being added each year, with curling, ice fishing, windsurfing, and a downhill skiing exhibition also on the program. Various entertainment events are also lined up for the festival, including the off-site Saturday Night Shindig. (For a schedule of festival events, contact the Fond du Lac Convention & Visitors' Bureau, which produces the Lakeside Winter Celebration.)

In the midst of all the snow and ice, there's something hot cooking: the annual Chili Cookoff is held on Saturday. Twenty finalists concoct their own special creations, with the winner going on to compete at the state and national levels.

A recent team effort produced this first-prize winner for four buddies.

CHILE CHILI

In a large pan sauté the onions, pepper, and meats in olive oil, adding lemon juice and garlic salt as they cook. When brown add Chili-O and chili powder, and stir in beer. Remove to a large pot, add mushrooms, stewed tomatoes, and tomato sauce, and heat to simmer. Stir well, add beans, and mix gently, continuing to simmer for at least 1 hour; 2 is better. Just before serving add Negrita spice and hot pepper sauce.

by Clint Moore, Dick Cusik, Alex Gonzales, and Tony Lumpkin

2 large yellow onions, diced

1 small bell pepper, diced

2 lb. ground round

1 lb. lean ground pork

½ lb. country sausage

3 fatty slices bacon, chopped

Meat from 2 chicken breasts, diced

Olive oil, sufficient to brown meat

Juice of 2 large lemons

Garlic salt to taste

3 pkg. French's Chili-O seasoning

3 oz. chili powder (or more, to taste)

1 can beer

10 oz. mushrooms, chopped

30 oz. stewed tomatoes

10 oz. tomato sauce

12 oz. Campbell's pork & beans

12 oz. light red kidney beans

12 oz. dark red kidney beans

Negrita spice (Chilean) to taste

Hot pepper sauce to taste

Back in 1885 the consensus of most Americans seemed to be that St. Paul was the North American equivalent of Siberia. So, "trying to prove something," some St. Paul citizens organized the first St. Paul Winter Carnival: a two-week midwinter extravaganza of skating, wild toboggan rides, parades, dances, a Sioux Indian village set up on carnival grounds, and the first ice palace in the United States (20,000 ice blocks culminating in a 106-foot tower).

More than a hundred years later, the yearly midwinter celebration continues. Each year St. Paul breaks out of its staid, snowbound mold and, for two weeks, revels in winter sports, games, parades, and parties.

Originally the focus of the carnival was the mythological clash between Winter and Spring, played out in the ritual battle of King Borealis (king of the winds, particularly the north wind) against his archenemy King Vulcanus (king of fire and heat). They sometimes fought for days in staged battles in and around the ice palace. This clash and its cast of characters inspired coronations, balls, and parades. Dog sled races, toboggan runs, ice skating, and other winter activities were added for fun and thrills.

The modern carnival features more than one hundred events (many of them free), both indoors and outdoors. Downtown there's the King Borealis Grande Day Parade and the Vulcan Victory Torchlight Parade, with every-thing from marching bands and clowns to a precision snowblower drill team. Or, for more majestic moments, there's the Sleigh and Cutter Parade held in scenic Como Park. Antique horse-drawn sleighs with drivers in period costumes glide across the snowdrifts through groves of frosty evergreens.

Recent carnivals have included major snow or ice structures, as well as a state snow sculpting contest and a national ice carving contest.

For conventional sports buffs, there's conventional competition. The Frozen 5-K and Half-Marathon, the Ten Thousand Lakes International Speedskating Championships, and hockey, cross-country ski races, and hot air balloon races are all part of the lineup of the usual snow and ice sports. A golf-in-the-snow tournament, car races on ice, snowmobile races, and the Softball on Ice Tournament (which has drawn as many as two hundred teams) are available for those with wackier interests.

Fine arts fans are catered to as well, with a multitude of events to choose from: exhibits, plays, music, dance, and storytelling. Among the performance sites are the world-renowned Ordway Theater, the historic Landmark Center, and the newly renovated World Theater, home of radio's "Prairie Home Companion."

To top it all off, there's the major indoor event, the Fun Fair. Known as the "indoor state fair of Minnesota," the Fun Fair includes a midway, zany foods, concerts, and booths of all sorts.

The St. Paul Winter Carnival is unusual in the length and richness of its history. There have been years when weather or other hardships prevented such extravagant festivities, and no carnival was held. The Depression years, World War II, and the age of television have each in their turn greatly affected the event—but still it survives, and thrives.

After more than a hundred winters, St. Paulites are still inviting people everywhere to join them, to celebrate, and to prove something: just how much fun winter in St. Paul can be!

CREAM OF MINNESOTA WILD RICE SOUP

Minnesotans are justly proud of their wild rice. Wild rice—which is actually a member of the grass family, not a rice—is a delicacy native to the state, cultivated and harvested by native Minnesota Indians. This recipe was created by a well-known St. Paul chef, Kazuhira Hishida (known as Kazoo), executive chef of the St. Paul Hotel, at 350 Market Street.

Sauté onion, bell pepper, celery, carrots, mushrooms, and garlic. Heat butter in a stockpot over medium heat and add flour; cook, stirring constantly, to make a roux. Slowly add chicken stock, stirring constantly. Add sherry. Add cooked wild rice and sautéed vegetables. Finish with heavy cream and diced pimiento. Season with salt and pepper to taste. Serves 8.

1 large diced onion

½ diced green bell pepper

1½ ribs diced celery

¾ cup minced carrots

2 large sliced mushrooms

1 clove chopped garlic

½ cup butter

1 cup flour

8 cups chicken stock

1 Tbspn. sherry wine

2 cups well-cooked wild rice (½ cup uncooked rice)

1 cup heavy cream

1 Tbspn. diced pimiento

Winterlude is part of an old tradition in Canada's capital. In the nineteenth century, when winter closed in and cut off the city from the rest of the world, people gathered for celebrations aimed at passing the winter in a mood of companionship and fun.

In the old days this meant an unending round of sleigh parties, curling competitions, singalongs, amateur theatricals, toboggan runs, and skating to music on rinks throughout the city. For a number of years, the capital even boasted an ice palace as the focal point of wintertime festivities. Then, as the country moved forward into the twentieth century and winter became less isolating and forbidding, these splendid customs were allowed to lapse.

In 1979 the National Capital Commission—a crown corporation responsible for the management and development of federally owned property in the capital—created Winterlude. In doing so, it restored some of the oldest and best wintertime traditions—and it continues to present new ones.

Much of the activity takes place on the Rideau Canal, an artificial channel that runs

WINTERLUDE BAL DE NEIGE

OTTAWA-HULL, CANADA, EARLY FEBRUARY

through the heart of Ottawa. Now known as the longest skating rink in the world, the canal was built between 1826 and 1832 for military purposes. For many years the locals have enjoyed winter activities there: family skating, sleighing parties, races to Dows Lake and back. Now figure skaters bring the grace of dancers and the courage of athletes to the Rideau Canal. Other skaters, thousands of them, in a rainbow of colored jackets, glide to and fro to music along the 7.8-kilometer waterway to Dows Lake. There they enjoy Ice Dream, a huge, white village of one hundred snow sculptures.

Children have many special treats at Winterlude. Piruvik is an ice and snow maze, a unique winter playground, where kids can clamber up snow towers and wriggle through snow tunnels. The Icebreaker Brigade, wandering troupes of clowns, acrobats, and jugglers, leap and tumble to delight children and adults alike. The Ice Hog family—Mr. and Mrs. Ice Hog and their children, Nuomi and Nuoma—are Winterlude's official mascots, and can these hogs hug! Look for them on any day during Winterlude, go up and say hello, and get a big hug. This is a warm and special part of Winterlude.

Sports are an important part of the festival; some of them are very new. Snolf? A new Canadian game—golf played in the snows of Gloucester. Ringette? Hockey for women, the fastest-growing Canadian sport. Athletes from Canada and abroad fly over the ice in the World Outdoor Barrel-Jumping Competition. Top-rated curling competitors from Scotland and Europe face Canadian stars on the ice in the Lord Elgin Challenge. There's an annual international dog sled race, a triathlon (running, skating, and skiing), and the Jack Barber Challenge world championship, in which the foremost long-distance skaters from Europe and Canada vie for the 100-kilometer championship. The Metropolitan Sledge Hockey Tournament features physically challenged athletes from all over North America. Strength and traditional lumberjack skills are on display in the lumberjack games.

The Crystal Garden Ice Carving Competition has more than seven hundred blocks of ice transformed into a world of glittering art. Winterlude Arts shows the work of Quebec and Ontario artists. There are outdoor performances on the ice at Dows Lake.

And in the night sky, fireworks exploding like brightly colored flowers of fire are a magnificent spectacle. An exciting new community project is the ice palace, designed and erected in response to a challenge from the creators of the ice palace at the St. Paul Winter Carnival. Night and day, this glistening three-towered pinnacle can be seen for miles around, a shining example of community spirit at work.

Winterlude offers more than two hundred activities for the whole family. Ottawa-Hull and a number of surrounding communities—Aylmer, Cumberland, Gatineau, Gloucester, Nepean, and Vanier—welcome visitors at festival events as well as in shops, restaurants, museums, and theaters.

Particularly noteworthy is Winterlude's warm and hearty welcome for people with special needs; there are hosts and hostesses at each festival site to help these visitors benefit from a wide range of services.

Food is part of the fun at Winterlude. Dozens of little food booths spring up on the ice at this time of the year to sell fudge, hot dogs, maple sugar, and chestnuts. Hungry souls might also be tempted to take refuge in the snoasis. This large, tentlike structure is a fine place to warm the toes while sampling ethnic food provided by numerous food vendors.

Of course a festival such as Winterlude is bound to give birth to some original food creations, forever after associated with the event. Winterlude has, among other official treats, its own official drinks and crepe. Recipes follow.

ICE HOG GROG COFFEE

1½ tspn. instant decaffeinated coffee

2 oz. boiling water

8 oz. hot chocolate

Whipped cream

Orange zest

Cherry

The Ice Hog Grog Coffee or Ice Hog Grog are just what you need after a day on the ice.

Place coffee and boiling water in a large mug. Stir, mixing well. Add hot chocolate. Top with a dollop of whipped cream, sprinkle with orange zest, and crown with a cherry. Serves 1.

ICE HOG GROG

½ oz. Canadian rye whiskey

1 oz. chocolate almond liqueur

½ oz. coffee liqueur

Hot black coffee

Whipped cream

Chocolate bits

Pour the whiskey and liqueurs into a large mug. Add coffee and top with whipped cream and a sprinkling of chocolate bits. Serves 1.

OFFICIAL WINTERLUDE CREPE

FILLING:
2 (14-oz.) cans bing cherries

2 oz. sugar

1 oz. fruit stabilizer or cornstarch

Water

Kirsch to taste

COINTREAU SAUCE:
4 oz. frozen orange juice concentrate

Juice and zest from ½ orange

The Official Winterlude Crepe was invented several years ago by Walter Krepski, owner of the Marble Works Restaurant, and chef Brian Donahue.

Filling: Drain cherries overnight. Place juice in large pot and boil. In a bowl combine sugar, stabilizer or cornstarch, and enough water to make 15 oz. Slowly add mixture to boiling cherry juice. Cool 10–15 minutes. Fold the whole cherries and kirsch into the thickened juice.

Cointreau Sauce: Combine frozen and

fresh orange juice, orange zest, water, and sugar, and boil for 20 minutes or until thickened. Add the Cointreau.

Preparation: Place 2½ oz. of filling in center of each crepe. Fold over twice and heat, basting with 1 oz. of Cointreau sauce. Top with fresh whipped cream and one whole cherry. Makes 12–15 crepes.

15 oz. water

8 oz. sugar

1 oz. Cointreau

PREPARATION:

12–15 crepes

Whipped cream

12–15 cherries for garnish

THE RITZ MUSSELS IN CREAM, GARLIC, AND WINE SAUCE

Customers line up at the canal-side Ritz for the restaurant's own freshly baked breads, wood-oven-fired pizzas, and these mussels—garlicky, creamy, and peppery.

Using stiff brush, scrub mussels under cold running water; cut off beards, discarding any mussels that don't close when tapped.

In heavy saucepan over medium heat, melt butter. Add leeks, garlic, bay leaf, and pepper flakes, cooking for 3–4 minutes, stirring occasionally, until leeks have softened.

Add mussels; cook, covered, for 2 minutes. Pour in wine; cook, covered, for 2 minutes or just until shells have opened. Stir in cream; increase heat to medium-high and bring to boil. Remove from heat, discarding any mussels that haven't opened. Season with salt and pepper to taste.

Arrange mussels in warmed shallow soup bowls. Pour sauce over; sprinkle with parsley. Makes 2 appetizers or light suppers.

Note: For a thicker sauce, remove mussels to warmed bowls. Continue boiling liquid for 2–3 minutes or until thickened enough to coat a spoon. Pour over mussels.

1 lb. mussels

2 Tbspn. butter

¼ cup sliced leeks

2 large cloves garlic, minced

1 small bay leaf

¼ tspn. hot pepper flakes

¼ cup dry white wine

½ cup whipping cream

Salt and white pepper

2 tspn. minced fresh parsley

NATIONAL ARTS CENTRE
SPLIT PEA SOUP

3 cups split green peas

8 cups water

½ tspn. dried savory

1 bay leaf

3 stalks celery

2 carrots

1 large potato

1 large onion

¼ cup olive oil

3 cloves garlic, minced

Salt and pepper

4 slices homemade-style bread

⅓ cup butter

Close your eyes and imagine you're sitting on the winter terrace of the National Arts Centre, spooning up steaming split pea soup, watching the flashing blades skate by.

Rinse peas; place peas with water in saucepan. Bring to boil, covered, skimming off foam. Stir in savory and bay leaf. Reduce heat; simmer until peas are tender, 55 minutes.

Meanwhile, chop celery. Then chop carrots, potato, and onion into bite-sized pieces.

In large skillet heat olive oil over medium-high heat. Add celery, carrots, potato, onion, and garlic, cooking for 5–7 minutes or until softened; add to saucepan. Simmer, covered, for 20–30 minutes or until all vegetables are tender. Remove bay leaf. For a chunky soup, leave as is. For a smoother soup puree in food processor, blender, or food mill. Or puree 1 cup of the mixture and stir back into soup. Season with salt and pepper to taste.

Trim crusts off bread; cut into bite-sized cubes. In large skillet over medium-high heat, melt butter. When foam subsides, toss in bread, stirring up with fork to coat cubes evenly. Cook, turning often, until crisp and golden.

Ladle soup into warmed bowls; sprinkle with croutons. Makes 6–8 servings.

The Coconut Grove Arts Festival, one of the largest outdoor arts festivals in the country, continues to represent to residents and visitors alike the high quality of outdoor events in Florida: safe, charming, and inviting.

The first sidewalk arts festival in Coconut Grove (tucked between Biscayne Bay and downtown Miami) was the scheme of a local publicist to draw attention to the Coconut Grove Playhouse production of *Irma La Douce*. A group of Grove residents, seeing interesting possibilities in the event, were inspired to form the Coconut Grove Association, dedicated to fostering culture in the village. A small group of association volunteers created the first Coconut Grove Arts Festival in 1964.

From a few artists and a few more spectators, the festival has grown to the present three-day event, with several hundred thousand people filling the

COCONUT GROVE ARTS FESTIVAL

COCONUT GROVE, FLORIDA, MID-FEBRUARY

lush, green village streets in the heart of Coconut Grove to browse, buy, eat, and drink. Live entertainment is presented each day in Peacock Park, featuring outstanding local and nationally known performers. Culinary artists offer a wide variety of ethnic and special foods, with something to tempt everyone's tastebuds.

The recent addition of an artist-in-residence program in area schools has meant that a number of artists have become closely associated with the community. A new activity in 1988 was a sculpture contest, with entrants from many parts of the country.

Here are some recipes from vendors who make the rounds of South Florida festivals.

SWEET AND SOUR SAUCE

Process apricots with their liquid in a food processor or blender until smooth. Put apricots, applesauce, vinegar, ginger, juices, and sugar or honey in saucepan and heat to boiling. Add cornstarch mixture and stir quickly until thickened. Add soy sauce. Serve at

1 (16-oz.) can unpeeled apricots

1 (8-oz.) jar unsweetened applesauce

½ cup vinegar

½ tspn. powdered ginger

1 (5½-oz.) can pineapple juice

½ cup frozen orange juice concentrate

3 Tbspn. sugar or honey

2 Tbspn. cornstarch mixed in ¼ cup cold water

2 Tbspn. soy sauce

room temperature. Makes about 6 cups.

From the creator: a delightful companion for tempura dishes.

by Lynn D'Andrea, First Place (Best-Looking Food Booth)

TEX-MEX FAJITA

PICO DE GALLO:
6 large ripe tomatoes, diced

1 large onion, diced

1 bunch fresh cilantro, coarsely chopped

4–5 garlic cloves, roughly chopped

Fresh jalapeño peppers, minced (optional)

Generous shake of salt

STEAK AND MARINADE:
6–8 cloves garlic, peeled and chopped

Juice of 6 limes

Generous shake of salt

Small amount of minced onion

3–4-lb. beef skirt steak

Flour tortillas

ico de Gallo: Put all ingredients in large bowl and mix well.

Steak and Marinade: Mix garlic, lime juice, salt, and onion in a large bowl. Put steak in the bowl, cover, and refrigerate overnight. The next day, grill or broil steak to desired doneness.

To assemble, wrap flour tortillas in foil and warm for 15 minutes in a 200° F oven. Chop or slice meat thin. Put a generous amount on each tortilla. Top with Pico de Gallo. Serves 10–12.

From the creator: "Texans take fajitas as seriously as their barbecue. *Fajita* means 'skirt,' which means we use a skirt steak—either an inside or outside skirt steak. It's a marbled meat and it's very tender." Add any topping you'd put on a taco: sour cream, avocado, and so on.

by Ward Deal

ZEPPOLES

4 cups self-rising flour

2 envelopes active dry yeast

4 cups water

ix flour, yeast, water, the 1 Tbspn. vegetable oil, granulated sugar, and salt in bowl and cover. Let mixture rise 15–20 minutes.

Pour 3–4 inches of vegetable or

peanut oil into large pot. Heat to 450° F. Take a tablespoon of dough and drop it into the hot oil. Brown about 1 minute on each side. Remove and cool completely. Sprinkle with powdered sugar. Makes about 25.

by Phil Falco
Falco's Pizzeria

1 Tbspn. vegetable oil

½ cup granulated sugar

½ tspn. salt

Vegetable or peanut oil for frying

Powdered sugar

TROPICAL DELIGHT

Fill blender ⅓ full of ice. Add strawberries and banana. Fill blender to within 1 inch from the top with orange juice. Blend at highest speed until thick and smooth. Serves 2.

by Larry Budnick
Strawberry Fields

Ice cubes

1 cup fresh or frozen unsweetened strawberries

1 banana, cut into chunks

Fresh-squeezed orange juice

"Celebrate the Rondy spirit!" And that's what they do. For ten wonderful days, all hours of the day and night, the myriad events of "Rondy" celebrate the spirit of the first settlers of the state. For the solitary trappers, the ingatherings for fur sales were a time of rejoicing, fun, and play—one of the few bright spots in lives otherwise filled with loneliness and deprivation. From its beginning as the Anchorage Sports Tournament in 1935, the festival included, along with fur trading, a queen contest, basketball competition, ice hockey, ice skating, and a one-dog children's sled race. In 1938 the name was changed to the Anchorage Fur Rendezvous, and Rondy has never slowed down since.

With more than 140 events, Rondy boasts something for everyone. See the Eskimo blanket toss. Rub elbows with Eskimos and trappers in sealskin and wolf parkas, who hail from Huslia, Skagway, and Nome. Picture yourself with world-famous mushers from around the globe, there to participate in the World Championship ship Sled Dog Race— right down the main street, before cheering crowds. A women's world championship sled dog race and junior racing for pint-sized mushers are also a part of the celebration. In the

ANCHORAGE FUR RENDEZVOUS
ANCHORAGE, ALASKA, MID-FEBRUARY

annual World Championship Dog Weight-Pulling Contest, pedigreed pooches with names such as Blood 'n' Guts strain to tug up to four thousand pounds.

In the midst of an Alaskan winter, who would expect to see a parade? During Rondy, those who brave the snow and cold are rewarded with marching units in bunny boots, clowns, floats of every sort, and such memorable sights as a forty-foot ice worm wriggling past. Yes, there are beautiful queens and princesses, dressed in furs as lovely as they are. A special feature of Rondy events is the presence of the Outstanding Military Persons of the Year. These enlisted women and men, selected from each branch of the service of the United States military, are guests of Rondy for the entire festival, and add dignity to the Rondy festivities.

Royalty abounds at Rondy: dignitaries, guests of honor, and VIPs chosen for many different reasons play an important role in Rondy events. Miss Anchorage Fur Rendezvous and her court reign over festival activities and later represent Rondy throughout the country for the year. The Anchorage business community chooses one man to be Lord Trapper, the personification of the rugged individualists who tamed the Alaskan wilderness; in his splendid fur regalia, he adds color to numerous gatherings. An outstanding couple is chosen each year by the Pioneers of Alaska, Anchorage chapter, to serve as King and Queen Regent. Honored at the Annual Regent's Tea, they hold places of honor in the parade, and serve as host and hostess during Rondy. Mr. and Mrs. Senior Citizen are also chosen from a group of outstanding senior citizens. And delighting the crowds everywhere is the huge and cuddly Pola Bear, Rondy's own Kahlua Bear. (A tradition during the annual International Festival Association Conference is the reception hosted by the Alaskan contingent, with Alaska State Fair and Rondy folk serving wonderful food flown in with them, and Pola presiding over silver cups brimming with the Kahlua concoction that will make you, or a bear, stand on your head.)

Spectacular evening events draw sell-out crowds. The Miners and Trappers Ball is a zany costume event, providing an outlet for creativity and demonstrating splendid Alaskan ingenuity. There's also the Minors Ball, sponsored by the International Jaycees, for people aged fourteen to twenty. The Masque Ball captures the pomp and splendor of an Old World *bal costume*, with gilded satin masks and elegant formal attire. The frontier spirit lives on in Monte Carlo Night. More than five thousand gamesters risk fortunes in funny money at roulette, cards, a wheel of fortune, and other games of chance. And each night a crowd cheers, boos, and hisses as the Rondy Players' melodrama entwines the audience in the classic conflict of good and evil.

Sporting events at Rondy range from speed skating, skiing, and curling to tennis, table tennis, power lifting, pool, and gymnastics. Indoor tournaments include masters swimming and diving competitions, bowling, darts, and judo. There's cribbage, basketball, an oyster-shucking contest, and, for the business crowd, a ten-key calculator keyoff. And everyone cheers on the contestants in the Rondy Outhouse Race, the NBA Frostbite Footrace, the Snowshoe Obstacle Race, and the GTE Snowshoe Softball Classic. There's even an Arctic soccer bowl and the Alaska rugby union's Frozen Oosik Rugby Tournament. Not to be missed, whether from trackside or hospitality rooms high in hotels nearby, is the incredible Grand Prix, on a track surrounded by snow.

The arts are very much a part of Rondy. Dance enthusiasts enjoy the international folk dance festival, a two-day event with colorfully costumed dancers from more than forty cultures. A round and square dance festival provides foot-tapping fiddle music for listeners and dancers alike. And for the superenergetic, there's the polka party produced by St. Patrick's Church. There's a wonderful snow sculpture event, Frozen Illusions, produced by the American Institute of Architects, Alaska chapter. All over town, there are competitions and exhibits of art, photography, stamps, antiques, antique autos, and model trains. The annual fur fashion show is spectacular. And the all-native crafts exhibition is a must-see.

The Sullivan Arena hosts the Rondy Trade Fair, where browsers and serious shoppers can linger over fine handcrafts, Alaskan native crafts, and other interesting merchandise. At the Egan Center there is the annual arts and crafts competition and the culinary arts exhibit.

Each year new events are added to the festival. For ten days in February, there are no strangers in Anchorage. Friends, neighbors, and visitors gather to mark the beginning of the end of dark days, frigid nights, and cabin fever. The initial Rondy spirit of fellowship and fun has remained through the years, and today the Anchorage Fur Rendezvous is a festival to delight everyone.

In 1988 the Anchorage Fur Rendezvous produced a collection of prize-winning recipes from 1986 and 1987. Titled *Prize-Winning Baked Goods*, this book contains several hundred recipes in the categories of yeast breads, quick breads, cakes, pies, cookies, desserts, candy, and junior recipes, this last from the younger set. There are even a few interesting recipes identified unashamedly as cake-mix recipes. The cookbook can be ordered from the Rondy office. (See Appendix B for the address.) Some of the following recipes are prizewinners, as identified; all of them are delicious.

FRUIT AND NUT BREAKFAST MUFFINS

3 cups flour (one-half white and one-half wheat)

1 cup oatmeal

½ cup oat bran or wheat bran

½ tspn. salt

1¼ tspn. baking soda

1¼ tspn. freshly ground nutmeg

1 Tbspn. freshly grated orange peel

Juice of 1 orange

2 Tbspn. oil

1 egg

¾ cup sweetener (honey or sugar)

2 cups buttermilk

1½ cups chopped dried fruit (raisins, apples, or apricots)

½ cups chopped nuts

Preheat oven to 350° F. Mix dry ingredients in large bowl. Put grated orange peel and orange juice into a 4-cup measure; add oil, egg, and sweetener and mix well. Add buttermilk and mix well. Add dried fruit and nuts to dry ingredients and mix to distribute. Add buttermilk mixture and mix only enough to moisten. Let stand 10 minutes.

Oil muffin pan and spoon batter into cups, being careful to disturb dough as little as possible. Fill cups to top. Bake 18–20 minutes. Remove muffins from pan to cooling rack. Wash pan and refill with more batter without stirring. Makes 18 muffins that freeze well.

by Dodie Nelson
First Place Division Winner

GARLIC-OAT CRACKERS

In small bowl combine rolled oats and water, and let stand 5 minutes. Lightly spoon flour into measuring cup; level off. In medium bowl combine flour, wheat germ, sugar, and garlic salt; blend well. Using pastry blender or fork, cut in margarine or butter until mixture is crumbly. Add oat mixture; stir until well blended. If necessary, add water by teaspoonfuls until mixture holds together. On floured surface, knead dough gently five or six times. Form into ball; cover with foil. Refrigerate overnight.

Preheat oven to 375° F. For each cracker form ½ tspn. of dough into ball; place on ungreased cookie sheet. With palm of hand flatten each cracker until very thin. Bake for 12–14 minutes or until edges brown slightly. Remove from cookie sheet; cool completely. Makes about 100.

by Arlene Hassell
First Place

1 cup rolled oats

½ cup water

¾ cup all-purpose flour

2 Tbspn. wheat germ

1 Tbspn. sugar

1 Tbspn. garlic salt

¼ cup margarine or butter

ZUCCHINI CAKE WITH GLAZE

Preheat oven to 350° F. Beat eggs until foamy; add sugar gradually. Add oil, zucchini, and vanilla and mix lightly. Combine flour, salt, baking soda, baking powder, and spices and add to mixture. Add nuts and raisins. Pour into greased tube pan and bake 1 hour.

Glaze: Mix confectioners' sugar, cream of tartar, and water until smooth. Pipe over cake.

by Mary Anne Bullock
First Place

4 eggs

2 cups sugar

¾ cup oil

2 cups grated, unpeeled zucchini

1 tspn. vanilla

3 cups flour

1 tspn. salt

1 tspn. baking soda

½ tspn. baking powder

1 tspn. each cloves, cinnamon, nutmeg

1 cup each nuts and raisins

GLAZE:
¾ cup confectioners sugar

⅛ tspn. cream of tartar

1 Tbspn. water

CHOCOLATE CHIP COOKIES

½ cup butter

½ cup margarine

1 cup brown sugar

2 eggs

1 tspn. vanilla

2 cups whole wheat pastry flour

2 cups oats

2 cups crispy rice cereal

1½ tspn. baking soda

¾ cup walnuts

½ cup dates

1 cup chocolate chips

Preheat oven to 350° F. In large bowl combine ingredients. Mix well. Drop by teaspoonfuls onto ungreased cookie sheets. Bake for 15 minutes.

by Barb Marsh
Second Place

MICROWAVE PEANUT BUTTER CRUNCH CANDY

1 cup peanut butter (creamy style)

⅓ cup warm water

⅓ cup light corn syrup

In a double boiler warm the peanut butter and set aside. Butter a cookie sheet and set this aside also. In a medium glass bowl stir the water, corn syrup, and sugar together and cook in the microwave on high without stirring until a candy thermometer registers 310° F (about 9½ minutes). Remove from microwave oven and quickly stir in the warm peanut butter. Spread thinly on the cookie sheet and immediately score into 1-inch pieces. When cool, break into squares and dip into coating chocolate. Store in airtight container.

by Lorna Reed
First Place

1 cup sugar
Coating chocolate

ADAM'S SUNFLOWER WHOLE WHEAT BREAD

Preheat oven to 350° F. Set aside 1 cup white flour. Mix remaining white flour and other dry ingredients, including yeast, in a large bowl. Heat water, butter, and milk until hot to touch. Stir into dry mixture. Mix in enough reserved white flour to make soft dough. On floured board knead dough 8–10 minutes. Shape into two loaves. Set into two greased loaf pans. Cover; let rise until doubled, about 40–50 minutes. Bake for 30 minutes or until done. Remove from pans and let cool on wire racks. Makes 2 loaves.

by Adam Chase
First Place Division Winner
Best of Show

3¼ cups white flour
3 cups whole wheat flour
1 cup sunflower seeds
⅓ cup sugar
4 tspn. salt
2 pkg. rapid-rise yeast
½ cups warm water
¼ cup butter
¾ cup milk

CINNAMON ROLLS

Preheat oven to 375° F. Dissolve yeast in warm water. Heat milk and shortening gently until shortening melts and then add with sugar, salt, eggs, and half of the flour to the yeast. Then add enough remaining flour to handle easily. Knead for about 5 minutes. Let rise in covered bowl in warm place

2 Tbspn. active dry yeast
½ cup warm water
1½ cups milk
½ cup shortening
½ cup sugar

2 tspn. salt

2 eggs

6–7 cups flour

Softened margarine

Cinnamon and sugar

Confectioners sugar

Vanilla

until double its size. Punch down and again let it rise until it is almost double its size. Roll dough into a 9-inch-by-15-inch rectangle. Spread with softened margarine. Sprinkle with cinnamon and sugar. Roll up tightly from wide side. Cut into 1-inch slices and place into greased pan. Cover and let rise until double. Bake for 25–30 minutes. While warm, frost with icing made of water, confectioners sugar, and vanilla to taste.

by Emily Kettleson
First Place Division Winner, Best of Show

ROCKY ROAD FUDGE

¼ cup milk

2 cups chocolate chips

2 cups miniature marshmallows

½ cup chopped nuts

Dash of salt

Grease baking pan with some butter or margarine. Heat milk and chocolate chips in saucepan over low heat, stirring constantly, until chocolate melts. Remove from heat. Stir in miniature marshmallows, chopped nuts, and salt. (The marshmallows will make little lumps in the candy.) Spread the candy in the buttered pan with spatula. Refrigerate about 1 hour or until firm. Cut into 1-inch squares.

by Jeremiah Cates
First Place

PLAIN BAGELS

14 oz. malt

4 oz. salt

12 cups water

6 oz. yeast

13 lb., 8 oz. high-gluten flour

Mix the malt and salt with 8 cups of the water until thoroughly blended. Dissolve the yeast in the remaining 4 cups water and set aside. Sift flour, add malt mix, stir slightly, and add the yeast solution. Develop into a smooth dough.

Allow the dough to relax for about an hour in a warm place. Keep covered. Place the dough on the table and make into pieces of about 3½ lbs. each. Allow

the pieces to relax before proceeding.
Do not use sifting flour or oil. Cut
into strips of about 3 oz. each and form
the bagels. Allow bagels to relax approximately 30 minutes. Preheat oven to
450° F. Drop bagels a few at a time into
boiling water for approximately 30
seconds, or until they float. Lift out,
place on baking sheet. Bake in oven for
10 minutes or until golden brown.

Raisin Bagels: Add ½ lb. raisins, ½ lb.
honey, and cinnamon to taste.

Egg Bagels: Add 12 oz. sugar and 1 lb.
whole eggs.

Onion Bagels: Add 1 lb. chopped
onion.

Pumpernickel Bagels: Add sugar,
brown vegetable coloring (enough to
color the dough), ½ lb. rye flour, 4 oz.
caraway seeds, and 3 oz. cocoa powder.

by The Bagel Factory
First Place Division Winner

SOURDOUGH BAGELS

Mix dry ingredients, including the
yeast, and add starter and water.
Form dough and allow to relax 15
minutes. Cut into pieces and form the
bagel shapes. Allow to rise approximately
30 minutes. Preheat oven to 450° F.
Drop bagels into boiling water for
approximately 30 seconds or until they
float well. Bake until golden brown.

by The Bagel Factory
First Place

10 lb. flour

8 oz. malt

3 oz. salt

2 oz. yeast

1 qt. sourdough starter

3 pints water

The arrival of spring in the city of Macon, Georgia, is a spectacular sight. Each year around the third week in March a soft pink blush spreads throughout this southern city as 130,000 Yoshino cherry trees burst into bloom with delicate pink and white blossoms. This grand explosion is cause enough for celebration—a true celebration of beauty, love, and international friendship.

The history of the cherry tree in Macon started back in 1952, when a local man, Mr. William A. Fickling, was mystified by a lovely tree with pink and white blossoms that appeared unbidden in his newly landscaped yard. On a trip to Washington, D.C., Mr. Fickling discovered that this tree, rare to the south, was a Yoshino (flowering) cherry tree, native to Japan. His delight in his find led him to learn to reproduce the trees, and he began sharing them with the community. Macon is now hailed as the "cherry blossom capital of the world."

The festival itself was the idea of Carolyn Crayton, Executive Director of the Keep Macon-Bibb Beautiful Commission. The purpose of the Cherry Blossom Festival is to honor Mr. Fickling's

MACON CHERRY BLOSSOM FESTIVAL

MACON, GEORGIA, MID-MARCH

generosity, to celebrate the beauty of the trees, and to foster a spirit of international friendship. Each year the festival features different countries; Australia and Japan are the honorees for 1990.

There's never a dull moment during cherry blossom time in Macon. Stroll in Third Street Park under a canopy of cherry blossoms while you enjoy cherry ice cream and beautiful music, or walk down Cherry Blossom Trail taking in breathtaking sights as the path winds leisurely through downtown. You can get lost in history as you tour the great antebellum mansions and historical homes of a bygone era. By night you can walk the ancient Ocmulgee Indian Mounds by torchlight, enjoy a play, or tap your toes to the music of one of the many concerts.

Many of the events involve music and entertainment. There are concerts, performances, and dances for all ages and tastes. Of course, there's royalty here, with a Little Miss and Mr. Cherry Blossom Pageant for preschoolers and a Coronation Ball for the queen and princesses who are selected in January to reign over the festivities. The Cherry Blossom Ball is the most elegant event of the festival.

The beautiful parks of Macon offer various events with art, music, food, storytelling, demonstrations of cooking, and an Easter egg hunt. The Mulberry Street Arts and Crafts Fair is staged by the Middle Georgia Art Association. The Nancy Hanks Excursion Line, departing from Terminal Station, offers several different rides on an authentic vintage train, with cars built between 1920 and 1950. The Loop Run winds through the town area for forty-five minutes, and the Line Run tours the countryside for two hours, while passengers visit from car to car and enjoy refreshments.

While many events for hot air balloons take place only in the early morning hours, Macon's Balloon Fest adds something for the evening: Balloon Glow, in Henderson Stadium, shows off the colorful balloons in illuminated beauty, allowing viewers and photographers a most unusual experience.

Exhibits in various locations cover a multitude of subjects, including an Ikebana Exhibit, a Bibb County Extension Service program on "Caring for Your Yoshino Cherry Tree," a show entitled "A Celebration of Photography," and a health fair. There are numerous fashion shows, luncheons and teas, and a magic show.

Of course there's a wonderful parade. The Cherry Blossom Parade is a highlight of the festival, with marching bands, colorful floats, antique cars, and costumed performers. Just for kids, there's the Children's Easter Parade, which gives kids from three to twelve an opportunity to decorate their bikes, trikes, wagons, or other non-motorized vehicles, and strut their stuff.

Sports have a real place in Macon, with the Cherry Blossom Golf Tournament, Pro-Am Tennis Tournament, Hickory Hill Skeet Shoot, a biathlon, and a Senior Walk for Wellness. And for zanier athletes, there's a bed race, sure to tickle the comic senses of all.

The religious organizations of Macon play an important role in the festival. Mabel White Memorial Baptist Church holds a worship service during the first Sunday of the festival, while Tabernacle Baptist Church has a community vespers service later that week.

One of the final events of the festival is the drawing for the grand prize winners of the Pin Contest. During the festival, a donation of $2 entitles you to a lovely cloisonné cherry blossom pin, and your name is entered in a drawing. Prizes have included trips abroad, shopping sprees, use of a car for a year, and diamond pins. But win, lose, or draw, your charming pin will always bring back memories of a delightful stay in a city blessed with beautiful surroundings and hospitable people.

First prize in the Cherry Dessert Contest went to this most unusual deep-dish pie. Gertrude Stallings is well known throughout the area as a superb cook and has won many prizes over the years. An octogenarian, Mrs. Stallings has been an active participant in the festival in numerous areas. Her artistry is not restricted to cooking: dignitaries and special festival visitors are given silk cherry blossoms that she has created. And though she gets around with the help of a cane, during festival time it is decorated with—what else—silk ribbons and cherry blossoms!

GERTRUDE STALLINGS'S OLD-FASHIONED CHERRY PIE

FILLING:

1 (21-oz.) can cherry pie filling

1 cup sugar

½ stick butter

1 tspn. vanilla

1 cup water

PASTRY:

¾ cup vegetable shortening

2 cups all-purpose flour

1 tspn. salt

5–6 Tbspn. water

Red food coloring

Green food coloring

Brown food coloring

Preheat oven to 400° F. Mix cherries, sugar, butter, vanilla, and water. Heat until sugar and butter melt. Pour into a well-greased deep-dish pie pan and set aside.

Make the pastry by cutting the shortening into the flour and salt with a pastry blender. Make a well in the center of this, and put 3 Tbspn. water in the well. Stir until a ball about the size of an orange forms. Remove and put aside.

Put 2 Tbspn. or more water into remaining flour and make a second ball. Roll out the first pastry ball until it is slightly larger in diameter than the pie pan, and then roll it up around the rolling pin and unroll it over the pie filling in the pie pan. Crinkle the edges of the pie crust.

Bake pie for about 45 minutes, and then use a fork to break up the baked crust and push the pieces down into the filling. Then roll out and put on the second crust. Crinkle edges as before and bake until pastry is lightly browned.

To make decorations, roll out leftover pastry and cut cherry shapes with a ¾-inch biscuit cutter. Cut shapes of leaves and stems with a knife, tracing around your own paper design. Mark veins in the leaves with a knife.

With a paintbrush that has been used only for cooking purposes, paint the designs with food coloring to resemble cherries, leaves, and stems. Arrange as desired on top crust and continue baking until lightly browned.

by Gertrude Stallings
First Prize Winner

The festival that celebrates the City Where Spring Begins exists because a dedicated citizen, Betty McCord, was concerned over some talk among legislators back in the 1960s. Seems there was a plan afoot to move the state capital from Tallahassee to Central Florida, so that it would be more convenient. Betty thought folks needed to realize what a jewel of a city Florida's capital was, so she and dedicated co-worker Ruth Yost (enlisting community support and a few volunteers) went to work to show them.

Springtime Tallahassee was incorporated in 1968 and has grown from its visionary beginnings into a year-round project that involves thousands of participants, including a nucleus organization of five hundred members (there's a waiting list to join).

Many festivals choose regional historical figures to be the standard-bearers for their events. Springtime Tallahassee focuses on Andrew Jackson

SPRINGTIME
TALLAHASSEE
TALLAHASSEE, FLORIDA, LATE MARCH/EARLY APRIL

and his wife, Rachel Jackson. (Jackson was the seventh president of the United States and the only person identified with Florida ever to hold that office.) Each year a prominent local man is chosen to represent Jackson, to promote the festival at meetings as well as other festive events throughout the South and to participate in Springtime Tallahassee activities.

Springtime Tallahassee takes place during two weeks, offering excitement, variety, and a myriad of events. A balloon rally, high school band festival, and the Springtime Tallahassee fashion show (featuring current styles as well as costumes from the Spanish, American territorial, antebellum statehood, Civil War and Reconstruction, and twentieth-century periods of Florida) are some of the usual offerings. Sporting events include the 500-Bicycle Criterium Race, a youth soccer tournament, an adult tennis championship, a 10K run, and a women's rugby tournament.

More unusual are the Springtime Spectacular car show (with an emphasis on classic Chevys) and the Riddle Rally, a road race designed to test a driving team's navigational, computational, and riddle-solving skills. A special event of growing interest is the annual North Florida Senior Games, with both competitive and noncompetitive activities, board games, and the Senior Smarts, similar to a high school Brain Brawl.

The kick-off event for Springtime Tallahassee is breakfast in the park, with General and Rachel Jackson as hosts; this is a bountiful southern breakfast of eggs, grits, sausage, ham, juice, and coffee served up by the Chaires-Capitola Volunteer Fire Department. The breakfast has become a tie-in with

Jackson's birthday celebration (he was born on March 7), and is a way to launch the festival with a touch of southern hospitality and welcome guests and dignitaries to the city.

At the time of the breakfast, the Great Grits Cookoff is held to honor an inspired local chef. Here is the recipe by the 1988 winner.

SLICED CHEESE GRITS

1 cup quick grits (uncooked)

¼ cup butter

3 cups milk

¼–½ tspn. salt

¾ cup grated Swiss cheese

¾ cup grated Cheddar cheese

Few drops Worcestershire sauce

⅓ cup grated Parmesan cheese

¼ cup butter, melted

Preheat oven to 350° F. Cook grits, butter, milk, and salt in a double boiler over boiling water for 25 minutes, stirring occasionally. Whip with electric mixer until fluffy. Pour into a 13-inch-by-9-inch-by-2-inch casserole dish. Allow grits to get firm. Cut firm grits into serving-size slices and stack slices in baking dish so cheese-butter sauce will penetrate. Spread Swiss and Cheddar cheeses evenly over grits. Mix Worcestershire sauce with Parmesan cheese and spread over grits. Drizzle ¼ cup melted butter on top of all. Bake for 25 minutes. Serve hot. Yields 8–12 servings.

by Elizabeth White
1988 Winner, Great Grits Cookoff

n Fond du Lac April brings jazz, and all the cats join forces. Two days of nonstop music, receptions, jam sessions, and performances by nationally known jazz artists—Dizzy Gillespie, Stan Getz, Buddy DeFranco, and Maynard Ferguson, to name a few from festivals past—delight the crowds at the Fond du Lac Jazz Festival. Visitors can snap and tap to a wide variety of styles, from straight-ahead jazz to Dixieland, and also enjoy more unusual groups, such as the Air Force Pacesetters. Proceeds from events underwrite student music scholarships, to continue the community's tradition of musical achievement.

The Fond du Lac Jazz Festival is produced by the Fond du Lac Convention and Visitors Bureau; contact it for the current schedule.

FOND DU LAC JAZZ FESTIVAL

LATE MARCH/EARLY APRIL

This recipe is simple but sophisticated. JoAnn Ward, executive director of the Fond du Lac Convention and Visitors Bureau, serves it for special friends who volunteer to work at the jazz festival. Easy to put together, it can be doubled or tripled for a crowd, and, combined with a tossed salad and warm, crisp French bread, makes a tasty buffet dish for a busy host or hostess.

FESTIVAL CASSEROLE

reheat oven to 350° F. Poach chicken breasts, remove bones, dice meat. Cut artichoke hearts into six pieces each. Reserving half of cheese for topping, mix all ingredients except paprika and place in unbuttered casserole. Top with reserved cheese and sprinkle with paprika. Bake for half an hour.

Note: This recipe cannot be frozen.

by JoAnn Ward

6 whole chicken breasts, split (12 pieces), skin removed

4 cans artichoke hearts

2½ cups grated fresh Parmesan cheese

5 cups mayonnaise

6 small or 3 large cans mushrooms (or like quantity fresh mushrooms, sautéed)

2 small jars pimientos, cut fine

Paprika to taste

One of the oldest festivals in Texas, this two-day event also has one of the largest grounds: eighty acres on the outskirts of town are owned by the Poteet Strawberry Association, which is planning to add more in celebration of its forty-third birthday in 1990.

Not only is this a Texas-sized festival, it is very much a Texas-style festival. The fun, hard work, and tradition of Texas rural life join forces to guarantee an exciting experience for old and young.

A couple of weeks prior to the festival date, there's a big coronation party at the high school for the festival king and queen. On Friday night there's a country and western dance, which is repeated on Saturday night. Somehow all the other activities are crammed into a Saturday and Sunday of events that only hardy folk can survive.

All this is in celebration of the strawberry, of which William Butler wrote in 1655, "Doubtless God could have made a better berry, but doubtless God never did." A member of the rose family, the strawberry is a unique fruit, the only one with seeds on the outside. It is one of the last remaining hand-cultivated crops, carefully planted, tended, picked, cleaned, and

POTEET STRAWBERRY FESTIVAL

POTEET, TEXAS, EARLY APRIL

packed by devoted farmers. Mid-season is a perfect time to celebrate the sunshine, balmy weather, and good earth which produce the delicacy.

In Poteet, the celebration really gets under way when the Rec-Vs start pulling into their spaces and campers begin setting up their tents. This festival is proud to offer free parking, public restrooms, public telephones, paved walkways, and many tent-covered activities—real Texas hospitality.

Saturday morning a parade kicks off the festivities, with floats, trail riders, bands, decorated cars, clowns, and celebrities. There's a carnival operating both days, with rides and other fun. Six large stages feature a wide variety of entertainment, with everything from an Old Fiddlers' Contest to musicians, dancers, and special acts for children. There are displays of antique engines, tools, and farm machinery, a perfect setting for demonstrations of blacksmithing. In other areas, dog lovers can watch the San Antonio Dog Training Club stage scent hurdle relays. You've got to save time for the rodeo, held both days, but you can have my place at the popular show put on by the Alamo Snake Handlers.

If you can keep up the pace, there are commercial exhibits and an arts and crafts show. Stagecoach rides and helicopter rides are available. Both evenings feature fireworks to close the show.

Spending two days at this festival will give you time to sample some of the variety of barbecue, sausages, and other Texan and Mexican food offered. Plenty of soft drinks and beer are served.

Of course, strawberries take pride of place at the festival. In addition to vendors selling every kind of strawberry delicacy you can imagine, there's a strawberry wine and food show. And most important, there's the strawberry judging, with well-known horticulturists doing the honors. When that is concluded, the crates of prizewinning berries are auctioned off. The grand champion crate of luscious fruit has brought as much as $4,700. Even if you can't afford to bid on one of the prizewinning crates, you can still buy fresh berries as you leave. Only Poteet berries, identified by the words "Farm Fresh" on the container, are sold here.

STRAWBERRY DUMPLINGS

Preheat oven to 450° F. In a saucepan, combine the ⅓ cup sugar and the water. Bring to boil, reduce heat, ꓒ simmer uncovered for 5 minutes. Stir in vanilla. Sift together flour, the 2 Tbspn. sugar, baking powder, and salt. Cut in butter or margarine until mixture is crumbly. Add milk and stir just until well combined. Place berries in a 1½-quart casserole; pour hot sugar-and-water mixture over them. Immediately drop dumpling dough in 8–10 spoonfuls over berries. Sprinkle with the 1 Tbspn. sugar. Bake for 25–30 minutes or till dumplings are done. Makes 4–5 servings.

⅓ cup sugar

⅔ cup water

½ tspn. vanilla

1 cup sifted all-purpose flour

2 Tbspn. sugar

1½ tspn. baking powder

½ tspn. salt

4 Tbspn. butter or margarine

½ cup milk

1 pint strawberries, hulled (about 2 cups)

1 Tbspn. sugar

STRAWBERRY CREAM CHEESE DELIGHT

Crust: Preheat oven to 400° F. Mix ingredients and press into pie pan. Bake for 12–15 minutes. Cool.

Filling: Soften cream cheese to room temperature. Whip until fluffy. Gradually

CRUST:
2 cups flour

½ cup brown sugar

1 cup chopped pecans

1 cup margarine, melted

FILLING:

2 (8-oz.) pkg. cream cheese

2 cans Eagle Brand milk

⅔ cup fresh lemon juice

2 tspn. vanilla

STRAWBERRY GLACÉ TOPPING:

1 quart strawberries

1 cup water

1 cup sugar

3 Tbspn. cornstarch

3–4 drops red food coloring

add Eagle Brand milk. Stir until well blended. Add lemon juice and vanilla; blend well. Pour into crust and chill.

Topping: Wash, drain, and hull strawberries. Simmer 1 cup berries and ⅔ cup water about 3 minutes. Blend sugar, cornstarch, and remaining ⅓ cup water; add to boiling mixture. Boil 1 minute, stirring constantly, and stir in red food coloring. Cool. Slice remaining berries on top of filling and cover with cooked strawberry mixture. Refrigerate until firm, about 2 hours.

STRAWBERRY BLACK BOTTOM PIE

½ cup half-and-half

1 (6-oz.) pkg. semisweet chocolate morsels

3 eggs, separated

1 9-inch pie shell baked

2 pints fresh Poteet strawberries, washed and stemmed

2 tspn. lemon juice

1 pkg. unflavored gelatin

1 cup cold water

¼ cup sugar

Heat half-and-half in saucepan over medium heat. Stir in chocolate morsels; beat smooth with wire whisk. Remove from heat; whisk in egg yolks one at a time, mixing until well blended. Return to heat. Cook, stirring, 1–2 minutes longer. Cool; pour into pie shell. Chill until set, 2–3 hours. Puree 1 pint of the berries with lemon juice (there should be about 1⅔ cups puree). Soften gelatin in water; warm over low heat to dissolve, then stir into berry puree. Chill until mixture begins to set. Meanwhile beat egg whites, gradually adding sugar, until soft peaks form. Fold in thickened berry mixture. Pour over chocolate layer; chill until set. To serve, slice remaining pint berries; sweeten if desired. Spoon over wedges of pie. Makes 6–8 servings.

CHOCOLATE-COVERED STRAWBERRIES

Mix powdered sugar, egg white, milk, and vanilla until smooth. Form into balls. Place whole berries on paper towel to absorb juice. Put one berry into each ball so as to be in the center. Refrigerate until firm. Melt chocolate and paraffin in small pan and, using toothpicks, dip each ball into it and let drain on waxed paper.

Let stand on waxed paper until firm.

1 lb. powdered sugar

1 egg white

3 Tbspn. milk

1 tspn. vanilla

Whole strawberry preserve for each piece

1 (6-oz.) pkg. chocolate morsels

½ block paraffin (½ of ¼ lb.)

STRAWBERRY SOUP

Blend all ingredients except water. Combine well-blended strawberry mixture with water and heat soup slowly. Soup may be served hot or cold. When serving cold, top with dollop of yogurt.

1 quart strawberries

¼ cup sugar

Pinch of salt

1 cup yogurt

1 cup dry red wine

4 cups water

A celebration unsurpassed in color and variety awaits you in the Lone Star State when Fiesta San Antonio embraces the city in a festive atmosphere of parades, pageants, festivals, fairs, concerts, sporting events, and a Mexican rodeo!

This tradition, begun in 1891 and renewed annually to commemorate the heroes of the Alamo, thrives today and provides nonstop fun for the entire family. Fiesta San Antonio's ten days of revelry are an entertainment bargain. Many events are free and those that are not are very affordable.

The only problem you'll have at Fiesta San Antonio is deciding where to go and what to do; with more than 150 events from which to choose, it's hard to make up your mind.

A must is the pilgrimage to the Alamo, which reminds everyone of the reason the celebration was established. Every year since 1925, on Fiesta Monday, the Alamo Mission Chapter of the Daughters of the Republic of Texas has staged a pilgrimage to the Alamo as a memorial tribute to the Alamo heroes and the patriotic heritage of Texas.

FIESTA
SAN ANTONIO
SAN ANTONIO, TEXAS, MID-APRIL

Three spectacular parades are included in the festivities. The Texas Cavaliers sponsor the one-of-a-kind River Parade, in which bedecked and brightly lit boat floats wind down the San Antonio River, alongside the downtown area. Then the Battle of Flowers Parade takes the spotlight, with beauties from San Antonio and surrounding areas waving from lavishly decorated floats and marching bands from all over the country strutting in style.

For the grand finale of parades, the city pulls out all the stops for the brilliantly lit Fiesta Flambeau Rey Feo Parade. The sponsors of this extravaganza are the members of Lulac Council Number 2, the founding council of the oldest Hispanic organization in the country, well known for its efforts in the advancement of education through scholarship programs. Beautiful floats, radiant queens, and tuneful bands are joined by El Rey Feo (the Ugly King), as well as King Antonio and Miss Fiesta San Antonio.

Festival music reflects the cultural blend that is San Antonio, with a variety of musical offerings. Because San Antonio is one of the nation's major military centers, there is much participation by musicians from the five military installations in the area, both in their own events and in various parades and ceremonies. A Battle of the Flowers band festival, world class jazz concert, mariachi festival, and German Beethoven Maennerchor are just a few of the events that keep a song in each person's heart. There's a fiesta square dance, and impromptu street dancing to local bands is one of the more captivating and memorable aspects of fiesta for many merrymakers.

Sports buffs have a great variety of activities from which to choose. There are several runs, a golf tournament, and a track meet for youths aged eight to fifteen. Soccer for women, rugby for men, and bowling tournaments for everyone are popular. The Fiesta Volleyball Classic, a coed, round-robin tournament, has divisions for almost every skill level. Cyclists compete in the Fiesta Grande bicycle race, one of the top races in the central United States. There's even a lacrosse tournament.

Children have lots to do at most fiesta events. There are also two events especially for them: the Fiesta para los Niños was started by the San Antonio Jaycees in 1985 just for young people, and children from kindergarten to fifth grade are invited to participate in the Shoe Box Float Parade. Contestants in this are asked to use shoe boxes and build miniature floats; after the judging, all participants take part in a miniparade, complete with mariachi band.

A number of art events are a part of fiesta, including the Randolph Art League's Alamo Plaza array of fine arts and crafts, and the Fiesta River Art Show, along beautiful River Walk, where artists are on hand to talk about their works. The Fiesta Arts Fair, on the historic grounds of the Southwest Crafts Center, offers art, entertainment, and family-oriented activity; of special interest here is the Craft Experience courtyard, where visitors of all ages can try their hands at a variety of crafts, including weaving, ceramics, painting, jewelry, and much more. The Texas Institute of Cultures features the collected works of a different Texas artist each year, in addition to special exhibits.

Ethnic special events include Fiesta Charra, the Israeli Festival, Day in Old Mexico, Mexican Charreada, and Hermann's Happiness, a German-style event that manages to include an oompah band, polkas, Hawaiian and contemporary dances, along with German, Texan, and Mexican food.

Gardeners and history buffs are actively involved at fiesta. The Women's Club combines a display of the best from area garden clubs with a fashion show. There is a San Antonio cactus and xerophyte show and sale. Antique lovers shouldn't miss the Gething house tour in the historic King William area, which also offers the King William Fair and tour of homes. One of the opening events for fiesta is the Patriotic and Historical Ball, held by the State Association of Texas Pioneers. The aim of this organization is to keep alive Texas history, perpetuate Texas traditions, and cultivate friendly relations between pioneers of Texas and their descendants.

The biggest and best fiesta party in town is called A Night in Old San Antonio, though it is held for four nights. The setting is La Villita, a restored eighteenth-century village. Frontier Town, Irish Flats, South of the Border, and Sauerkraut Bend are theme areas offering food, entertainment, and a feeling for the heritage of San Antonio. Using thousands of volunteers, the

San Antonio Conservation Society has been presenting this gala since 1937, to help in its efforts to save San Antonio's legacy of historical sites.

When you leave Fiesta San Antonio, you can relive the fun with mementos. Suitable for any party is the custom of breaking *cascarones* on the heads of your friends: the pastel-tinted eggs burst into a shower of confetti! Just as the spirit of fiesta explodes into a cascade of multicolored confetti when the *cascarón* is broken, so the spirit of San Antonio bursts forth in fiesta's multicultural events, which are brought to life by the heart of the celebration: fiesta volunteers. ¡Viva fiesta!

Fiesta San Antonio recipes were selected from a beautiful cookbook published by the San Antonio Conservation Society. A useful and charming addition to any collection, it is hardbound and illustrated with lovely watercolors of local historical sites. (For information on the cookbook, please write to Fiesta San Antonio.) The society's motto is "Shall I say, 'Yes, I remember it,' or 'Here it is, I helped to save it'?" What a wonderful way to make the past a part of the present.

CEVICHE

1 pound snapper, redfish, or other sweet white fish

Juice of 3 limes, or enough to cover fish

1 tspn. salt

1 Tbspn. fresh cilantro, chopped

3 serrano peppers (packed in vinegar), cut up

Juice of 1 orange

2 Tbspn. olive oil

1 large onion, finely chopped

2 fresh tomatoes, peeled and chopped

Cut fish into thin bite-sized pieces. Combine lime juice, salt, and cilantro. Pour over fish. Be sure there is enough juice to cover fish. Marinate in refrigerator 4 hours. Add serrano peppers, orange juice, olive oil, onion, and tomatoes. Serve in cups, along with juice; accompany with saltine crackers. Serves 6.

by Mrs. James N. Castleberry, Jr. (Mary Ann)

PICADILLO DIP

Sauté onion and garlic in oil. Stir in beef and brown lightly. Add tomatoes, chili powder, oregano, and cumin. Mix well. Stir in flour, salt, and pepper. Simmer slowly for about 20 minutes. Serve with corn chips. Yields about 2 ½ quarts.

Mrs. M. H. Nipper (Leatrice)

2 medium onions, minced

2 cloves garlic, crushed

3 Tbspn. oil

2 lb. ground beef

3 cups tomatoes, drained

2 tspn. chili powder

2 tspn. oregano

2 tspn. cumin

2 Tbspn. flour

Salt and pepper to taste

BLACK BEAN SOUP "MOROS Y CRISTIANOS"

Soak beans in water overnight; drain. Cover with fresh water. Add ham hock, garlic, onion, and salt. Simmer until very tender, adding more water if necessary. Serve soup in individual bowls over white rice. Top each serving with chopped onion and a dash of Tabasco. Serves 12–14.

by Mrs. William P. Francisco (Nancy)

1 (1-lb.) pkg. black beans

3 quarts cold water

1 (1½-lb.) small ham hock

1 clove garlic

1 onion, chopped

1 tspn. salt

White rice

Chopped onion

Tabasco sauce

WHITE GAZPACHO

3 large cucumbers, peeled, sliced lengthwise, seeds removed, coarsely chopped

1 cup seedless grapes

1 avocado, diced

2 large cloves garlic

3 cups chicken stock or 2 (13¾-oz.) cans chicken broth

1 cup plain yogurt

2 cups (1 pint) sour cream

3 Tbspn. white vinegar

2 tspn. salt

2–3 drops Tabasco sauce

ACCOMPANIMENTS:

2 tomatoes, peeled, juiced, seeded, chopped

½ cup scallions, finely chopped

1 green pepper, seeded, finely chopped

1 cup almonds, slivered, toasted

½ cup parsley, finely chopped

1 cup garlic croutons

Place cucumber, grapes, avocado, and garlic in blender or food processor and puree. Add chicken stock or broth, yogurt, sour cream, vinegar, salt, and Tabasco sauce. Process until smooth. Cover, refrigerate until thoroughly chilled, at least 1 hour. Before serving, whisk to blend, taste for seasoning. More salt or Tabasco sauce may be added. Serve in chilled soup bowls. Pass accompaniments in separate bowls. Serves 20–22.

by Mrs. W. Grant Bechtel (Helen)

BEBE'S JALAPEÑO SPINACH

2 Tbspn. margarine

½ cup onion, chopped

1 Tbspn. flour

¾ cup drained liquid from 1 (15-oz.) can spinach

1 (8-oz.) jar Jalapeño Cheez Whiz

2 Tbspn. Worcestershire sauce

2 (15-oz.) cans spinach, drained

Melt margarine in skillet; add onion. Sauté onion until glossy. Add flour, stirring well to remove any lumps. Slowly pour in spinach liquid, stirring constantly. When mixture is slightly thickened, add cheese and Worcestershire sauce. When cheese has melted, fold in spinach. Great accompaniment for game, beef, or poultry. Serves 6.

by Mrs. Sherwood W. Inkley (Bebe)

SOUTH TEXAS HOT SAUCE

Place all ingredients in blender. Blend until vegetables are finely chopped. Makes 1 quart.

by Mrs. Stephen W. Albert (Lanie)

1 (16-oz.) can stewed tomatoes

1 medium green pepper

1 medium onion

1 tspn. garlic powder

1 tspn. salt

5 jalapeño peppers

MOTHER'S CHOW-CHOW

Combine ingredients for dressing and cook over medium heat, stirring constantly until dressing is thick and smooth. Add chopped vegetables. Stir, mixing well; bring chow-chow to a boil. This does not need to be cooked but must be heated thoroughly. Pour into sterilized pint jars and seal. Yields 9–10 pints.

by Mrs. Gene M. Patton (Tance)

DRESSING:

1 cup flour

2 cups sugar

3 pints vinegar

2 Tbspn. dry mustard

2 Tbspn. celery seed

1 Tbspn. salt

1 Tbspn. turmeric

CHOPPED VEGETABLES:

1 quart green tomatoes

1 quart onions

1 quart celery

1 quart green cabbage

1 pint (combined) red and green bell peppers

2–3 hot peppers

PICKLED OKRA

Wash okra. Pack into sterilized pint jars. To each jar add 1 pepper and 1 clove garlic. Bring water, vinegar,

3 cups okra

1 pepper, per jar

1 clove garlic, per jar
3 cups water
1 cup vinegar
¼ cup salt

and salt to a rolling boil. Fill jars with boiling mixture. Seal caps immediately. Allow to stand for 3 weeks before using. Yields about 4 pints.

by Mrs. Charles E. Cheever, Jr. (Sally)

CITRON CUSTARDS

Pastry, for 9-inch pie
1 cup butter
12 egg yolks, beaten very light
2 cups sugar
1 cup citron, cut up fine
1 tspn. vanilla extract

Preheat oven to 350° F. Make enough very rich pastry for 9-inch pie. Roll pastry very thin. Line small individual tart pans with pastry. Cream butter. Add egg yolks, sugar, citron, and vanilla. Mix well. Place 1 tspn. custard in each pan and bake for 15 minutes or until crust is golden and tops nicely browned. Cool. Store in tin box in cool place. Yields 5 dozen.

by Mrs. Robert C. Murray (Eloise)

FLAN

1¾ cups sugar
6 eggs
3 cups milk
1 tspn. vanilla extract

Preheat oven to 350° F. Melt ¾ cup of the sugar in skillet over medium heat; cook until syrup is golden brown. Pour into 6 buttered custard cups. Set aside. Beat eggs well; gradually add remaining sugar. Heat milk almost to boiling point; add gradually to egg mixture, stirring until sugar dissolves. Add vanilla. Pour into caramel-lined cups; place cups in pan of hot water, and bake for 1 hour or until knife inserted in center of custard comes out clean. Cool. To serve, unmold onto dessert plates. Serves 6.

by Mrs. Sherwood W. Inkley (Bebe)

The Stockton Asparagus Festival is a phenomenon that has developed into one of the major food and entertainment events in California.

Asparagus has long been recognized as the most distinguished and elegant vegetable of the San Joaquin Delta region. The purposes of the Stockton Asparagus Festival are to celebrate the asparagus harvest, promote tourism in the city of Stockton and San Joaquin County, and serve as a fundraiser for local nonprofit organizations.

The focal point of the Stockton Asparagus Festival is a shameless, joyfully orchestrated orgy of culinary ecstasy. Festival visitors are tempted with the mouth-watering aromas and flavors of, for example, asparagus bisque, asparagus and shrimp salad, asparagus pasta, beef and asparagus sandwiches, deep-fried asparagus, and steamed asparagus. All are prepared by volunteers; all are fixed fresh, on site, with an emphasis on presentation and flavor.

One of the highlights of the Stockton Asparagus Festival is the Concours d'Elégance: more than two hundred cars of all makes and vintages spread through a beautiful oak grove in the park. Whether you're a bona fide car buff or a casual admirer, you will delight in the Asparagus Festival Concours d'Elégance.

STOCKTON ASPARAGUS FESTIVAL

STOCKTON, CALIFORNIA, FOURTH WEEKEND OF APRIL

Fine arts and crafts are major parts of the festival. Exhibitors are selected each year on the basis of the originality and craftsmanship of their work and its relevance to the theme of the festival. Shoppers may select from a variety of arts and crafts, including jewelry, pottery, textiles, leather, and wood, as well as paintings and photography.

Everything from the hottest oldies to the greatest big band sounds are featured on the Stockton Asparagus Festival's main entertainment stage. The country entertainment pavilion features country music at its best. There's even a dance floor on which to swing your partner and do-si-do. A five-hundred-seat children's entertainment amphitheater, complete with a picturesque lake between seating and entertainers, features everything from puppet shows to theatrical presentations. There's even a stage featuring Dixieland entertainment and other popular music. Strolling entertainment is also provided at the festival by the likes of barbershop quartets, mascots, and magicians.

The Stockton Asparagus Festival Fun Run is one of the most widely attended three-mile runs in the area, with approximately eight hundred participants. The run winds through the festival grounds and the picturesque Oak Grove Regional Park nature trails. Entrants receive official Stockton

Asparagus Festival Fun Run T-shirts, as well as postrace refreshments and free admissions to the festival.

The following selection of recipes includes winners from the 1987 and 1988 festivals, as well as excerpts from the Stockton Asparagus Festival's own *Asparagus Cookbook*. Published after the first annual festival, the cookbook is a unique collection of wonderful recipes, and includes the history and folklore of asparagus, as well as tips—pun intended—for cooking asparagus. For more information or to order a cookbook, write to the Stockton Asparagus Festival office (see Appendix B).

ASPARAGUS LASAGNA

1–2 lb. fresh asparagus, cleaned, trimmed, and cut into pieces (may use frozen asparagus)

¼ cup butter

½ cup diced onions

12 oz. fresh mushrooms, chopped

¼ cup flour

1 tspn. salt

¼ tspn. cayenne pepper

2½ cups milk

1 (8-oz.) pkg. lasagna noodles

Pepper (optional)

2 cups cottage cheese

8 oz. jack cheese, shredded (more may be used)

½–1 cup grated Parmesan cheese (more may be used)

Preheat oven to 325° F. Cook asparagus and drain; let cool.

Melt butter in medium-size saucepan. Add onions and mushrooms to butter. Cook over medium heat, stirring occasionally, until tender, about 5 minutes. Blend in flour, salt, and cayenne pepper. Gradually stir in milk; cook until thickened, another 5 minutes.

Cook lasagna noodles, following package directions.

Spread ½ cup creamed mushroom sauce in greased 13-inch-by-9-inch baking pan. Layer noodles (seasoned with pepper for pungent flavor), asparagus, cottage cheese, jack cheese, ⅓ remaining mushroom sauce, and Parmesan cheese. Repeat to make three layers.

Bake in preheated oven for 45 minutes. Let stand 20 minutes before cutting to serve. Serves 6–8.

by Liz Rotert
First Prize, 1987

SAN JOAQUIN VALLEY ENCHILADAS

Preheat oven to 425° F. In large fry pan heat oil and cook tortillas one at a time to soften. Set aside to cool and drain.

In saucepan melt butter, then blend in flour. Add chicken broth and cook until thick and bubbly. Add sour cream and taco sauce. Heat thoroughly.

On one tortilla at a time, place a serving of jack cheese, chicken, some onion, plenty of asparagus to extend to both ends of tortilla, and 3 Tbspn. of the sauce. Roll tortilla, place seam side down in glass dish.

Sprinkle with any remaining jack cheese, cover with a layer of Parmesan cheese, and then cover with remaining sauce. Bake for 25 minutes. Makes 12 enchiladas.

by Liz Rotert
First Prize, 1988

½ cup oil
1 dozen flour tortillas
½ cup butter
½ cup flour
3–4 cups chicken broth
1 cup sour cream
½ cup green taco sauce
3 cups grated jack cheese
3 cups cooked, shredded chicken
½ cup chopped onions
2–3 lb. cooked asparagus
Parmesan cheese, freshly grated

LEMONY ASPARAGUS GOUGÈRE

Preheat oven to 375° F. In medium saucepan, bring water, butter, salt, lemon rind, and pepper to a boil. Add the flour and cheese; stir well to make a dough. Remove from heat and beat in eggs well, one at a time. Smooth dough over bottom of large greased au gratin pan or 10-inch pie plate. Make a well in the center of the dough, building up the edges. Sprinkle center with ham. Bake for 30 minutes.

Meanwhile prepare the Fluffy Lemon Sauce.

Fluffy Lemon Sauce: Melt butter in small saucepan; blend in flour until

1 cup water
½ cup butter
½ tspn. each salt and finely grated lemon rind
½ tspn. pepper
1 cup each flour and grated Swiss cheese
4 eggs
¼ lb. chopped ham
8 oz. fresh asparagus, trimmed into 4-inch to 5-inch spears, steamed and hot

2 Tbspn. grated Parmesan cheese

1 Tbspn. each fine bread crumbs and melted butter

FLUFFY LEMON SAUCE:
1 Tbspn. butter

1½ Tbspn. flour

½ cup chicken broth

2 Tbspn. lemon juice

2 egg yolks

2 egg whites

smooth. Gradually stir in chicken broth. Cook over low heat, stirring, until thickened. Stir in lemon juice. Slowly beat small amount of hot mixture into beaten egg yolks, then slowly add egg yolks to remaining mixture, stirring constantly until bubbly. Remove from heat. Beat egg whites until stiff, and gently fold into sauce.

To serve, take the gougère out of the oven and arrange the freshly cooked asparagus on top of the ham. Spoon Lemon Sauce over asparagus and sprinkle with Parmesan cheese and bread crumbs tossed with melted butter. Broil just to brown. Serve immediately.
by Janet Hill

ASPARAGITO

½ cup finely chopped onion

1 clove garlic, minced

4 cups asparagus, chopped

1 (4-oz.) can chopped green chilies

1 tspn. basil leaves, crushed

½ tspn. oregano leaves, crushed

¼ tspn. ground cumin

¼ tspn. salt

1 Tbspn. cooking oil

1 cup grated mozzarella cheese

¾ cup wheat bran

½ cup water

6 to 8 flour tortillas

Small amount of cooking oil (optional)

Sour cream (optional)

Parsley, minced (optional)

Sauté onion, garlic, asparagus, chiles, basil, oregano, cumin, and salt in cooking oil over medium heat 5 minutes. Add cheese, bran, and water, stirring until cheese melts. Spoon vegetable mixture onto tortillas. Roll to enclose filling.

Optional: Pan fry burritos in cooking oil until golden, turning once. Top with sour cream and minced parsley if desired. Makes 6–8 burritos.
by Brenda Alastra

ASPARAGUS BISQUE

In stockpot melt butter, and add flour to make a roux, stirring constantly so mixture doesn't burn.

Add 1 quart milk slowly to the roux, stirring constantly. When combined and thickened, add remaining milk and chicken stock. Add bay leaf, white pepper, and salt. Add asparagus, and cook soup slowly for 1 hour, adding instant mashed potatoes if needed.

To serve, top each serving with croutons and sour cream, and then sprinkle with dill weed. Makes 1 gallon.

1 cube butter (¼ pound)

¾ cup flour

2 quarts whole milk

1 cup chicken stock (made from bouillon cube)

1 bay leaf

1 tspn. white pepper

1 tspn. salt

3 cups cleaned and cooked asparagus, tips and center cuts only, cut into ½-inch pieces

Instant mashed potatoes (use to thicken bisque if needed)

Large sourdough croutons

Sour cream

Dill weed

Begun in 1956 as a single event, the Pegasus Parade, the Kentucky Derby Festival has grown into a whirlwind of more than seventy colorful events in the ten days leading up to and including the day of the Kentucky Derby. It is one of the nation's largest civic celebrations, and one of the top twenty annual events in North America in terms of attendance and participation.

The Kentucky Derby Festival's ten days of activities highlight the drama and excitement leading up to the Kentucky Derby, "the greatest two minutes in sports," while showcasing Louisville's pride and traditions. (The Kentucky Derby Festival, Inc., does not sponsor or produce the Kentucky Derby race.) A wide variety of festival events offer fun for every age and interest, and participation in many of them is free, due to the support of numerous sponsors.

One of the most popular sports events, McDonald's Kentucky Derby Festival Basketball Classic, takes place several weeks before the start of the festival. Featuring twenty of the finest high school players in the United States, this classic confrontation fills the nineteen-thousand-seat

KENTUCKY DERBY FESTIVAL

LOUISVILLE, KENTUCKY, LATE APRIL/EARLY MAY

Freedom Hall. Another popular event, and a Louisville tradition, is the mini-marathon, a thirteen-mile footrace run along a scenic route from a suburban park through city streets to the heart of downtown Louisville. Local residents gather in their neighborhoods to cheer on the runners, both local and out of town; more than 50 percent of the entrants are from out of town, representing as many as thirty-three states and several foreign countries.

Minutes before the Pegasus Parade takes place, a stellar field of Olympic-class runners competes in two footraces along Broadway: the Pegasus Women's Mile and the men's Renegade Mile. A soccer tournament offers a chance for women and men of all ages to participate in a round-robin competition. The "Take It to the Bucket" West End Shootout measures the skills of girls and boys. Several hundred anglers rise before dawn to compete in the Bass Fishing Classic, which offers more than $3000 in prizes. The Tennis Carnival is an all-day event that showcases tennis skills, fitness conditioning tasks, and knowledge and awareness of tennis. A pro-am golf tournament matches local golfers with professionals.

The most heartwarming Kentucky Derby Festival event is the Don Fightmaster Golf Tournament, which offers physically and mentally disabled children a chance to take active part in a sporting event.

Fun at this festival is everywhere, from chow wagons serving up barbecue and continuous entertainment to clogging and square dancing exhibitions at a number of shopping malls. Puppetry pageants, including shows by a variety of performers such as puppeteers, jugglers, mimes, clowns, and a Mark Twain impersonator, are held at various festival sites and at youth centers, hospitals, and elder homes.

Festival in the Park, held in scenic Cherokee Park, gives families a day of fun, picnicking, and entertainment. Festival at Riverport, held in Riverview Park on the banks of the Ohio River, has costumed characters, displays, live music, and horseshoe-pitching contests, and finishes with a fireworks display.

The Great Balloon Race is regarded by its participants as the premier ballooning event in the United States, with fifty colorful hot air balloons taking to the sky over Louisville in pursuit of a "hare" balloon, and as many as forty thousand children and adults watching in the dawn light. Another event that has everyone craning their necks is the air show, which takes place just before the Great Steamboat Race.

The Great Steamboat Race dates back to 1964. In the only remaining annual river race for authentic sternwheelers in America, the *Belle of Louisville* is matched against the *Delta Queen*. Thousands of spectators line the Kentucky and Indiana shores as the two boats race to see who will take home the coveted gilded antlers that year.

Car enthusiasts have two days of must-see activities: the first day offers the Porsche Concours d'Elégance, a display of Porsche sports cars that are judged for their authenticity and preservation. On the second day an autocross is held, with a race course set up on which Porsche owners can test performance and handling against a time clock.

For those interested in flesh-and-blood horsepower, the Rock Creek Spring Horse Show, adjacent to pastoral Seneca Park, has riders and gaited horses competing in twenty-eight classes.

The Cavalcade of Bands contest is held on the night prior to the parade. Top high school marching bands from all over the country take part in a field competition and are judged on their music and precision marching routines. All the bands then march in the parade, which offers some of the finest band music heard anywhere.

The most popular of all the events on the festival schedule is the magnificent Pegasus Parade. Considered one of the top parades in the United States, it is a wonderful array of animated floats, top-notch marching bands, celebrities, and specialty and equestrian units. The Kentucky Derby Festival is unique within the special events world for the participation of sponsoring organizations, who have their employees or volunteers design and build their floats. Their pride, and the quality of the floats, are examples of laudable civic involvement. An estimated quarter of a million parade fans line the

1.7-mile route in downtown Louisville. The parade is seen live on Louisville's WAVE-TV, and is a focal point of the Kentucky Derby Festival's syndicated network television special, viewed by hundreds of thousands more fans.

The next best thing to living in Louisville in the spring is visiting there during the Kentucky Derby Festival. Be sure to check on accommodations well in advance, and learn to hum a few bars of "My Old Kentucky Home."

The Kentucky Derby Festival has a lowercase but high-class official cookbook: *fillies flavours*. The Fillies, Inc., one of the most active volunteer groups to support the Kentucky Derby Festival, devoted much energy to this project, and the result is a charming and very usable cookbook.

Editors-in-chief Frances Harding Mengel and Barbara Harding Mengel, assisted by a large publication staff, a long list of contributors, and friends of fillies, have produced a book that is a mélange of sophisticated and down-home recipes, truly representative of the cuisine of the Land of the Beaten Biscuit. The dust jacket says, *"fillies flavours* is a collection of treasured recipes from many outstanding culinary artists in our region. While these recipes may not be original, they were donated by many talented chefs as favorites."

If the eight hundred recipes aren't all original, the outrageous names must be: Middle Age Spread, Sweet Kentucky Knights, Eve's Tart, Fat Ladies, and the all-time kids' favorite, Pasghetti. And where else can you find a recipe for turkey carcass soup, not to mention a recipe for a splendid casserole called Pumpernickel Pudding? This delightful book can be ordered from The Fillies, Inc., c/o Kentucky Derby Festival, Inc., 137 West Muhammad Ali Boulevard, Louisville, KY 40202. For current price and postage, call (502) 584–6383.

FULL OF BEANS SOUP MIX

1 lb. dried navy beans

12 oz. dried split peas

12 oz. dried lentils

1 lb. dried Great Northern beans

1 lb. dried black-eyed peas

1 lb. dried pinto beans

1 lb. dried red beans

1 lb. dried black beans

1 lb. barley pearls

12 oz. dried large lima beans

Combine all ingredients. Divide into 12 2-cup packages. For gift giving, place in plastic bags and tie with bright ribbon, or place in glass jars and cover lids with calico. Include the recipe for Full of Beans Soup. Dried lentils are a sign of good luck!

FULL OF BEANS SOUP

Wash beans thoroughly, place in a large saucepan, and cover with water, adding the 2 Tbspn. salt. Soak overnight. Drain beans and put back in saucepan, adding the 8 cups of water. Add ham, onion, tomatoes with their juice, garlic, salt, chili con carne seasoning, and lemon juice. Simmer for 3 hours, stirring occasionally. You'll be proud of this easy soup.

2 cups of bean mix

Water, enough to cover beans

2 Tbspn. salt

8 cups water

1-lb. slice of ham, cubed

1 medium onion, chopped

1 (28-oz.) can of tomatoes, cut up (reserve juice)

2 cloves garlic, pressed

¾ tspn. salt

1 tspn. chili con carne seasoning

2 Tbspn. lemon juice

FLOWER PETALS

Cut a slice off the top and bottom of each onion; remove the outside skin. Make 3 cuts in each onion about ¾ of the way through, making 6 sections. Onion will open like "flower petals." Make a small core in center of onion and place in it 1 Tbspn. of butter and 1 Tbspn. Worcestershire sauce. Cut 1 slice of bacon in half and crisscross over top. Wrap completely in foil. Repeat with remaining onions. Place on barbecue grill over hot coals and let cook for 45 minutes. Serves 6.

6 medium red onions

6 Tbspn. butter

6 Tbspn. Worcestershire sauce

6 slices bacon, uncooked

COUNTRY HAM SPREAD

Make a cream sauce by melting butter in a saucepan and then adding flour and half-and-half. Cook,

2 Tbspn. butter

1 Tbspn. flour

1 cup half-and-half

1 Tbspn. plus 1 tspn. unflavored gelatin

¼ cup Burgundy

2½ lb. country ham, cooked and ground

¼ cup mayonnaise

2 tspn. Dijon mustard

½ cup whipping cream, whipped

stirring, until thickened. Dissolve gelatin in wine, add to hot cream sauce, and stir well. Cool, fold in ham. Combine mayonnaise and Dijon mustard, add to cream mixture. Chill until slightly thickened. Fold in whipped cream. Pour into a 1-quart greased mold. Refrigerate until set. Unmold on a serving platter. Pass beaten biscuits or party rye.

EDEN SHALE'S CHEESECAKE

6 Tbspn. butter

8 double graham crackers, crushed

3 Tbspn. sugar

1 cup butter

3 oz. unsweetened chocolate

2 cups light brown sugar

1 cup sugar

2 Tbspn. flour

4 eggs

4 tspn. milk

2 tspn. vanilla

3 (8-oz.) pkg. cream cheese

1¼ cups sugar

⅛ tspn. salt

3 eggs

1 tspn. vanilla

2 cups sour cream

¼ cup sugar

1 tspn. vanilla

Melt the 6 Tbspn. butter. Add crushed graham crackers and the 3 Tbspn. sugar. Press into bottom and sides of a 10-inch springform pan. Set aside. Melt butter with chocolate. Remove from heat. Add light brown sugar, the 1 cup sugar, and flour. Beat in the 4 eggs, one at a time. Add milk and the 2 tspn. vanilla. Pour into prepared crust. Cream the cream cheese with the 1¼ cups sugar and ⅛ tspn. salt until fluffy. Add the 3 eggs separately. Add the 1 tspn. vanilla. Layer over chocolate mixture. Do not stir or mix layers. Bake at 350° F for 1 hour. Check every 5 minutes thereafter until center is soft set. Allow to rest for 15 minutes. Combine sour cream, the remaining ¼ cup sugar and 1 tspn. vanilla. Spread over top of cake, return to oven for 10 minutes. Allow to cool for 1 hour, then refrigerate for at least 4 hours. Freezes well. Simply divine! A well-guarded secret until now! Serves 16–20.

RED VELVET ROBE CAKE

Preheat oven to 350° F. Cream butter and sugar. Add eggs. Make a paste of red food coloring and cocoa. Add to butter mixture. Add buttermilk alternately with sifted flour and salt. Add vanilla. Combine baking soda with vinegar (this will foam), then add it to cake mixture, blending instead of beating. Pour into two 8-inch greased pans. Bake for 25–30 minutes. Cool on a rack. Split each layer into 2 layers and frost with Red Velvet Robe Frosting (next recipe).

½ cup butter

1½ cups sugar

2 eggs, beaten

2 oz. red food coloring

2½ Tbspn. cocoa

1 cup buttermilk

2¼ cups cake flour, sifted

½ tspn. salt

1 tspn. vanilla

1 tspn. baking soda

1 Tbspn. white vinegar

RED VELVET ROBE FROSTING

Cook flour and milk until very thick, stirring constantly. Cool. Cream butter and sugar until very light, add vanilla. Add to flour-and-milk mixture. Blend well. It should have the texture of whipped cream. Add red food coloring for a pink tint. Frost Red Velvet Robe Cake between layers and on top and sides. Fit for a queen!

3 Tbspn. flour

1 cup milk

1 cup butter

3 cups granulated sugar

1 tspn. vanilla

Few drops red food coloring

OH! KENTUCKY BURGOO

2 chickens, 4 lb. each

2-lb. breast of lamb

5-lb. beef chuck

2 smoked ham hocks

1 tspn. liquid smoke

2 bay leaves

Salt to taste

3 lb. green beans, chopped

6 medium onions, chopped

1 bunch celery, chopped

1 head cabbage, chopped

2 medium turnips, diced

2 parsnips, diced

2 green peppers, diced

2 bunches carrots, chopped

1½ lb. fresh okra, sliced

4 (10-oz.) boxes frozen peas

4 (10-oz.) boxes lima beans

4 (28-oz.) cans tomatoes with juice, cut up

4 potatoes, peeled and cubed

6 ears of corn (kernels cut from cob)

½ cup fresh parsley, chopped

1 Tbspn. liquid smoke

¼ cup lemon juice

1 Tbspn. Worcestershire sauce

1 Tbspn. sugar

Salt to taste

Put all the meat in a very large kettle. Cover with water. Add the 1 tspn. liquid smoke, bay leaves, and salt to taste. Simmer slowly, about 4 hours, until meat is tender. Cool. Take out meat. Strain broth and return broth to kettle. Cut the meat fine, remove all skin, fat, and bones and discard. Return meat to broth. Enough for one day! Refrigerate. Next day add vegetables and remaining ingredients to meat and broth. Simmer very slowly until vegetables are tender and broth is thick. Usually takes all day. At this point you may want to tie a bandanna around your head! You have to stir often and watch to ensure against scorching. Now freeze the burgoo, or, if you wish to serve it the next day, refrigerate it overnight and reheat, so that the flavors fully develop. Makes about 60 servings.

What's an admiral doing in Kansas? If it's Admiral Windwagon Smith, he's inspiring the folk in Wichita to buy buttons and to celebrate his remarkable invention.

Part of the Wichita River Festival's magic is spun in a legend about a seafaring man named Admiral Windwagon Smith, who had a dream of revolutionizing transportation on the plains by building a large prairie schooner, rigged with mast and rudder, and sailing the prairie grasses. Unfortunately, the evening before his planned maiden voyage, a great gust of Kansas wind caught the "windwagon" and swept it into the sunset, never to be seen again.

Each year a Wichitan is chosen to portray the admiral and act as ambassador for the festival. The admiral dons his red and silver jacket, climbs aboard the windwagon, and sets sail for ten days of adventure and magic.

There's a potpourri of events; something for every age group, interest, and nationality. There's the Sundown Parade, the major lead-off event, with marching bands, floats, clowns, and other colorful characters parading through Wichita's downtown streets. The excitement continues as brightly

WICHITA RIVER FESTIVAL
WICHITA, KANSAS, EARLY MAY

colored hot air balloons float in the sky and thousands of runners jam the streets to participate in the ten-kilometer run and the two-mile river run.

Sports enthusiasts gear up for the numerous sporting events: golf, tennis, softball, rugby, soccer, horseshoes, and the tug-of-war. Music lovers can listen to Wichita's premier high school bands playing familiar tunes and church choirs singing patriotic melodies. There's also bluegrass, jazz, country, and blues, each adding its special touch to the festival atmosphere.

The excitement of the aquatic events crests on the Arkansas River as spectators overflow the banks to watch a barefoot waterski tournament, canoe race, raft race, rowing regatta, and—a highlight for many—the antique bathtub race.

Then there's the resounding finale: the Twilight Pops Concert featuring the Wichita Symphony Orchestra. Thousands of people watch and listen as F-4 Phantom jets streak across the evening sky, church bells toll, and cannons boom their climactic thunder to Tchaikovsky's *1812 Overture*. Fireworks light up the sky, casting a brilliant glow over the city, as its people and their guests share the pleasure of this wonderful community celebration, the Wichita River Festival.

Oh, about the buttons! For a $1 donation to Wichita Festivals, Inc., you can enjoy all seventy-plus events at the Wichita River Festival. In return for your donation, you receive a colorful button that you can wear as a symbol of your support. The board of directors states, "A festival is an expression of the lifestyle of a community and its people: of their past, present, and promise. Each year at the Wichita River Festival, we relive our past aboard a barge crossing the Big Arkansas, in the outdoor legend of Windwagon Smith, and in the streets of the old town section of our city. Our present and our promise is in you, the $1 River Festival Button buyer. When you wear the button, you support the Wichita River Festival. You make it happen!" This festival is a fine example of the diversity and the enthusiasm of community festivals, rewarding to volunteers and spectators alike.

The first recipe is the contribution of Kathleen Kelly, the lifestyle home economist of the *Wichita Eagle-Beacon*. She is a popular writer, well known throughout the area for her column and her features on food.

WHOLE WHEAT BREAD

SPONGE:

2 cups lukewarm water

2 envelopes dry yeast, regular or quick rise

2 tspn. salt

2 Tbspn. sugar

2 cups white flour (bleached or unbleached)

½ cup water

⅓ cup butter, margarine, or shortening

⅓ cup honey, molasses, or sorghum

5–6 cups whole wheat flour

Prepare the sponge in a large bowl. Place the 2 cups lukewarm water in bowl and sprinkle in yeast, salt, and sugar. Stir with wire whisk or electric mixer until yeast dissolves. Add flour and beat with whisk or mixer until mixture is smooth. Cover with plastic wrap and towel and set in a warm spot until light and bubbly, 30 minutes to 1 hour.

Meanwhile, combine the ½ cup water, butter, margarine, or shortening, and honey, molasses, or sorghum in a small saucepan or glass measure; heat on stovetop or in microwave until butter, margarine, or shortening is almost melted; stir and cool to lukewarm. When the sponge is bubbly, add the butter-honey mixture and stir. Stir in whole wheat flour 1 or 2 cups at a time, using a heavy wooden spoon, a hand-held mixer, or a stand mixer with dough hooks. The dough should be somewhat sticky, but soft and workable. Turn out on a smooth surface lightly dusted with white or whole wheat flour, and knead until

smooth and bouncy, about 10 minutes.
Place dough in a warm, greased bowl,
turning to coat entire surface. Cover
loosely with plastic wrap and a towel.
Let rise in a warm spot about 1 hour, or
until doubled in bulk. Turn dough out
on work surface and divide into 3
portions for pan loaves (or portions
desired for loaves or rolls). Knead
lightly, cover with towel, and let rest for
10 minutes. Shape as desired and place
in pans. Cover lightly with plastic wrap
and let rise until pan loaves reach tops of
pans or other shapes are puffy, about 30
minutes. Bake in preheated 350° F
oven 20–45 minutes or until loaves
sound hollow when tapped. Baking time
will vary according to size and shape of
loaves or rolls. If soft crust is desired,
brush with melted butter or margarine
while warm. Makes 2 standard whole
wheat pan loaves.

From the creator:

Wheat is the heart of Kansas agriculture,
the grain that makes us the "wheat state"
and the "breadbasket of the world."

While white bread—from the bakery
or homemade—is a nutritious . . . food,
emphasis in recent years has been on
whole-grain breads for the fiber they bring
to our diets. They also add color, texture,
and old-fashioned goodness to our meals.

In my experience, many home bakers
are reluctant to prepare whole-grain
breads because mixing can be tricky and
they take a little longer to rise. Mixing mis-
takes come when too much flour is added.
The dough should be somewhat sticky
when kneading begins, and care should be
used not to knead in too much extra flour.

To speed rising, use a "sponge." This
sounds very culinary, but in fact it is just a
simple mixture of yeast, flour, and water.
The yeast gets growing in this mixture
so that it has the head start needed to set
the whole wheat flour mixture to rise. This
method is an excellent one for the beginning bakers to use.

The dough can be shaped into pan loaves, french-style loaves, round loaves, dinner rolls, or cinnamon rolls.

Kansas farmers, millers, and bakers (both professional and amateur) take great pride in the "staff of life." In their behalf, I invite you to share the pleasure and pride of baking.

The following recipes come from a most unusual woman, Lucia Jenney, a superb local cook who enjoys cooking for friends and who delights in preparing and donating the food for a large list of local cultural, civic, and church affairs. Much of the produce comes from the garden tended by her husband, surgeon Charles Jenney.

Several years ago Lucia, a former River Festival Button chair, dropped by the office a few days before the festival opened. She says, "They were so stressed out, they couldn't decide what they wanted for lunch. I offered to bring something in the next day so they wouldn't have to worry."

This sublime state of affairs has continued, and for ten days each May, this is the best-fed festival staff in the world. Lucia says she just loves to cook, and can't understand people who say it is boring. She gets lots of thanks, some of them out of the ordinary. "Someone I had cooked for came out and gave me a hot air balloon ride. How many people can say they have gone up in a balloon right from their own front yard?"

CHICKEN CASSEROLE

8 oz. wide noodles

2 whole chicken breasts, poached, boned, and cut in ½-inch pieces

2 cans artichoke hearts, quartered

1 can cream of mushroom soup

1 can cream of chicken soup

1 soup can of sour cream

½ cup broth or wine

⅓ cup Parmesan cheese

Preheat oven to 350° F. Boil noodles and put on bottom of 9-inch-by-13-inch casserole. Mix the rest of the ingredients except cheese; arrange on top of the noodles, sprinkle cheese on top, and bake 1 hour or till hot and bubbly.

REUBEN CASSEROLE

reheat oven to 350° F. Mix together sauerkraut, onions, and sour cream and spread in 9-inch-by-13-inch casserole. Shred corned beef and place on sauerkraut mixture. Sprinkle Swiss cheese on top of meat. Top with broken or crumbled *fresh* rye bread pieces. Dot with butter and bake for 30 minutes.

1 lb. drained sauerkraut

½ cup chopped onions

1 cup sour cream

1½ lb. sliced corned beef

3 cups grated Swiss cheese

Rye bread

Butter

CHICKEN TACOS

auté onion in oil for 5 minutes; add tomatoes for 2 minutes; add chicken, mix well, and set aside to cool.

Microwave tortillas in their package, about 6 at a time, until soft and flexible, about 30–60 seconds.

Place 1 Tbspn. meat mixture at one end of each tortilla, and roll the tortilla. Fry in hot oil, flap side down, until golden, then turn over and fry other side. Drain and serve with sour cream, Salsa, and Guacamole.

Salsa: Mix all ingredients.

Guacamole: Mash avocado and add some of the Salsa to taste.

1 medium onion, chopped

1 tablespoon oil

2 tomatoes, chopped

1 (4-lb.) chicken, boiled with onions, carrots, celery, and salt for flavor (bone and shred chicken when cold)

3 pkg. (12 each) corn tortillas marked *soft* on packages—these work best

1 inch of oil, for frying

Sour cream

SALSA:
1 onion, chopped

2 tomatoes, chopped

1 jalapeño pepper or less (to taste), finely chopped

2 Tbspn. cilantro, chopped

Juice of 1 lemon or more, to taste

1 clove garlic, minced fine

Salt or chicken bouillon to taste

Pepper to taste

TACO SALAD

1 lb. cooked hamburger

1 medium onion, diced

2 tomatoes, chopped

1 #2 can Mexican-style pinto beans

1 cup shredded Cheddar cheese

1 cup Russian dressing

1 lb. lettuce, broken for salad

1½ cups cheese-flavored nacho chips

Mix all ingredients except for the last 2. When ready to serve, toss with lettuce and nacho chips.

Oxnard's fruitful annual event, the California Strawberry Festival, combines an incredible array of arts and crafts with exciting entertainment, a strawberry blonde competition, pie-eating contests, and specially created strawberry dishes. The festival is located in the beautiful Marina resort at Channel Islands Harbor. It is sponsored by the City of Oxnard and produced by Terry Pimsleur & Company.

These recipes were created by a well-known amateur chef, Dennis Allison. Kate Allison is his talented daughter, and she sometimes works with him.

CALIFORNIA STRAWBERRY FESTIVAL
OXNARD, CALIFORNIA, EARLY MAY

STRAWBERRY FENNEL SEA BASS

In this dish the flavor of the strawberries blends and contrasts with the fish and its cream sauce, to provide an unusual and pleasant effect.

Slice the strawberries into thin, even slices.

Finely dice the vegetables and sauté slowly in olive oil, until soft. Add fish and cook slowly until the fillets are barely cooked through. Remove fish to a warm platter.

Over high heat, add Pernod and wine and reduce the liquid to 3 Tbspn. Allow to cool briefly and add cream. Add salt and pepper to taste, strain sauce, and dress the fish with the sauce.

To serve, place a layer of strawberries on top of the fish. Garnish the platter with any remaining strawberries. The strawberries are an integral part of this dish, not merely a garnish. The intent is to have a mixture of strawberry, cream fennel sauce, and fish in every bite.

Serve with boiled new potatoes and a green vegetable such as broccoli or green beans.

1 box very ripe, large strawberries

1 bunch green onions

1 small head fennel

1 small carrot

Small amount of olive oil

4 fillets of sea bass or other oily white fish

1 Tbspn. Pernod

¼ cup white wine

¼ cup heavy cream

Salt and pepper to taste

CHICKEN CURRY WITH FRESH STRAWBERRY CHUTNEY

STRAWBERRY CHUTNEY:

1 small onion

1 lime

1 small apple

1 clove garlic

1 small hot chili, seeds and membranes removed

1/4 cup chopped ginger root

3/4 cup brown sugar

1/4 cup raisins

1/4 cup sultanas

3/4 cup cider vinegar

1/4 tspn. salt.

1/2 cinnamon stick

1/8 tspn. coriander seed

1/8 tspn. mustard seed

2 cloves

1 box fresh strawberries

1 fresh pineapple

CHICKEN CURRY:

3 onions

1 pint yogurt

2 tspn. grated ginger root

Toasted and crushed poppy seeds

2 cloves garlic

1 Tbspn. good quality curry powder

A few grinds of black pepper

12 chicken thighs

1 Tbspn. lemon juice

The central theme of this dish is an unusual chutney which, unlike most, is made with fresh, uncooked fruits. Like all chutneys, it provides a counterpoint to the other flavors in the dish.

Strawberry Chutney: Medium-dice onion, lime, and apple. Finely dice garlic, hot chili, and ginger root. Add all remaining chutney ingredients except strawberries and pineapple and simmer until fruits are tender. Cool.

Clean and dice strawberries and dice an equivalent quantity of pineapple. Blend with the chutney mixture to make a thick mélange.

Chicken Curry: Start the day before. Make a marinade by mixing 2 of the onions, finely chopped, yogurt, ginger root, poppy seeds, 1 of the cloves of garlic, crushed, curry powder, and black pepper. Cover the chicken with this mixture and refrigerate overnight. The next day allow the chicken mixture to reach room temperature. In a casserole with a tightly fitting lid, sauté the remaining onion and garlic clove, finely diced, then add the chicken and its marinade. Bring it to a boil, then turn down the heat and simmer covered until done (25–30 minutes). Add the lemon juice to get a bright yellow color.

Serve the Strawberry Chutney with the Chicken Curry, plain or saffron rice, and a leafy green vegetable. Serves 6.

MICROWAVE STRAWBERRY UPSIDE-DOWN CAKE

This easy-to-make dessert is quick, looks good, and tastes great.

Use a glass pie pan. Generously butter the bottom and sides. Slice the strawberries about ⅛-inch thick and cover the bottom and sides of the pan in an attractive pattern. Sprinkle berries with the 1 Tbspn. of sugar, heat jelly until it is liquid, and drizzle onto berries.

Cream butter and the ½ cup of sugar together, add egg. Add dry ingredients, milk, and aromatics. Mix until blended.

Pour batter into pie pan. Cook the cake for 9 minutes on medium, stopping and rotating the cake 90° every three minutes. Then cook the cake for 4 minutes on high. (Microwave cooking times will vary depending upon the particular microwave unit used.) Allow the cake to remain in the microwave oven for an additional 5 minutes or so to set.

While the cake is still warm, unmold onto a large serving plate. (Place the plate on top of the cake, then flip it over. Sometimes a sharp rap on one edge is necessary to release the cake onto the serving plate.) Serve slices with sweetened whipped cream.

Butter, for greasing pie pan

1 box strawberries

1 Tbspn. sugar

2 Tbspn. red currant jelly

¼ cup butter

½ cup sugar

1 egg

¼ tspn. salt

1 tspn. baking powder

1 cup flour

⅓ cup milk

¼ tspn. almond extract

¼ tspn. vanilla

Sweetened whipped cream, for topping

The Indy 500 is one of the grand spectacles of America, eagerly anticipated by millions. Countless kids—and more than a few parents—dream of one day being there as the engines roar and the race is on.

For those living in the Indianapolis area, there's much more fun and excitement than the television viewers ever know. The 500 Festival Associates, Inc. (a nonprofit civic organization that does not produce the actual five-hundred-mile race), thinks of the Indianapolis 500 Festival as the city's annual party. Each year more corporations, businesses, and individuals are joining forces to produce a growing number of events.

Each festival begins with the preliminary selection of thirty-three princesses, who will be honored guests at all 500 Festival events. This day-long event takes place in late February; in March the queen and four members of her royal court are selected at a coronation pageant, which has grown to be so popular that it is televised.

One of the most popular events is the 500 Festival Mini-Marathon, the largest of its kind in the nation. It actually begins in late February, with a maximum of 7500 partici-

INDIANAPOLIS 500 FESTIVAL

INDIANAPOLIS, INDIANA, LATE MAY

pants embarking on a thirteen-week training and information program designed to prepare them to finish the race, as well as to aid in their long-term running and walking programs. The Mini-Marathon takes place on the Friday of Memorial Day weekend, as contestants run the official 13.1-mile course from the Circle in downtown Indianapolis to the finish line on the track at the Indianapolis Motor Speedway.

In early May the Mayor's Breakfast kicks off the month of special events with a distinguished guest speaker and gala entertainment. Attending are mayors from across the state, local and state government officials, the 500 Festival board of directors, and visiting celebrities. Following the breakfast all guests join a caravan (complete with police escort) to opening day ceremonies at the Indianapolis Motor Speedway.

Carburetion Day, on Thursday before the race weekend, honors those important people behind the drivers. The chief mechanics and crews of the thirty-three qualified cars are greeted by the queen, her court, and the princesses (that's a total of thirty-three young women, remember) at this picnic party. A pit-stop contest and tours of the garage area are included for guests.

On Friday, in a moving and beautiful event, time is taken out of the busy festival weekend to observe the real meaning of Memorial Day. Preceded by a band concert, the memorial service honors those Indiana men and women who gave their lives in the service of our country. The 74th Army Band performs, and Gold Star mothers and many other groups lay wreaths in honor of the dead.

On Saturday of Memorial Day weekend, the 500 Festival Memorial Parade delights more than 400,000 people in downtown Indianapolis, and is internationally televised to more than 30 million viewers. The parade typically features more than twenty-eight floats and bands, sixty-five-foot balloons, Indy 500 drivers, and many nationally known celebrities, all reflecting the theme of the festival for that year. There is reserved seating for about 41,000 people; tickets go on sale in early April.

The Indianapolis 500 Festival recipes were contributed by members of the board of directors and their spouses. Jo Hauck, executive director and one of the "first ladies" of the festival world, says, "I asked that they send recipes that they use during the month of May, knowing how very busy everyone here is at that time." I think you will agree that no one needs to brown bag it in Indianapolis in May.

PEA AND PEANUT SALAD

Mix all ingredients except peas and refrigerate. Add peas an hour before serving. Serves 6–8.
by Sharon H. Weedman

3 celery ribs, chopped

6 green onions, chopped

1 cup salted red Spanish peanuts with skins

⅓ cup mayonnaise

2 Tbspn. Italian salad dressing

1 (10-oz.) pkg. frozen peas

CHEESECAKE CUPCAKES

5 eggs

3 (8-oz.) pkg. cream cheese

1 cup sugar

1 tspn. vanilla

TOPPING:

1 cup sour cream

¾ cup sugar

¾ tspn. vanilla

Preheat oven to 300° F. Beat eggs into cream cheese, one at a time. Beat sugar and vanilla into the mixture. Pour in muffin cups. Bake for 40 minutes. Cool 5 minutes. Mix Topping ingredients, frost cupcakes, and bake an additional 5 minutes.

These cupcakes may be frozen.

From the kitchen of
Gloria Riggs

CRAB MEAT SPREAD

12 oz. cream cheese, softened

2 Tbspn. mayonnaise

2 Tbspn. Worcestershire sauce

1 tspn. lemon juice

1 small onion, minced

1 garlic clove, minced

½ bottle (or 6 oz.) chili sauce

1 (6½-oz.) can crab meat, drained and minced, or 6½ oz. frozen crab meat, thawed

Lemon juice

Pepper

Parsley, chopped

Blend cream cheese, mayonnaise, Worcestershire sauce, the 1 tspn. lemon juice, onion, and garlic. Spread in shallow serving dish. Spread chili sauce over cream cheese mixture. Top with crab meat and sprinkle with lemon juice, pepper, and parsley.

Serve with your favorite crackers. Serves 10–12.

by Verletta King

MARINATED BEEF TENDERLOIN

Rub tenderloin with butter and wine. Let tenderloin sit in marinade 2–3 hours. Bake at 400° F for 25–30 minutes, no longer. Cool and slice thin. Discard juice. Mix together oil, tarragon vinegar, dry mustard, dry horseradish, and salt. Pour over sliced tenderloin. Refrigerate overnight. Arrange on serving tray and garnish with mushrooms, onion, olives, and lemon. Serve with a dish of sour cream on the side. Perfect for entertaining, because it is all done the night before!

by Karen Hebert

5 lb. beef tenderloin

Butter and wine for marinade

¾ cup cooking oil

½ cup tarragon vinegar

¼ tspn. dry mustard

1 tspn. dry horseradish

1 tspn. salt

½ lb. mushrooms, sliced

1 onion, sliced

24 stuffed olives

Lemon, sliced

Sour cream

PORTUGUESE TOAST (RABANADAS)

Mix together milk, the 2 Tbspn. of sugar, and port wine.

Fold in the egg whites, beaten until they hold a peak, then add the egg yolks, well beaten, and continue beating the mixture until it is smooth.

Soak the French bread in the mixture, brown the slices on both sides in heated butter or oil, and drain them on absorbent paper.

Blend the 2 cups of sugar with cinnamon and a pinch of salt, and sprinkle the mixture on the bottom of a wide baking dish. Add the sautéed bread and sprinkle the slices of bread with the remaining spiced sugar. Keep warm in oven until ready to serve.

by Bill Carr

2 cups milk

2 Tbspn. sugar

2 Tbspn. port wine

3 eggs, separated

8 slices French bread

Butter or oil

2 cups sugar

2 Tbspn. cinnamon

Pinch salt

CINNAMON LOAF CANDY

2 cups sugar

1 cup coffee cream

2 Tbspn. butter

1 Tbspn. vinegar

½ tspn. cream of tartar

1 tspn. vanilla

⅔ cup pecans, broken up

Cinnamon

Boil sugar, cream, butter, vinegar, and cream of tartar until mixture forms a soft ball in cold water (234° F–238° F). Add vanilla and let cool until barely warm. Add pecans and beat until mixture hardens. Divide into 4 or 5 parts. Make into rolls and roll each one in cinnamon. Let sit in cool place until solid, then slice. Enjoy!
by Joyce Parke

500 CHICKEN

8 boneless chicken breasts, skinned

6 Tbspn. butter

¼ cup vermouth (dry)

2 cups sour cream

8 oz. blue cheese

1½ Tbspn. Worcestershire sauce

3 small garlic cloves, crushed

¼ cup chopped black olives

Preheat oven to 350° F. Brown chicken in butter in heavy skillet about 4 minutes per side. Brush 9-inch-by-13-inch baking dish with butter from skillet. Transfer chicken to baking dish. Deglaze skillet with vermouth and reduce to 2 Tbspn. of liquid over medium heat. Combine sour cream, blue cheese, Worcestershire sauce, garlic, and reduced vermouth in bowl. Spoon mixture over chicken and bake until juices run clear, approximately 50 minutes. Garnish with black olives and serve over rice, for black-and-white presentation. Makes 6 servings.
by Ellen Frist

500 FESTIVAL POPPY SEED CAKE

Soak poppy seeds overnight in the ¾ cup milk. Preheat oven to 350° F. Mix sugar and butter. Sift dry ingredients and add alternately to butter mixture with the ½ cup milk. Add vanilla and soaked poppy seeds. Fold in egg whites. Bake 25 minutes.

Custard Filling: Mix all ingredients except nuts and cook in a double boiler until thick. Cool. Add nuts. Spread between cake layers.

Frosting: Boil corn syrup and pour slowly into beaten egg whites, while continuing to beat. Add vanilla. Frost cake.

Optional: Decorate with chocolate race car and a checkered flag or two!

by Mrs. Dale Scott (Mary Jane)

¾ cup poppy seeds

¾ cup milk

1½ cups sugar

1½ cups butter

2 cups flour

2 tspn. baking powder

½ cup milk

1 tspn. vanilla

3 egg whites, stiffly beaten (save yolks for Custard Filling)

CUSTARD FILLING:

½ cup sugar

1 cup milk

3 egg yolks

1 Tbspn. flour or more, to make desired thickness

1 cup chopped walnuts or pecans

FROSTING:

1½ cups white corn syrup

2 egg whites, beaten

1 tspn. vanilla

RASPBERRY WALNUT TORTE

1¼ cups flour

⅓ cup powdered sugar

½ cup butter, softened

2 (10-oz.) pkg. frozen red raspberries, thawed

¾ cup chopped walnuts

2 eggs

1 cup sugar

½ tspn. salt

½ tspn. baking powder

1 tspn. vanilla

SAUCE:

1 cup water

Reserved raspberry liquid

¾ cup sugar

4 Tbspn. cornstarch

2 Tbspn. lemon juice

Preheat oven to 350° F. Combine 1 cup of the flour with powdered sugar and butter and blend well. Press into bottom of 9-inch-by-9-inch pan. Bake for 15 minutes. Cool. Drain raspberries; reserve liquid for Sauce. Spoon berries over crust; sprinkle with walnuts. Beat eggs with sugar in small bowl until light and fluffy. Add the remaining ¼ cup flour, salt, baking powder, and vanilla; blend well. Pour over walnuts. Bake for 30–35 minutes until golden brown. Cool. Cut into squares. Serve with ice cream and Sauce.

Sauce: Combine water, raspberry liquid, sugar, and cornstarch in a pan. Cook, stirring constantly, until thickened and clear. Stir in lemon juice. Cool.

by Jackie Morris

WINNER'S CIRCLE PIE

¼ cup butter

1 cup sugar

3 eggs, beaten

¾ cup light corn syrup

1 tspn. vanilla

¼ tspn. salt

½ cup chocolate chips

½ cup black walnuts, chopped

2 Tbspn. bourbon

Unbaked deep-dish pie shell

Preheat oven to 375° F. Cream butter and sugar. Add eggs, light corn syrup, vanilla, and salt. Add chocolate chips, walnuts, and bourbon. Stir well. Pour into pie shell. Bake for 40–50 minutes. May be served warm or cold.

by Helen Schatzlein

Celebrating the delicious harvest of Sonoma County berries, the Jumbleberry Jubilee in Santa Rosa turns Fourth Street into a berry patch full of outstanding arts and crafts, with garden cafés, street performers, continuous entertainment, and a fabulous array of berry treats. It was started just two years ago by the Downtown Santa Rosa Development Association, and is produced by Terry Pimsleur & Company.

These recipes were created by Mary Bettencourt, a resident of Half Moon Bay, California, who is a well-known local cook and recipe developer.

JUMBLEBERRY JUBILEE IN SANTA ROSA
SANTA ROSA, CALIFORNIA, EARLY JUNE

STRAWBERRY POPPY SEED PIE

Combine graham cracker crumbs, ¼ cup of the sugar, and melted butter. Press mixture firmly into the bottom and sides of a 9-inch pie plate. Refrigerate while preparing the filling.

In the top of a double boiler, combine another ¼ cup of the sugar, gelatin, salt, and poppy seeds. Gradually stir in milk or cream. Cook over hot (not boiling) water until mixture thickens and gelatin is dissolved. Pour small amount of hot mixture into beaten egg yolks. Mix well and stir egg yolk mixture into remaining hot mixture. Cook, stirring constantly for 2 minutes. Remove from heat and stir in vanilla. Cool until mixture mounds slightly. Beat egg whites with cream of tartar until soft peaks form, and gradually add the remaining ½ cup sugar, beating until stiff peaks form. Fold cooled poppy seed mixture into egg whites. Set aside. Arrange the sliced strawberries over the

1¼ cups graham cracker crumbs

1 cup sugar

6 Tbspn. melted butter

2 Tbspn. unflavored gelatin

¼ tspn. salt

⅓ cup poppy seeds

2 cups milk or cream

4 eggs, separated

2 tspn. vanilla

¼ tspn. cream of tartar

2 cups sliced strawberries

½ cup sweetened whipped cream, for garnish

Whole strawberries, for garnish

crust. Spoon the poppy seed filling over the strawberries. Chill at least 4 hours or overnight. Before serving, garnish with whipped cream and whole strawberries. Makes 10–12 servings.

STRAWBERRY CAKE ROLL

3 eggs, separated

1 cup sugar

1 tspn. vanilla

¼ cup water

¾ cup sifted flour

1 tspn. baking powder

¼ tspn. salt

Powdered sugar

1 pint strawberries, washed, hulled, and sliced

2 cups whipped cream, sweetened to taste

CREAM CHEESE FILLING:
6 oz. cream cheese

1 cup powdered sugar

4 Tbspn. butter

1 tspn. vanilla

Preheat oven to 375° F. Beat egg yolks until very light and fluffy, and gradually beat in sugar. Add vanilla and water. Sift together flour, baking powder, and salt; stir into egg mixture. Beat egg whites until stiff peaks form. Carefully fold into first mixture. Spread onto a greased 15-inch-by-10-inch-by-1-inch pan lined with waxed paper that has also been greased. Bake for 15–20 minutes or until done. Loosen edges and turn out on towel sprinkled with powdered sugar. Carefully peel off waxed paper. Trim off stiff edges. While still hot, roll up cake and towel together. Cool on cake rack. Unroll and spread with Cream Cheese Filling; top with sliced strawberries. (Save 6 strawberry halves for garnish.) Roll up cake and frost with whipped cream. Garnish with reserved strawberries. Refrigerate until time to serve. Makes 8 servings.

Cream Cheese Filling: Cream together all ingredients.

STRAWBERRY CHEESE SOUFFLÉ

2 pints strawberries

Sugar to taste

½ cup almond-flavored liqueur

1 lb. ricotta cheese

Mash, hull, and slice strawberries. Add sugar to taste and the almond-flavored liqueur. Cover and chill while preparing soufflé.

Preheat oven to 375° F. For the soufflé, combine ricotta cheese, sugar, 3 eggs plus 1 yolk, flour, bread crumbs, and vanilla. Beat until well mixed. Beat the remaining egg white until stiff but not dry. Then carefully fold the beaten egg white into the cheese mixture. Pour into an 8-inch buttered soufflé dish. Bake for 45 minutes or until golden brown and edges begin to pull away from dish.

Cool about 2 minutes on a rack, until soufflé begins to fall. Loosen with a knife and invert onto a large serving dish with a deep rim.

Sprinkle with almonds and dust with powdered sugar. Surround with the strawberries, reserving some. Serve warm, cut into wedges. Top each serving with some of the reserved strawberries. Serves 8.

½ cup sugar

4 eggs (1 egg separated)

2 Tbspn. flour

3 Tbspn. dry bread crumbs

1 tspn. vanilla

½ cup chopped almonds, toasted

Powdered sugar

The Union Street Festival Arts and Crafts Fair, a Victorian garden party, opens the street festival season in San Francisco. Featured are arts and crafts, an uphill writer's race, a fashion show from Union Street boutiques, and a tea dance to big band sounds. Jugglers, clowns, and puppeteers amuse and entertain the crowd. Food is a prominent part of this festival, as garden cafés feature fine California wines accompanying gourmet foods.

The Union Street Association sponsors this event, which is produced by Terry Pimsleur & Company.

This recipe is contributed by the Blue Light Café, 1979 Union Street, San Francisco, California.

UNION STREET FESTIVAL ARTS AND CRAFTS FAIR

SAN FRANCISCO, CALIFORNIA, EARLY JUNE

BLUE LIGHT CAFÉ'S CHICKEN FAJITAS

4 chicken breasts (approximately 8 oz. each)

1 medium red bell pepper

2 medium green bell peppers

1 large white onion

Corn oil, for sautéing

1 lime

1 dozen flour tortillas

Guacamole

Sour cream

Salsa

MARINADE:

1 cup corn oil

¼ cup white wine

¼ cup soy sauce

2 cloves chopped garlic

Salt and pepper to taste

Skin and bone the chicken breasts and cover with the Marinade. Refrigerate for 2–6 hours. Core the red and green bell peppers; slice peppers and white onion into ¼-inch strips. Sauté the peppers and onion in corn oil—do not overcook. Grill the marinated chicken breasts over high heat or charcoal for approximately 3 minutes each side. Chicken should not be overcooked, but springy to the touch. Slice into ¼-inch strips. Combine chicken with onion and bell pepper mixture in a large iron skillet. Squeeze lime over the mixture and serve in warmed flour tortillas. Serve with guacamole, sour cream, and salsa.

Marinade: Mix all ingredients.

For more than a quarter of a century, the town of Clarkson has been celebrating the heritage of its founders with the Czech Festival, three days of fun, frolic, and wonderful food.

A pork barbecue supper starts the festivities on Friday afternoon with rock and country bands entertaining, followed by a polka concert, talent contest, and square dance.

On Saturday and Sunday the entertainment begins at 1 P.M. with the playing of the Czech national anthem. There are a number of dancing groups of all ages, most featuring the polka and other Czech dances; there's also a maypole dance. The entertainment is continuous and varied, from trick roping and magic acts to an accordion concert.

Saturday begins with a coed softball tournament. Polka bands perform during the afternoon and evening, and there is a polka street dance until the wee hours of Sunday morning.

CZECH FESTIVAL
CLARKSON, NEBRASKA, MID-JUNE

On Sunday several area churches hold special services, notably a Czech folk service at New Zion Presbyterian and a Polka Mass at SS. Cyril and Methodius Catholic Church. Later there is a ten-year reunion and a horseshoe tournament. The street parade takes place at 5 P.M., followed by more entertainment and another street dance.

The Clarkson Women's Club art fair is open all weekend in the Opera House, where members of the club also demonstrate the culinary arts of preparing strudels, poppy seed doughnuts, listy, kolaches, horn rolls, and other traditional foods.

The Clarkson Historical Museum offers another cultural opportunity. Many fine art objects that were brought from Czechoslovakia are on display here, along with exhibits on the history of Clarkson.

Czech dinners are available from 11 A.M. to 3 P.M. on Saturday and Sunday. The Commercial Club also has an open-air stand serving their famous buchta sandwich—slices of lean pork with Swiss cheese and sauerkraut—and other Czech and American food.

Czech-American Recipes was compiled by the GFWC Women's Club for their 1986 centennial celebration and contains fine traditional recipes. This small book is dedicated "to the loving memories of our Great-Grandmothers, Grandmothers and Mothers, who diligently and faithfully preserved our heritage." The women are now at work on another cookbook; you may want to add both to your collection of specialty recipes. Information is available from Diane Uher, President, GFWC Clarkson Women's Club, Box 414, Clarkson, NE 68629. (This festival is a member of Nebraska Events.)

KOLACHE–CESKE KOLACE

2 pkg. dry yeast

¼ cup sugar

1½ cups lukewarm milk

5 cups flour

2 beaten eggs

1 Tbspn. salt

½ cup lard, melted and cooled

1 cup mashed potatoes (unsalted)

In a large bowl dissolve yeast with two Tbspn. of the sugar, ½ cup of the lukewarm milk, and 1 cup of the flour. Mix together, cover with a cloth, and allow to rise in warm place until bubbly—about 10 minutes. Add eggs, salt, remainder of sugar, lard (reserve some to brush on dough and then on baked kolache), potatoes, and remainder of milk. Beat well and gradually add remainder of flour, mixing well after each addition. Cover and set in warm place, and let rise until double in bulk. When dough is light place on floured bread board and cut off pieces to make balls the size of medium-sized eggs, and place on well-greased baking pan about 1 inch apart. Brush tops with melted lard. Allow to rise in warm place till double in bulk. In center of each bun, make an indentation and fill with prepared filling (recipes follow). Allow to rise about 15 minutes. Bake in 375° F–400° F oven until golden brown, approximately 12–15 minutes. Remove from oven and brush with lard. Remove kolache from pan and place on bread board. Cover with cloth and allow to cool completely. Store in tight container. Makes 3 dozen.

What is better than a good cup of coffee and a kolache!

COFFEE MADE WITH EGG

25 cups water

25 tspn. coffee grounds

1 egg

2–3 more Tbspn. water, if needed

Bring to boil, in a large kettle, the 25 cups of water. Measure the coffee grounds into a 3-cup bowl, break a raw egg into the coffee, and stir. If rather dry add the 2–3 Tbspn. water. When water is boiling add the coffee-and-egg mixture

gradually, stirring, and stir for 2–3
minutes. Then boil slowly until foam
disappears. Allow to set for 10 minutes.
Strain into a coffee pot and stir. Delicious!

COTTAGE CHEESE FILLING– TVAROH

Mash cottage cheese with potato masher. Add the other ingredients and stir all ingredients together. (Do not prepare until ready to use.)

A heaping tspn. of prune filling is very good on top of this filling. Spread with a spoon.

1 lb. dry curd cottage cheese

¼ tspn. salt

1 egg yolk

½ cup raisins

⅛ tspn. cinnamon

¾ cup sugar

½ tspn. vanilla (or lemon flavoring)

CHERRY FILLING– POVIDLY TRESENE

Sprinkle sugar over cherries. Allow to set while dough is being prepared. Especially good as pie filling.

1 can pitted red sour cherries, drained

½ cup sugar

STREUSEL TOPPING

Rub ingredients together until crumbly.

⅓ cup flour

⅓ cup sugar

3 Tbspn. butter

POPPY SEED FILLING– MAKU POVIDLA

½ cup seedless raisins

Water, enough to cover raisins

1 can prepared poppy seed filling

1 Tbspn. butter

2 Tbspn. brown syrup

¼ cup sugar

Crushed sugar cookies, if necessary, for thickening

Chopped nuts, if desired

Rinse raisins in a saucepan. Then cover with water, simmer until almost dry. Combine raisins, poppy seed filling, butter, brown syrup, and sugar. (If necessary to thicken, add crushed sugar cookies and, if desired, chopped nuts.)

CELESTIAL CRUSTS–LISTE

5 egg yolks

1 Tbspn. melted butter or margarine

Pinch of salt

6 Tbspn. rich milk

2 cups flour, more or less, to make stiff dough

Fat for frying

Powdered sugar, for sprinkling on top

Mix ingredients except for powdered sugar, roll thin, cut in squares, make small slashes in centers, and deep fry in fat. Sprinkle each with powdered sugar.

MAHOGANY CHIFFON CAKE

¾ cup boiling water

½ cup cocoa

¾ cups sifted cake flour

1¾ cups sugar

1½ tspn. baking soda

Preheat oven to 325° F. Combine boiling water and cocoa and let cool. Sift together flour, sugar, baking soda, and salt. Make a well in the flour mixture and add oil, egg yolks, cooled cocoa mixture, and vanilla. Beat until smooth. Then measure egg whites and

cream of tartar into large mixing bowl
and beat until very stiff.

Pour flour-and-egg yolk mixture over
entire surface of egg whites, gently
cutting and folding in with a rubber
spatula until blended. Pour into
ungreased 10-inch tube pan. Bake for
65–70 minutes. Let cool. Do not
underbake.

1 tspn. salt
½ cup corn oil
8 unbeaten egg yolks
2 tspn. vanilla
1 cup egg whites (usually 8)
½ tspn. cream of tartar

FROSTING–POLEVA

Beat butter or margarine on high
speed of electric mixer until light
and fluffy. Gradually add confectioners
sugar, vanilla or milk or cream, and egg
white, beating on medium speed. If
frosting is too thick for spreading, add
evaporated milk, a teaspoon at a time.
Frosts a 2-layer cake.

For chocolate frosting, add 3 squares
melted unsweetened chocolate.

This is a very good frosting. It will
keep in the refrigerator, in a tightly
covered container, for 3 weeks or more.

⅔ cup butter or margarine, softened
6 cups sifted confectioners sugar
1 tspn. vanilla, milk, or cream
2 Tbspn. egg whites (or 1 small egg)

MORAVIAN CABBAGE

Drop cabbage into 2 cups boiling
water. Add 1 of the diced onions
and the caraway seeds. Simmer 10
minutes. Sauté remaining onion in bacon
grease. Blend in flour; continue cooking
and stirring until browned. Add salt,
sugar, vinegar, and 1 cup cabbage water,
stirring to make sauce.

Drain cabbage. Add flour mixture and
bacon. Simmer 20 minutes.

1½ lb. cabbage, shredded
2 onions, diced
½ tspn. caraway seeds
½ cup bacon grease, from the frying of the bacon (below)
⅓ cup flour
Salt to taste
4 tspn. sugar
⅓ cup vinegar
4 slices bacon, diced and fried

91

W ith the North Beach Fair, the North Beach Chamber of Commerce continues the tradition of the Upper Grant Street Fair, which started in 1954. This revived event features arts and crafts, a literary fair, and an Italian art exhibition, to the musical accompaniment of rhythm and blues. Wine and Italian gourmet foods are featured. There are contests to establish the best of North Beach foods, including pizza, calzone, gnocchi, bread, gelato, Italian cake, cappuccino, and, for a touch of eclecticism, fortune cookies!

These two recipes are the works of art of Dennis Allison, a notable amateur chef who lives in San Francisco.

NORTH BEACH FAIR
SAN FRANCISCO, CALIFORNIA, MID-JUNE

OSSO BUCO
SAN FRANCISCO

VEAL:

4 veal shanks cut into 2½-inch lengths

8 thin slices pancetta

Olive oil

SAUCE:

1 carrot

1 medium onion

2 small stalks celery with leaves

A little olive oil, for sautéing

½ cup white wine

1 cup tomato sauce

2 sprigs fresh thyme or ½ tspn. dried thyme

1 bay leaf

1 stalk fennel (sweet anise), finely chopped

T his is a traditional Italian veal dish. The aromatic braising sauce thickens during the cooking process, heightening and enhancing the flavor of the veal. The ingredients listed here are for 4 servings.

Wrap and tie the veal shanks in the pancetta slices. Brown over medium heat in olive oil. Remove to a plate while preparing the vegetables.

Preheat oven to 300° F. Finely dice the vegetables and sauté them in a little olive oil in the same pan in which the veal was browned. Add wine and reduce over high heat until only a couple of tablespoons of liquid remain, then add ¼ cup of the tomato sauce, the herbs, fennel, and salt and pepper. Choose a casserole that will just contain the veal shanks sitting upright. Place the vegetable-tomato sauce on the bottom of the casserole, and then add the browned veal shanks, removing the strings. Add the remaining tomato sauce until the level of liquid is at the middle of the shanks. Bring to a simmer on the top of the stove, then bake covered for 45 minutes. Uncover and cook for an additional 30 minutes, basting every 10 minutes with the sauce in the casserole. In the meantime prepare the Gremolata Garnish by finely chopping the chervil or parsley, garlic, and lemon rind.

To serve, use white plates. Serve 1 shank, 2 pieces, to each person. Dress with the Sauce and top with the Gremolata Garnish. Pass additional Gremolata Garnish. Serve with polenta and a green vegetable for color and flavor contrasts. Ideal vegetable choices would be rapini (a kind of bitter Italian broccoli), broccoli, kale, red or green Swiss chard, or Italian beans. A robust red wine goes well with this dish.

Salt and pepper

GREMOLATA GARNISH:
4 Tbspn. chervil or parsley

2 cloves garlic

1 tspn. lemon rind

GARLIC PASTA WITH RED AND GREEN SAUCE

This is a garlic lover's delight. Fresh pasta with a subtle garlic flavor is coated with two sauces, one red and the other green, each perfumed with the flavor of garlic.

Pasta: Mix the eggs, olive oil, water, salt, and pressed garlic together. Put the flour on a pasta board, make a hole in the center, put egg-mixture in the hole, and incorporate into a dough. Knead for about 10 minutes or until smooth and elastic. Allow it to rest in the refrigerator for 30 minutes.

Roll out into sheets using a pasta machine, and then cut to the desired width. The shape of the pasta should match your mood.

Bring 4 quarts of lightly salted water to a rolling boil. Add pasta and cook until al dente, about 5 minutes. Drain. Return

PASTA:
2 eggs

1 tspn. olive oil

1 Tbspn. water

½ tspn. salt

2 cloves garlic, pressed

1¾ cups flour

RED SAUCE:
1 onion

1 carrot

½ Japanese eggplant

1 stalk celery

1 small stalk fennel, finely chopped

1 clove garlic, finely chopped

1 slice pancetta

½ tspn. dried basil

½ tspn. dried oregano

¼ tspn. red pepper flakes

Salt and pepper, to taste

1 cup tomato sauce

1 bay leaf (preferably European)

GREEN SAUCE:

1 stalk broccoli (about 2 lb.)

Handful of spinach leaves

1 onion

1 clove garlic

Olive oil

Salt and pepper to taste

CHEESE GARNISH:

Dry Asiago cheese

to the cooking pan and dress with a small quantity of the cooking liquid and a little butter or olive oil.

Red Sauce: Cut all the vegetables into fine dice (⅛-inch cubes). Sauté them in olive oil until tender. Add fennel, garlic, pancetta, and seasonings, except for bay leaf; saute 1–2 minutes more. Add tomato sauce and bay leaf. Simmer over very low heat for 20 minutes to meld the flavors.

Green Sauce: Italian broccoli (rapini) is preferred, but ordinary broccoli will serve. Clean and chop the broccoli into uniform pieces and steam in a small quantity of water. When barely done remove from heat, and stop its cooking by plunging it into cold water. Drain. Steam the spinach until it is just limp, and then plunge it into cold water. Drain.

Meanwhile, sauté the onion and garlic in a little olive oil until translucent. Do not let the garlic or the onion burn. Put the broccoli, spinach, onion, and garlic into a blender and puree to make a thick sauce. Turn out sauce into a saucepan. Add salt and pepper.

Serve pasta in shallow bowls; decorate with a large spoonful of Red Sauce, a large spoonful of Green Sauce, and a small handful of freshly shredded Asiago cheese.

"**V**alkommen!" say the hospitable folk of Stromsburg, a town otherwise known as the Swede capital of Nebraska. For nearly forty years they've been celebrating midsummer with gusto, good food, and good times at the Swedish Festival.

During the two days of the festival, there are parades, dances, an air show, a variety of free entertainment, a midway, and special exhibits and displays of crafts.

The festival emphasizes all things Swedish. An honorary Swede is named, a king and queen are crowned, and Swedish costumes are worn. Visitors can enjoy performances by Swedish dancers or browse through a Swedish craft shop with authentic local and imported articles for sale.

For the athletically inclined, there is a 10K as well as a Fun Run, horseshoe-pitching contests, and a mud volleyball contest. Special games are planned for children.

SWEDISH FESTIVAL
STROMSBURG, NEBRASKA, MID-JUNE

Free camping is provided (available only if you arrive early) in Stromsburg's beautiful Buckley Park, south of the city, which also has a picnic area, and tennis, baseball, basketball, swimming, and playground facilities.

The three major events of this festival feature food. On Friday night local businesspeople and farmers join forces to offer a chicken barbecue, enjoyed by several thousand people. Both Friday and Saturday the Women's Civic Improvement Club operates a Swedish coffee shop called Grandma's Kitchen, serving all sorts of Swedish goodies. And on Saturday there is an incomparable smorgasbord, which gets more popular each year. It has already outgrown two previous locations and is now served at two seatings in the high school gym. For twenty-five years a group of volunteers, led by Mrs. Donald Rystrom, has served an awe-inspiring assortment of authentic Swedish food; the menu, printed in English and Swedish, fills two pages, and the smorgasbord women boast that they serve "nothing but the best, and plenty of it."

Swedish Festival is a member of Nebraska Events. The following recipes are taken from *Food Favorites*, a nice down-home cookbook that has been updated and republished every few years since its first edition in 1965. Order from Mrs. Donald Rystrom, Box 411, Stromsburg, Nebraska 68666. Income from the smorgasbord and the cookbook goes to various community improvement projects. The dedicated volunteers say "Tack sa mycket" (Thanks so much).

PICKLED SALT HERRING- INLAGD SILL

3 large salt herring

DRESSING:
1 cup white vinegar (or more)

½ cup sugar

½ cup chopped or sliced onions

3 bay leaves

12 whole peppercorns

GARNISH:
Dill or chives

Clean fish, removing head, and soak 8–12 hours. Bone and fillet. Cut in thin strips crosswise. Arrange like whole fish on glass plate or place in glass jar. Mix ingredients for dressing, pour over herring. Garnish with dill or chives.
by Mrs. Donald Rystrom

SILL SALAD-SILLSALLAD

4 medium potatoes, cooked

1 bunch carrots, cooked

1 bunch beets, cooked, or 1 can beets

1 good-sized raw onion

2 salt herring (soak onion and herring overnight)

Sliced hardboiled eggs

Chop all vegetables. Skin and bone and grind the herring. Mix well, let stand for several hours. Serve with hardboiled eggs as garnish.
by Mrs. Ralph Larson

ROSETTES-STRUVOR

1 Tbspn. sugar

2 eggs, slightly beaten

1 cup milk

1 cup flour

¼ tspn. salt

1 tspn. vanilla or lemon extract

Add sugar to eggs, and then add milk. Sift flour before measuring, and then, together with salt, stir into first mixture and beat only until smooth (about the consistency of heavy cream). Add flavoring. Fry in rosette iron as directed below. When cool, dust with powdered sugar.
Hints: Do not use electric mixer. Flour

and milk may be well beaten, and then blended with slightly beaten eggs. Blisters on rosettes indicate eggs have been beaten too much. If iron or fat is not the correct temperature, either too hot or too cold, batter will not adhere to the forms. If your rosettes are not crisp, the batter is too thick and should be diluted with milk. For extra nice rosettes, allow batter to stand 2 hours, covered in refrigerator, before frying.

Use of rosette iron: Place at least 4 inches shortening in deep fryer and heat to 375° F. Immerse rosette forms in fat until thoroughly heated. Lift iron out, shaking off excess fat, and dip into prepared batter. Dip only to depth of the form, not over the top of it. Dip forms back into the hot fat. When foamy bubbling stops or rosettes are a delicate brown, lift iron out of fat, allowing excess fat to drip off iron back into fryer, and remove the rosette cookies. It is usually necessary to give a tap on the top of each form with a wooden spoon to make cookie release. Continue cooling on paper toweling, open side down, so excess fat will run out. Reheat iron as necessary in the hot fat before making more rosettes.

by Mrs. Donald Rystrom

FOR FRYING:
Oil or melted shortening

GARNISH:
Powdered sugar

OVEN PANCAKES—UNGPANKAKA

Preheat oven to 400° F. Melt butter or bacon grease in two large pans, 9 inches by 13 inches. Mix remaining ingredients into a thin batter and pour into pans. Bake until batter puffs up in peaks. Cut in large squares. Serve with butter and syrup.

by Mrs. Myrtle Johnson and
Mrs. Dana Shostrom

4 Tbspn. butter or bacon grease with fried bits of bacon

4 well-beaten eggs

2 cups milk

1 cup flour

Sprinkle of salt

2 tspn. sugar

PEPPARKAKOR

3½ cups flour

1 tspn. baking soda

1½ tspn. ginger

1½ tspn. cinnamon

1 tspn. cloves

¼ tspn. ground cardamom

2 tspn. grated orange rind

½ cup butter or margarine

¾ cup sugar

1 egg, unbeaten

¾ cup light molasses

Blanched almond halves, 1 for each cookie

Sift together flour, baking soda, spices, and orange rind. Cream butter or margarine with sugar, add egg and molasses, and then mix in dry ingredients. Cover and chill overnight.

Preheat oven to 375° F. Roll out ⅓ of dough at a time, to ⅛-inch thickness. Cut into desired shapes with cookie cutter. Place blanched almond half in each center. Bake for 10 minutes.

by Mrs. L. O. Graves and
Mrs. Myron G. Johnson

RYE BREAD–LIMPA

1 pkg. dry yeast

4 cups warm water

11–12 cups sifted white flour

1 cup sorghum

¼ cup melted lard

2 cups sifted rye flour

1 Tbspn. salt

1½ Tbspn. seasoning mixture of anise, fennel, and caraway seeds, ground

Dissolve yeast in water. Let stand 5 minutes. Add 2 cups of the white flour and sorghum to make a sponge. Beat until smooth and let rise in warm place until bubbly. Add the rye flour and remaining white flour, salt, and seasoning and mix well. Turn out on floured board and knead until smooth and elastic, about 10 minutes, adding more flour if necessary. Put into greased bowl and let rise until doubled in bulk. Punch down and shape into 4 loaves. Let rise until doubled in bulk. Bake in preheated 375° F oven 50–60 minutes.

by Mrs. Leo Larson

SWEDISH MEATBALLS–
KOTT BULLAR

Mix all ingredients, form into meatballs, and fry in skillet. When brown, pour on some water and let simmer until cooked through.

by Mrs. Lavelle Lamoree

1 lb. lean ground beef

½ lb. ground pork

1 raw potato, ground

1 egg

¾ cup bread crumbs

½ tspn. pepper

1 tspn. salt

1 small onion, minced

3 Tbspn. milk

CHEESE CUSTARD–OSTLADA

Preheat oven to 350° F. Beat eggs slightly, add salt, stir until well mixed. Gradually add milk, stir in grated cheese. Bake in shallow greased dish for 25–30 minutes or until a silver knife inserted in center comes out clean.

by Mrs. Myron G. Johnson

2 eggs

¼ tspn. salt or to taste

1⅓ cups rich milk

3 Tbspn. grated cheese

Walleye Weekend showcases the Mercury Marine National Walleye Tournament, with more than three hundred fishers participating in the competition. Walleye Weekend, produced by the Fond du Lac Convention and Visitors Bureau, welcomes visitors with great music, a variety of food specialities, exhibits, and more than forty special events. There is no admission charged for the entertainment, and there is fun for the whole family in Lakeside Park, the lovely four-hundred-acre park along Lake Winnebago.

Highlights include milk carton boat races, sporting dog shows, world championship lumberjack events, an art exhibit, a volleyball tournament, Familyland, and a Sports Olympics.

Water-related activities are a big draw, of course. There's a junior fishing tournament, MerCub boat demo rides, fishing clinics with the pros, boat exhibits, and the Midwest Invitational Sailboard Regatta.

The festival utilizes the vast resources of the beautiful Lakeside Park, located at the northern-most end of Main Street in Fond du Lac. There are more than one thousand camping sites

WALLEYE WEEKEND

FOND DU LAC, WISCONSIN, MID-JUNE

in the area, and visitors at Lakeside Park have easy access to shopping malls, boutiques, restaurants, and other area attractions.

One of the most popular events of the weekend is "the world's largest fish fry," prepared by Chef Ron Speich (assisted by the Lakeside Evening Kiwanis) and served to more than one thousand happy eaters.

An instructor in the restaurant and hotel cookery program at Moraine Park Technical College, Ron Speich is a graduate of the University of Wisconsin, Stout, and has a master's degree in hotel and restaurant management. He has worked in numerous restaurants during the past fourteen years. He offers us his famous fish fry recipe, along with some how-to and how-not-to advice for preparing deep-fried fish:

> The three most common problems are batter not sticking to the fish, an oily taste, and rubbery batter. Once you understand basic procedures for deep-fat frying, you can easily make a delicious product: 1) The fish should not be frozen, and should be coated with seasoned flour before being dropped into batter; 2) the fish pieces should be the correct size; 3) the batter should be the proper consistency; and 4) the oil should be at the correct temperature.
>
> To make seasoned flour, mix flour with salt (or garlic salt), white pepper, and onion salt. Fish fillets should be no larger than 3 inches long and ¼ inch to ½ inch thick. The batter must be thin; if it is thick,

it takes longer for the fish to cook. Use a deep-fat frying thermometer to make sure the temperature is 350° F. It is important to use a batter mix that contains corn flour; it has a much better taste than regular flour and a yellow color that aids in the browning of the batter.

RECIPE FROM THE WORLD'S LARGEST FISH FRY

Combine flours, baking powder, and powdered milk and mix well. Add lemon juice. Beat eggs lightly, add water and beer, mix. Add liquid to dry ingredients to get a consistency a little thinner than that of pancake batter.

Heat oil in container deep enough so that fish will be totally submerged and will float easily. Temperature: 350° F.

Dust fillets with seasoned flour, dip into batter, allow excess to drain off before dropping into deep fat. As fish fries it will become golden brown. Do not drop too many pieces into the oil at one time; it is important that the temperature remain at 350° F.

1 cup corn flour (not cornmeal)

1 cup regular flour

½ Tbspn. baking powder

1 Tbspn. powdered milk

¼ tspn. lemon juice

2 eggs

2 Tbspn. water, plus 1½ to 2 cups beer, depending on consistency

Oil for frying

Flour seasoned with salt, onion powder, white pepper, and garlic powder, to taste

3 Tbspn. salad oil

A hush of anticipation settles over the crowd. There! Off in the distance . . . parade sirens echoing down Milwaukee's grandest avenue . . . the first strains of the marching bands. . . . One of the world's largest "people parades" is nearly here!

It's a celebration of Milwaukee and of Milwaukee's festival season, the season to enjoy cultures from every corner of the world. And you are there, enjoying a cast of thousands, as celebrities, costumed dancers and musicians, and colorfully clad clowns march before you.

The City of Festivals Parade means marching bands from all over the world. And plenty of fun. It means jugglers and roller skaters, high-wheeling bicyclists, cartoon heroes, funny cars, and, of course, fabulous floats—all offered up free.

And most of all it means a certain spirit. A spirit of friendship, of togetherness. It's the spirit of Milwaukee, a city known for its rich cultural and ethnic traditions. And the City of Festivals Parade is a mighty, moving spectacle that you won't want to miss, in a great place on a Great Lake.

The City of Festivals Parade was initiated in 1983 by Mayor Henry W. Maier to honor Milwaukee's strong cultural and ethnic heritage.

CITY OF FESTIVALS PARADE

MILWAUKEE, WISCONSIN, LATE JUNE

The parade officially opens the summer season, and is a salute to Milwaukee celebrations such as Summerfest, Rainbow Summer, Festa Italiana, Germanfest, Afrofest, Irishfest, Festa Mexicana, Polishfest, Holiday Folk Fair, and many others.

The parade is organized and directed by several hundred dedicated community volunteers and sponsored by civic-minded individuals and businesses. In 1985 a float competition was begun among Milwaukee's three engineering schools, Marquette University, the University of Wisconsin, and the Milwaukee School of Engineering. A 5K run along the parade route also was started that year.

A weekend of events begins with the parade kick-off luncheon on Friday. On Saturday a 5K run takes place along the parade route, which is already lined with spectators, most of them picnicking and waiting for the 3 P.M. parade start. In the evening crowds move on to the nearby Summerfest grounds for a full evening of free entertainment, featuring national and international bands, musical groups, and ethnic dancers, topped off with a gigantic display of fireworks. What a wonderful way to open the summer season in Milwaukee, the "festival capital of the world."

Parade-goers have learned all sorts of ways to pack tasty food and drink for curbside consumption during that long period between staking out a spot and cheering the first band. Three veterans share their tips and recipes with us.

MICKEY DOUCETTE'S TURKEY SALAD

Cut melon balls in refrigerator container and cover with French dressing; marinate 2 hours or overnight in refrigerator.

Combine melon balls with all remaining ingredients except lettuce. Serve on lettuce bed or in hollowed-out cantaloupe halves. Makes 6 servings.

Mickey Doucette's Turkey Salad can be chilled in the cantaloupe halves, wrapped in foil, and carried in a cooler for an unusual picnic treat.

1 whole cantaloupe, cut into melon balls

French dressing

2 cups cooked, cubed chicken or turkey

1 cup mayonnaise

1 Tbspn. grated onion

½ cup sour cream mixed with 1½ tspn. curry powder

1 tspn. salt

2 cups chopped celery

2 Tbspn. lemon juice

Lettuce, optional

MARGARET NELSON'S FIRESIDE SANDWICHES

Preheat oven to 350° F. Combine ham, cheese, onion, mustard, horseradish, and mayonnaise. Divide mixture evenly and spread on buns. Wrap buns individually in foil. Heat in oven for 20 minutes. Serve with pickle slices and tomato wedges. Makes 8 sandwiches.

Margaret Nelson says her family has always loved parades, and she learned that one good idea was to pack a lightweight ice chest with plastic bottles

2 cups finely chopped, fully cooked ham

1 cup shredded sharp cheese

2 tspn. grated onion

2 tspn. prepared yellow mustard

½ tspn. horseradish

2 tspn. mayonnaise

8 hamburger buns

filled with frozen liquids. "These aren't as messy as ice cubes, but are just as effective in keeping food and drinks chilled." Fireside Sandwiches are a family favorite. They can be served hot in cold weather, by wrapping them in foil and then in newspapers and rubber bands or insulated bags. (In summer, pack them on ice.)

BARBARA CLAYBAUGH'S FROTHY ORANGE COOLER

1 (6-oz.) can frozen orange juice

3 (6-oz.) cans water

2 Tbspn. powdered sugar

1 egg

1½ cups crushed ice

ombine all ingredients in a blender container; whip until smooth and frothy. Makes about 4 servings.

Barbara Claybaugh, the parade's executive director and a parade expert, knows how thirsty folks can get: she recommends making her thirst-quenching Frothy Orange Cooler. It can be frozen, taken along, shaken up, and then served in its own container.

For nearly twenty years a small army of dedicated volunteers has staged this wonderful mid-America festival, the Fourth of July Festival, which entertains more than 300,000 people during five days, culminating in a grand celebration of Independence Day.

There's a real commitment to the family on the part of the festival organizers. They want everyone to take part, so they have imaginative events for all ages and interests.

One of the biggest draws, attracting both participants and spectators in increasing numbers, is the rodeo. A three-day event sanctioned by the international professional association for rodeo cowboys, it is the second largest in the country. It is sponsored and produced by the Edmund Roundup Club, which offers money and trophies. Contestants, both men and women, come from about thirty states and a number of foreign countries to partici-

JULY FOURTH
FESTIVAL
EDMUND, OKLAHOMA, EARLY JULY

pate. Serious rodeo events are interspersed with entertainment such as trick roping.

For those who want to combine a different sort of horsepower with a whole lot of brain power, the road rally is the choice. Anyone may enter, in any vehicle, and so far they've had everything from Model Ts to Maseratis. The driver and navigator must decipher about 125 clues and cover about 55 miles; last year seventy-five vehicles were involved, and this year they are expecting more than three hundred.

Golfers are offered a tournament with prizes, including a hole-in-one contest with a new car as first prize. In 1990 a pro-am tournament will be introduced, with two days of pro-am activity and a four-day pro tourney.

Park activities for children of all ages include bull frog jumping (BYOF—bring your own frog), a largest bubble bubblegum contest, and a greased pole contest, with the crew of the local fire department placing a $20 bill on top of each of four poles, which they keep well greased. The technique for climbing the pole includes a dunking in the creek and then rolling in sand, to offer some friction. (The parents must be a patient lot.)

Everyone enjoys the fiddling contest, horseshoes, and other games. There is a wide variety of entertainment on stage, including spots for inspired speakers to make patriotic speeches. Local officials are present to pull the plug if and when the remarks become political. And there is free watermelon in the park, all you can eat.

The town population is 62,000, but more than 150,000 people come to the parade. There are about 250 parade units involved, with many units having as many as 30 separate parts. Shriners and other organizations appear in the parade, and a growing number of entries are made up of families, friends, and other groups who get bitten by parade fever, build their own floats, make their own costumes, and strut. This is the only place in the state to see the wonderful big balloons made famous in the Macy's Thanksgiving Day Parade. Commercial and noncommercial floats compete for numerous awards. One of the most popular marchers in the parade is a huge Brahma bull named Tall Man, who is believed to be the only tame Brahma in the country; he is also present at other events, and folks can climb on his back and get photos made.

On July 4 the activity in the park begins at 5:00 P.M. There is a variety of entertainment until dusk, when a community choir sings a program of patriotic songs, parachutists bring in the flag, and the choir sings the national anthem; the "bombs bursting in air" signal the beginning of a spectacular fireworks show.

The recipes offered here are favorites of some of the people who are involved with the festival.

MALT SHOP PIE

1 pint vanilla ice cream

½ cup crushed malted milk balls

2 Tbspn. milk

1 (9-inch) graham cracker pie crust

3 Tbspn. instant chocolate-flavored malted milk powder

3 Tbspn. marshmallow topping

1 cup whipping cream

Additional crushed malted milk balls

In a chilled medium bowl, stir ice cream to soften. Blend in the ½ cup crushed malted milk balls and 1 Tbspn. of the milk. Spread in graham cracker pie crust and freeze. Meanwhile, in medium mixing bowl, combine the malted milk powder, marshmallow topping, and the other 1 Tbspn. milk. Add whipping cream. Whip until soft peaks form. Spread mixture over layer in crust. Freeze several hours or until firm. Sprinkle with additional crushed malted milk balls before serving. Makes 8 servings.

TROUT WITH ORANGE-RICE STUFFING

Preheat oven to 350° F. In a medium saucepan combine the celery, orange juice, onion, butter, lemon peel, lemon juice, water, and salt. Bring to a boil. Add long grain rice and cover saucepan. Reduce heat and simmer the mixture about 20 minutes, or until the long grain rice is tender. Remove from heat. Add orange pieces and almonds to rice mixture, stirring lightly until combined. Stuff each fish cavity loosely with about ⅓ cup stuffing. Place fish in a 13-inch-by-9-inch-by-2-inch baking dish. Brush fish with cooking oil and cover with foil. Bake for 30 minutes or until fish flakes easily when tested with a fork. Use two large spatulas to transfer fish to serving platter. Serves 6.

½ cup finely chopped celery

3 Tbspn. orange juice

2 Tbspn. finely chopped onion

2 Tbspn. butter

½ tspn. shredded lemon peel

1 Tbspn. lemon juice

½ cup water

½ tspn. salt

¼ cup long grain rice

1 medium orange, sectioned and coarsely chopped

¼ cup toasted chopped almonds

6 (5-oz.) fresh or frozen pan-dressed trout, heads removed

2 Tbspn. cooking oil

CARAMEL CORN

Preheat oven to 250° F. Mix brown sugar, corn syrup, salt, and butter. Bring to boil, stirring constantly. Boil for 5 minutes. Remove from heat. Add baking soda and vanilla. Pour over popcorn in a large casserole or pan and bake for 1 hour, stirring every 15 minutes.

Keep popped corn in a warm oven until ready to use.
by Doris Conley

2 cups brown sugar

1 cup corn syrup

1 tspn. salt

1 cup butter

½ tspn. baking soda

1 tspn. vanilla

6 qt. popped corn

TOMATO SOUP CAKE

½ cup shortening

1½ cups sugar

2 eggs, well beaten

1 tspn. baking soda

2 Tbspn. water

2¼ cups sifted flour

½ tspn. ground cloves

1 tspn. cinnamon

1 tspn. baking powder

1 can tomato soup

1 cup nuts

½ cup raisins

Preheat oven to 350° F. Cream shortening; add sugar and eggs. Add baking soda, dissolved in water. Sift 2 cups of the flour with spices and baking powder. Add alternately with tomato soup. Add nuts and raisins, dredged in the ¼ cup remaining flour. Bake in bundt pan for about 1 hour.

by Doris Conley

CEVICHE

3 lb. small to medium shrimp

Juice of 6–8 large limes

½ cup salad oil

1 tspn. dry basil

1 tspn. dry tarragon

2 medium onions, chopped*

6–8 jalapeño slices*

2–3 Tbspn. jalapeño juice*

2 Tbspn. Tabasco*

*These ingredients may be varied to your taste. If you don't want it hot, then leave them out, but always use a little onion. The end result still tastes great, but is not hot.

Bring water to rolling boil, then boil shrimp for 1 minute. Take off heat, and place shrimp in cold water immediately; the cold water will stop all cooking. Peel shrimp.

Place peeled shrimp in large nonreactive pan or pot. Mix in all other ingredients, and add enough water to cover. Place in refrigerator, with or without lid, for 18 hours. Drain liquid *but save it*, as you may want to use it later. The lime juice will cook the shrimp perfectly. Some people don't boil the shrimp, but it is easier to peel them if you do.

Serve cold with crackers.

If you have shrimp left over, cover them with some of the liquid that you have saved, and put them in the refrigerator. The leftovers will keep approximately 1 week.

by Peter L. Scott and Paul J. Kessler

The folks in Lawrence, Kansas, make this promise of Independence Days: "Good old-fashioned family fun with a nineteenth-century flair!" Nearly a decade of smart planning, attention to historical detail, and the hard work of more than five hundred volunteers have combined to make good the claim.

Two days and two nights of festivities in Burcham Park, on the shores of the Kansas River, feature activities for all ages, historical exhibits, entertainment, and a crafts show that includes an old-fashioned auction of turn-of-the-century crafts. Canoe races, river rides, and historical sidewalk tours are balanced by the Sheep-to-Shawl contest and the Milk-a-Goat event.

An unusual experience is a visit to the Mountain Fur Men Campsite. There a fire glows welcomingly while dulcimer players serenade passersby with soft, sweet sounds. Magicians and roving entertainers mingle with the crowd, and one night features a spectacular fireworks display on the levee across the river, in honor of Independence Day.

INDEPENDENCE DAYS

LAWRENCE, KANSAS, EARLY JULY

A big part of the event's "nineteenth-century flair" comes from the demonstrations of authentic crafts of the period. Watch the blacksmith work in the shade of the century-old cottonwood trees that line the riverside, and then enjoy the woodworker carving traditional art objects or observe wheat weavers as they handcraft unusual decorations. All craftspeople and volunteers are encouraged to wear period clothing.

Special attention is paid to children, with creative crafts workshops, puppet shows and other entertainment, pony rides, traditional relays and contests, fence painting, and a petting zoo, all there especially for them.

No July 4 celebration would be complete without a parade. Lawrence's features the traditional bands, dignitaries, elected officials, and clowns, as well as some added attractions: the Best-Dressed Dog and Most-Decorated Bike contenders, for example, and a number of antique carriages.

Independence Days organizers have focused on history to create some unusual events. As part of the Tent Show, visitors have watched a reenactment of the 1890s women's suffrage debate. At the League of Women Voters' Front Porch Politics forums, they've had a chance to discuss current issues with political figures. And those who'd rather avoid politics altogether have taken up their mallets and had a civilized game of croquet instead. But without a doubt the special event that stamps the authentic American heartland seal on this festival is the watermelon seed–spitting contest!

The following recipes have been developed by various groups and organizations specifically for the festival. All the food, representative of the Midwest at the turn of the century, is prepared and served outdoors in Burcham Park, which is nestled in a grove of 100-year-old cottonwood trees on the shores of the Kansas River.

COOK'S PORK SKINS

An historical art alive in Kansas, this process is *not* recommended for amateurs, and should *not* be done indoors.

The Cooks use a large cooking kettle, to allow enough space for the skins to expand properly.

Heat cooking oil to 360° F. Cut pork skins into small squares. Carefully add approximately four cups of skins to the oil, stir constantly while cooking for 16 to 18 seconds. When the pork skins have tripled in size, lift out, drain carefully, then remove to a table to cool before serving or packaging. They may be served plain or with barbecue sauce.

by Harold and Muriel Cook

COOK'S HOMESTYLE HICKORY RIBS

½ tspn. each chili powder, thyme, paprika, garlic salt, and onion salt

½ tspn. pepper (optional)

¼ cup Worcestershire sauce

1 Tbsp. cider vinegar

Beef shortribs

Barbecue sauce

Combine spices and sprinkle over ribs, rubbing in well. Mix together Worcestershire sauce and cider vinegar. Place ribs in marinade and refrigerate overnight.

Use a smoker-type grill cooker with a vented cover, small hickory wood chunks and charcoal. Soak hickory chunks in water for one hour. Prepare charcoal in cooker, and add presoaked hickory chunks when the coals are hot. Place ribs on the wire grill, and adjust smoke vent so that meat cooks at a very low temperature (approximately 170° F) for 5 to 6 hours. The meat should be turned periodically, and basted with the marinade, diluted with ½ cup water. During the final hour, increase heat, adding barbecue sauce just before ribs are done. Also serve sauce with ribs at the table.

by Harold and Muriel Cook

HOMEMADE ROOT BEER

A thirst quencher for the nostalgic is this specialty from the Church of Jesus Christ of Latter-Day Saints.

Stir extract, water, and sugar in large container. Add 2 lb. of dry ice, crumbled, mix well, and serve with NO ice in the glass. Add more dry ice as needed to maintain carbonation. Makes 5 gallons of ice-cold root beer.

Note: Handle dry ice with care always. Ask at the ice company where you buy ice for further information.

2 oz. Hires Root Beer Extract

4 gallons water

4 lb. sugar

10 lb. dry ice

FUNNEL CAKES

O ne of the most popular vendor foods nationwide is served by the Reorganized Church of Jesus Christ of Latter-Day Saints.

In a skillet, heat ¾ inch salad oil to 370° F, using deep-fat thermometer to check temperature frequently. With wire whisk, mix well flour, milk, baking powder, salt, and egg. Hold a narrow-spouted funnel (½-inch spout) with one finger closing spout, and pour scant ¼ cup batter into funnel. Over hot oil, carefully remove finger and allow batter to run out in a stream, making a spiral about 6 inches in diameter. Fry 6 to 8 minutes until golden brown, turning

Salad oil

1 cup plus 2 Tbspn. all-purpose flour

¾ cup milk

1 tspn. double-acting baking powder

Dash of salt

1 egg, beaten

Confectioners sugar

Maple syrup

once with tongs. Drain well on paper towel. Stir batter before making each fritter. Serve with sugar or maple syrup. Makes 6 cakes.

BUFFALOBURGERS!

Cook patties over a hickory fire, about 2 minutes each side, turning only once. Serve on a bun, topped with barbecue sauce and accompanied by an ear of fresh sweet corn and baked beans. Everyone will enjoy a very lean sandwich.

Buffalo: a funny-looking North American animal related to an oxlike Old World animal of the family Bovidae. It often has curved horns and lots of hair, which are not edible. We find buffalo in Kansas, Nebraska, and Colorado; we caution you against the Colorado, which (depending on the time of year) may have a nasty taste. Meat packers provide the buffalo in round patties about 4 inches in diameter, weighing between one-quarter and one-third pound.

BBQ TURKEY DRUMSTICKS AND CORN IN THE HUSK

TODAY, Inc. stands for Teenagers of Douglas County and You. In addition to working in construction and maintenance all year, these kids can feed hundreds of happy eaters. Here is their recipe for feeding a large crowd:

We use an open barbecue pit that measures 7 feet by 4 feet by 3 feet, made of cinder blocks with iron grates. We get a hot, flameless wood fire going. Remember to have oven mitts, long tongs for turning, and plastic squirt bottles of water to put out any flames over 6 inches high.

To serve about 1500 people: 1500 turkey legs (approximately one pound each) and 90 dozen ears of corn, in the husk. (Get more corn if you think everyone will want an ear.)

Place 80 drumsticks on the grates; watch them carefully and turn continually. Look out for flame flare-ups. After about an hour of careful turning, you have perfectly smoked turkey drumsticks; add barbecue sauce just before serving. We use K. C. Masterpiece BBQ Sauce.

Place corn, in the husks (about 4 dozen ears at a time), along the outer edges of the grates and cook, turning frequently, until the husk turns slightly brown on all sides. Peel the husk back and you have a perfectly roasted ear of corn. Don't forget the butter and salt.

CARRIE NATION PEACH COBBLER

The women of the Xi Gamma chapter of Beta Sigma Phi serve this for the perfect finish to an outdoor feast.

Filling: Drain peaches, reserving juice, and place in a 9-inch-by-12-inch pan. Mix brown sugar, cornstarch, salt, lemon juice, almond extract, and ⅔ cup of the reserved juice; pour over fruit. Dab butter over all.

Crust: Preheat oven to 350° F. Mix ingredients with fork until moist. Place between layers of wax paper, and roll out to size of 9-inch-by-12-inch pan.

FILLING:

7 cups peaches (2 2½-lb. cans)

1 cup brown sugar

¼ cup plus scant 1 Tbspn. cornstarch

¼ teaspoon salt

4 tspn. lemon juice

½ tspn. almond extract

½ cup butter

CRUST:

1¾ cup flour

1 tspn. salt

½ cup oil

3 Tbspn. cold water

Sugar

Cinnamon

Cover fruit mixture with crust, and sprinkle crust with sugar and cinnamon. Bake for about one hour, until golden brown.

HOMEMADE ICE CREAM

2 eggs, beaten

Pinch of salt

1 cup sugar

2 Tbspn. vanilla extract

½ pint whipping cream

1 can sweetened condensed milk

½ gallon milk (approximately)

Mix first six ingredients in order given. Place in freezer container, and add milk to fill line. Churn till frozen. Makes one gallon.

On July 4, 1961, Victor Jory led the first WSB-TV "Salute 2 America" Parade down Peachtree Street. The theme that year was patriotism, and the red, white, and blue celebration has since become a tradition, America's largest regularly scheduled Independence Day parade.

The parade is produced entirely by WSB-TV, as a way of demonstrating its pride in being part of the North Georgia community for more than forty years.

Like a number of other events, the parade began as a response to a negative situation. An Atlanta television reporter produced a documentary on the presence, or rather absence, of the American flag in Atlanta. "The flag just didn't fly over Atlanta," he said. "In fact, you would have been surprised at the places the flag didn't fly."

Two WSB-TV staff members decided that it was time Atlantans did a little flag-waving. Jean Hendrix, then director of special events and public relations, and producer Guy Waldron (best known as the creator of "The Dukes of Hazzard") launched the parade, which has grown into a major midsummer event for hundreds of thousands of Georgians.

SALUTE 2 AMERICA PARADE (WSB-TV)

ATLANTA, GEORGIA, JULY 4

Although the two originators have gone on to other activities, the parade has flourished and grown. The current parade coordinator, Don Whiteley, has brought to the event participation of more international-class musical units and an emphasis on the enhanced appearance of the floats that are such an important part of a parade. As a well-known consultant and judge for numerous parades and band events in the United States and other countries, Whiteley has the experience that makes it possible to put on a spectacular special event. From high-school marching bands and nationally ranked drum and bugle corps to bands of the United States military, the groups who play in this parade are outstanding.

Beautifully decorated floats, dazzling specialty groups, and a host of marching musical units from all over the United States, Canada, and abroad are joined by mammoth character balloons. Elaborate and colorful floats carry local and national celebrities, political figures, and lovely beauty pageant winners. Some of the stars who have appeared in past years are John Wayne, Bob Hope, Burt Reynolds, Carol Channing, and Roy Clarke.

Beginning at the CNN Center at the Omni Hotel at 1 P.M., the parade follows its traditional 1.4-mile route up Marietta Street to Woodruff Park.

After a left turn onto famed Peachtree Street, the parade continues through downtown Atlanta to Ralph McGill Boulevard. More than 300,000 spectators line the parade route, while an estimated 200,000 viewers watch the live TV coverage, which starts at noon with pre-parade news. And for a wonderful two hours, not a toe is left untapped in Georgia!

The recipes in this section represent several aspects of the good food of the South. Georgia's Vidalia onions are becoming well known throughout the world for their superb flavor; only onions grown in a special area in and around Vidalia, Georgia, can be called by that name. Apples are another fine Georgia product. I've combined the two to make a savory side dish which goes well with pork, country ham, or turkey, also good Georgia products.

APPLES AND ONIONS

6 large, tart cooking apples

3 large Vidalia onions

1 cup brown sugar

¾ tspn. cinnamon

¼ tspn. nutmeg

1 tspn. ground cardamom

Pinch of salt

4 Tbspn. sausage or bacon fat, melted

Preheat oven to 350° F. Peel and core apples, peel onions, and cut in small chunks. Place in casserole. Mix together brown sugar, spices, and salt and sprinkle over apples. Pour melted fat over all. Cover tightly and bake for about one and a half hours. Uncover just before serving, and stir once to blend contents.

This is a very forgiving recipe: you may vary the amount and kind of apples and onions; you may experiment with white sugar, honey, or molasses; you may use butter or margarine instead of sausage or bacon fat; you may change, add, or delete most of the spices. But *you cannot leave out the cardamom!*

The recipe may be cooked several days ahead and reheated; this will enhance the flavor. And you may want to forget to mention "onions" until after it is tasted. But on a chilly day, this will scent your house and tease your taste buds. Just remember the cardamom.

PECAN PIE

A favorite Southern dessert is pecan pie. There are dozens of variations on the theme of crust, filling, and pecans: some recipes add chocolate, some add peanut butter, some "tart it up" with tarts topped with whipped cream. Our family favorite is this simple, classic, and delicious light version, given to me years ago by my Aunt Kitty, Catherine Yates Reynolds.

Preheat oven to 450° F. To keep the crust from getting soggy, prick it gently with a fork once or twice, brush it gently with whipped egg white, and put in oven for 3–5 minutes to set. Cool before adding filling mixture.

Reduce oven temperature to 350° F. Mix together remaining ingredients and pour into pie crust. Bake for about 30 minutes. It will take just a bit longer, but you need to watch so that the nuts don't burn. My mother, Maysie Beller, makes a super edition of this by doubling the amount of nuts!

Crust for single pie, unbaked ("short" pastry is best)

1 egg white, whipped

3 eggs

1 cup sugar

1 cup Karo Crystal syrup

4 Tbspn. butter

1 cup pecans

1 tspn. vanilla

CANDIED GRAPEFRUIT PEEL

One of the traditional Christmas specials in my family was this time-consuming but delicious citrus treat. When I was a child, I couldn't understand why we didn't have it more often. Since all my aunts were busy working women as well as fantastic cooks, I marvel at the quality and variety of food they served. Thanks to my aunt Carolina Yates Bojar for many fine recipes, and the patience in preparation.

Put grapefruit peel in a pan with water to cover and bring to a boil. Boil 15 minutes. Drain and cover with water

Peel from 1 grapefruit, pith removed, cut in thin julienne strips

½ cup sugar

Bittersweet chocolate (optional)

again. Boil 10 minutes. Drain and taste. If peel is not too bitter, it is not necessary to boil again; otherwise, boil 10 more minutes. Drain well.

Combine peel with sugar and ¼ cup water, and cook over high heat until the liquid has almost completely evaporated. Do not let sugar caramelize. Remove peel from pan, and drain on wire rack.

If you want to gild the lily, you can drizzle the candied peel, when cool, with melted bittersweet chocolate.

BARBA'S CHOCOLATE POUND CAKE

½ lb. butter
3 cups sugar
3 cups flour
6 Tbspn. cocoa
5 large eggs
1 cup sweet milk
2 tspn. vanilla
⅛ tspn. salt

For family gatherings and church bake sales, this cake has been the first choice for many years. My role model, inspiration, and mentor in the ways of good food has been my god-mother, my aunt Martha Yates Drew. This is only one of the hundreds of recipes that this remarkable lady, now in her nineties, has passed on to me. Like most of her "receipts," it is simple but marvelous.

Preheat oven to 325° F. Cream butter and sugar thoroughly. Sift flour and cocoa together. Beat eggs into sugar and butter one at a time. Add flour mxiture alternately with sweet milk. Bake in a large tube pan for one hour, or until cake leaves side of pan and is firm on top. This makes a large cake, and is very good.

The size and spirit of Seward's Fourth of July Celebration have earned it not only the title of Nebraska's Official Fourth of July City, but also the honor of being one of only four cities chosen as "star cities" during the 1986 centennial celebration of the Statue of Liberty.

The history of the event is a good example of grassroots patriotism. Back in 1967 there happened to be a big July 4 celebration that everyone enjoyed. The following year nothing special happened on the holiday. Three high school seniors were disappointed. They coordinated the first Fourth of July Committee and in 1969 presented special events and an Independence Day parade.

Now, many years later, the goal of the committee is still to provide families with a wholesome good time, mostly free of charge. Seward's Fourth of July Celebration draws a large crowd of visitors from the immediate area, and each year more visitors come from other states and even other countries. (One visitor from New Orleans called it an "extra-small Mardi Gras.") And appropriately, it seems, the current committee chair is Clark Kolterman, one of the three seniors who started the whole thing back in 1969!

FOURTH OF JULY CELEBRATION

SEWARD, NEBRASKA, EARLY JULY

These days the celebration begins at 7:00 A.M. with a community pancake breakfast. The day is filled with old-fashioned fun suitable for all ages. Events include a horseshoe-pitching contest, a men's slow-pitch round-robin tournament, and a competition of the Seward Volunteer Fire Department.

The area around Courthouse Square is filled with all sorts of activities and entertainment. There are dancers and singers representing various national and ethnic groups. Also popular are puppet shows and magicians. There is a large arts and crafts exhibit, with many demonstrations.

Representatives from more than sixty community groups take part in a grand parade that tops off the daytime festivities. When night falls a grand-stand show and a giant fireworks display end the celebration.

Seward's Fourth of July Celebration is a member of Nebraska Events, an organization whose members are involved in various civic and community special events. Members help and support each other in a variety of ways, including sharing their recipes.

FOURTH OF JULY MEXICAN PIZZA

1½ cups Bisquick baking mix

½ cup yellow cornmeal

½ cup cold water

1 lb. ground beef

1 (4-oz.) can whole green chilies, drained, seeded, and chopped

1 (1¼-oz.) envelope taco seasoning mix

¾ cup water

1 (16-oz.) can refried beans

1½ cups shredded Cheddar cheese

1 cup shredded lettuce

2 medium tomatoes, chopped

½ cup chopped onion

Taco sauce for topping, if desired

Preheat oven to 425° F. Grease 12-inch pizza pan. Mix Bisquick, cornmeal, and the ½ cup cold water until soft dough forms; beat vigorously 20 strokes. Pat into pan with floured hands, forming ½-inch rim. Bake 10 minutes. Cook and stir beef until brown; drain. Stir in chilies, taco seasoning mix, and the ¾ cup water. Heat to boiling, stirring frequently. Reduce heat. Simmer uncovered, stirring frequently until thickened, 5–10 minutes.

Spread beans over baked crust, top with beef mixture, and sprinkle with cheese. Bake 10 minutes longer. Top with lettuce, tomato, and onion. Serve with taco sauce if desired. Makes 6 to 8 servings.

A GOOD PIE CRUST RECIPE

2 cups flour

1 tspn. salt

⅔ cup Crisco

2 Tbspn. melted butter

5 Tbspn. cold water

1 Tbspn. vinegar

Mix flour and salt. Cut in Crisco and butter until mixture is like coarse crumbs. Add water and vinegar. Mixing with fork, form into ball and chill. Roll out to form two crusts. This is foolproof.
by Della Miers
Seward, Nebraska, Past Parade Chairman

PERFECT APPLE PIE

This pie is used for the July 4 Apple Pie Eating Competition held every year in Seward, Nebraska!

Preheat oven to 400° F. Pare apples and slice thin. Combine sugar, flour, spices, and salt. Mix with apples. Line 9-inch pie plate with pastry, fill with apple mixture, dot with butter, adjust top crust, sprinkle with sugar. Bake for 50 minutes or until done.

Red Hot Apple Pie: omit cinnamon and nutmeg in "Perfect Apple Pie." Combine 3 Tbspn. red cinnamon candies with sugar, flour, and salt.

by Della Miers

5 to 7 tart apples

¾ to 1 cup sugar

2 Tbspn. enriched flour

1 tspn. cinnamon

¼ tspn. nutmeg

Dash of salt

Pastry for 2-crust, 9-inch pie

2 Tbspn. butter or margarine

CHEESE SPARTA

Cut each piece of bread with doughnut cutter. Line the bottom of a 9-inch-by-13-inch pan with the bread with holes in it, and top this with layers of ham, cheese, and broccoli. Place cut-out circles of bread on top. Mix together the eggs, milk, and any dry mustard, and pour mixture into pan. Place in refrigerator overnight. Bake 1 hour at 350° F. Let stand for at least 5 minutes before cutting and serving. Serves 12.

This is a good recipe for a luncheon. It can be served with a fruit salad. It can be made the night before, leaving you with time to visit with your guests.

by Clark Kolterman, President
Nebraska Events, Inc., Seward, Nebraska

12 slices bread

2½ cups chopped ham

1 lb. chopped Cheddar cheese

1 pkg. frozen chopped broccoli, cooked enough that it breaks apart

6 eggs

6 cups milk

1 tspn. dry mustard

FORGOT STEW–
REMEMBER NEBRASKA

2 lb. beef stew (or round steak)

4 carrots, in chunks

4 potatoes, in chunks

2 stalks celery, coarsely chopped

1 large onion, quartered

1 green pepper, slivered

1 large (3½-lb.) can tomatoes

1 large (3½-lb.) can tomato juice

3 Tbspn. whole pearl tapioca

1 scant Tbspn. sugar

1 Tbspn. salt

Preheat oven to 300° F. If the stew will be in the oven all day, set it at 200° F.

Stir all ingredients together. Put in roaster with lid. *Do not lift lid until serving time.*

by Irma Ourecky, Vice-President
Nebraska Events, Inc., Nebraska Czechs of Wilber

J azz and All That Art on Fillmore was started several years ago to capture the essence of Fillmore Street in the heyday of jazz music. San Franciscans are invited to celebrate their jazz roots with three days of outstanding arts and crafts, gourmet food, fine California wines, and continuous musical entertainment in an outdoor setting. The festival is sponsored by the Fillmore Street Merchants and Improvement Association and produced by Terry Pimsleur & Company.

Zell Trippsmith is originally from Scotland and now lives in Jacksonville, Florida. She commutes to California frequently to create delicious food at local festivals.

JAZZ AND ALL THAT ART ON FILLMORE

SAN FRANCISCO, CALIFORNIA, EARLY JULY

CHICKEN ZELL

P reheat oven to 400° F. Cut cheese into 8 equal pieces. Cut chicken breasts in half and flatten. Roll chicken breasts around the cheese and secure with toothpicks. Dip in eggs and then bread crumbs, and brown in butter. Dissolve bouillon cube in boiling water. Sauté onion and green pepper in the ⅓ cup butter till tender. Add flour, seasonings, and dissolved bouillon and cook until thick. Sauté mushrooms in butter. Add mushrooms and rice to bouillon mixture. Pour into 8-inch-by-10-inch baking dish. Top with chicken and bake for 20 minutes. Garnish with fresh parsley.

1 lb. Cheddar cheese

4 whole chicken breasts, boned and skinned

2 eggs, beaten

¾ cup dried bread crumbs

Butter for browning chicken

1 chicken bouillon cube

1 cup boiling water

½ cup chopped onion

½ cup green pepper

⅓ cup butter

2 Tbspn. flour

½ tspn. salt , ¼ tspn. black pepper

¼ lb. fresh mushrooms

Butter for sautéing mushrooms

2 cups cooked white rice

1 cup cooked wild rice

Fresh parsley, for garnish

Welcome to Heritagefest, a unique Old World festival in which the entire city of New Ulm comes alive with reflections of times past. Gemütlichkeit abounds as the residents welcome thousands of visitors to a colorful celebration of the history and culture of the German immigrants who first settled here in the early days of this country.

The festival lasts four days; they are days filled with an exciting variety of entertainment, food, and cultural events. The Heritagefest parade features bands from the United States, Germany, and, increasingly, all over Europe and Scandinavia.

Most important, Heritagefest is an opportunity to explore the lives, arts, crafts, and pastimes of earlier generations. Both the entertainment and the crafts at Heritagefest reflect the year-round devotion of New Ulm citizens to keeping alive the best of German culture.

HERITAGEFEST

NEW ULM, MINNESOTA, MID-JULY

For more than fifty years, there has been strong community involvement with vocal and instrumental music. The Concord Singers, officially founded in 1931, has become the foremost amateur German-language male chorus in the country. The Original German Band plays the music that German and Austrian brass bands and town bands play, some of it passed on from German bands who performed at Heritagefest in prior years. Musikverein 88, nine young musicians who began playing together in high school in 1984, plays ethnic music and has become very popular all over the state. Though its members graduated from high school in 1988, they make time in their college lives to practice and perform, and plan to tour Germany in the future.

Other popular entertainers are The Oddballz, a troupe of jugglers, acrobats, and comedians, the Children's Theatre and Puppet Wagon (a group of youngsters aged seven to fifteen), the New Ulm Civic Orchestra, the New Ulm Municipal Band, and The Menagerie (a group of teenage performers from the area who have a tradition of including all AFS exchange students as members). Schell's Hobo Band, started in 1948, Wendinger Brothers Band, featuring twin concertinas and performing in German costume, and Johnny Helget's Band add to the nonstop fun.

More unusual talents also abound at Heritagefest. Offstage and onstage, American and European entertainers share their joy and expertise in yodeling, alphorn playing, and whistling. A group of men performs traditional English Morris dances, and the Bavarian Club Enzian, a four-generation family group, performs and teaches the varied dances of the villages in the Bavarian Alps.

Children have some special treats to enjoy. There are two groups of animated characters present: the Heinzlemannchen family, patterned on German gnomes, and the Morel Mushroom characters, Meta, Max, and Moritz. And for a fun look at how their lives compare with those of their great-grandparents, children (as well as adults) can visit a schoolhouse from Leavenworth that has been preserved intact and is typical of the late 1800s and early 1900s. Next to the schoolhouse is an authentic log cabin that was originally built near the Cottonwood River, south of New Ulm, in 1865. Both are furnished authentically and are open to the public through the courtesy of the Brown County Historical Society.

A fascinating part of the history on display at Heritagefest is the arts and crafts exhibit, which includes an impressive number and variety of exhibitors. A partial list of traditional crafts includes rosemaling, quilting, kloeppling (Bohemian lace making), hardanger, spinning, sheepshearing, soap making, snowshoe making, glassblowing, and German folk painting. Woodcrafts, folk art, whittling, whistle making, and doll and toy making are on display.

Many exhibitors demonstrate their skills, answer questions, and share information with visitors. Two popular working exhibitors are a blacksmith and a craftsperson who makes barrels from logs, an ancient craft called coopering. There are also demonstrations of (among other skills) sausage making, horseradish making, butter making, and, for those with a sweet tooth, beekeeping.

The Heritagefest recipes are from a small booklet called *Es Schmeckt Gut at Home in New Ulm, Minnesota*, collected by Margot Albensoeder for the New Ulm Tri-Centennial Committee. The translation is "It's Tasting Good . . . ," and if the recipes in this charming collection are a sample, New Ulm is blessed with good cooks. The book is still in print; write to the festival office for information.

SAUERBRATEN

Put meat in large crock or pot. In a separate pan, bring the next 9 ingredients to a boil, and simmer for 10 minutes. Let mixture cool and pour over meat—it should cover it—and let stand for 3–4 days in a cool place or the refrigerator. Then remove meat, wipe dry, rub with pepper. Drain carrots and onions, saving marinade.

Brown meat on all sides in a Dutch

4-lb. beef (rump)
1½ tspn. salt
2 cups vinegar
4 bay leaves
12 peppercorns
4 cloves, whole

6 onions, sliced

5 carrots, cut in strips

1 cup water

1 Tbspn. sugar

Pepper

12 ginger snaps, crushed

Brown sugar, to taste (optional)

oven and add carrots and onions. Cover tightly and roast until tender (just as you would usually do for a beef roast). Baste as often as needed with marinade.

When the meat is done, take out, let cool, and slice.

To juices in pan add marinade and crushed ginger snaps. (If you prefer you can use 3 Tbspn. flour and 1 cup sour cream instead of ginger snaps to thicken the gravy.) Add a little brown sugar, depending on taste.

Put meat back in gravy and heat through. Serves 10.

A bit of wisdom in home cooking: When making gravy for Sauerbraten (or the dressing for German Potato Salad), inhale the aroma as you are cooking it; if it makes you cough or your eyes water, it's too sour!

GERMAN ONION SOUP

2 Tbspn. butter or margarine

2½ large onions, sliced into rings

1 Tbspn. flour

4½ cups hot beef stock

Salt and pepper to taste

2 slices white bread, cubed

1 Tbspn. butter or margarine

2 egg yolks

2 Tbspn. white wine

4 Tbspn. heavy cream

Fresh parsley or chives, to sprinkle on top

Heat the 2 tablespoons butter or margarine in kettle, add onion rings, and brown a nicely nutty brown. Sprinkle with flour, heat, and stir for approximately 1 minute, and then slowly add hot stock while stirring. Season with salt and pepper. Simmer for about 20 minutes.

In the meantime toast bread cubes in frying pan in the 1 Tbspn. butter. Set aside.

In a cup blend the egg yolks with wine and cream. Add a little salt and pepper. Pull soup off burner and stir in the egg mixture.

Cover and let sit for 2 minutes. Serve in preheated soup bowls. Sprinkle each serving with toasted bread cubes and parsley or chives.

This soup is just a bit different and milder than the other (French) onion soup!

APPLE RINGS

Peel the apples and remove the cores with an apple corer. Cut the apples into ½-inch rings and place the rings in a bowl.

Sprinkle with the sugar, pour the lemon juice over the rings, and cover. Let stand while you prepare the batter.

Sift the flour into a large bowl. Add the wine or soda water in a steady stream and beat well to mix. Add the egg yolks and vegetable oil and mix slowly.

If you have time it's best to let this sit for ½ hour—although no difference was noted by just going to the next step.

In a separate bowl beat the egg whites with the salt until the whites hold stiff peaks. Fold the egg whites into the wine or soda water mixture.

In a wide, flat saucepan or a deep frying pan (at least 2 inches deep) heat the shortening. Dip the apple rings into the batter and fry them, a few at a time, until golden brown. Do not let the shortening get too hot!

Drain the fried apple rings on paper towels, sprinkle with sugar and cinnamon, and serve hot. These are good with coffee or tea.

6–7 medium apples

3 Tbspn. granulated sugar

1 Tbspn. fresh lemon juice

9 oz. flour (1 cup plus 1 oz.)

1 cup wine or soda water

4 egg yolks

2 Tbspn. vegetable oil

3 egg whites

½ tspn. salt

Shortening or oil for frying

Sugar and cinnamon, for sprinkling on top

ROAST PORK WITH CARAWAY

Preheat the oven to 450° F. Wash and dry the meat and rub with salt and pepper. Using a sharp knife, cut into the rind in a diamond pattern. Fill a roasting pan with approximately 1 inch water, and add the meat with the rind down. Cut onions into rings, thinly slice garlic, add to the meat. Sprinkle with caraway seeds.

Roast meat for ½ hour, and then turn the meat over so rind is on top, and

2-lb. pork (shoulder or ham)

Salt and pepper

2 medium onions

3 garlic cloves

2 Tbspn. caraway seeds

Hot broth

Cold water or beer

continue to roast for about another 1½ hours at a somewhat reduced temperature. Baste frequently and gradually add some hot broth. Toward the end of roasting time, brush the rind with cold water or beer to make it crisp.

GERMAN POTATO SALAD

4 lb. firm red potatoes, boiled

6 slices thick bacon, cubed

3 small onions, chopped

3 Tbspn. flour

1 cup water

½ cup vinegar

¼ cup sugar

Salt and pepper to taste

Cook potatoes in jackets. Don't overcook. You don't want them to fall apart when you peel and slice them. Set aside in large mixing bowl.

Fry bacon until nice and brown and crumbly. Remove bacon from pan. Add onions, flour, water, vinegar, and sugar. Boil together until glossy. Pour over and mix into potato slices. Add salt and pepper. If desired also add the crumbly bacon bits.

P.S. This recipe comes in quite a few variations with regard to measurements. As is common with recipes that have been handed down, you will have to play around a bit, depending on how sour or sweet you prefer this salad.

For dinner, a fruit compote and any type of dark bread accompany the salad really well.

OMA'S SCHMIERKUCHEN

1 pkg. dry yeast

¼ cup warm water

1 cup milk

3 Tbspn. plus 1½ tspn. sugar

2 eggs, beaten

1½ cups flour

3 tspn. lard

2 cups flour

Dissolve the yeast in the warm water. Let stand for 10 minutes. Scald the milk and pour over the sugar. Let it cool down to about lukewarm. Now add the yeast and into all of this stir the 2 eggs. Add the 1½ cups of flour.

Stir until very smooth. Then add the lard and again beat until smooth. Now add the 2 cups of flour, and stir until the dough forms a rough ball. If needed add a little bit more flour.

Grease bottom and sides of a bowl, and also grease the dough ball. Set dough into bowl. Cover and set in a warm place. Let sit until dough doubles in size.

Preheat oven to 350° F.

Cook the prunes until tender. Mash the prunes together with the ¼ cup sugar, cinnamon, and nutmeg.

Divide the dough into 4 (9-inch) pie tins. Make a well in the dough in each tin, working the dough up the edges of the tin.

Fill each tin with ¼ of the cheese mixture and dot with ¼ of the prune mixture. Sprinkle with a little more sugar and cinnamon. Bake for 30–35 minutes. Make 4 pies.

FILLING:

1½ lb. (24 oz.) cottage cheese (small curd)

¼ cup cream

¾ cup sugar

2 Tbspn. flour

1 tspn. salt

2 eggs, beaten

1 lb. prunes

¼ cup sugar

1 tspn. cinnamon

½ tspn. nutmeg

LINZER TORTE

Sift the first 7 ingredients into a medium-sized bowl. Cut in the butter or margarine. Stir in egg, kirsch or cherry brandy or wine, almonds, and lemon rind and juice until well blended. Chill 1 hour. Cut the dough in half, and fit ½ into the bottom of a 10-inch greased and floured springform pan. Spread ½ cup jam or preserves over dough.

Preheat oven to 350° F.

Sprinkle a board with flour and roll finger-thick strips of other half of dough. Arrange strips lattice fashion over preserves. Bake for 50 minutes or until pastry is firm. Cool in pan on wire rack. Remove from pan. Fill lattices with the remaining jam or preserves. Sprinkle with some powdered sugar.

1¾ cups sifted all-purpose flour

¾ cup sugar

2 tspn. dry cocoa (not a mix)

2 tspn. baking powder

¾ tspn. ground cinnamon

¼ tspn. salt

¼ tspn. ground cloves

½ cup butter or margarine

1 egg, beaten

2 Tbspn. kirsch, cherry brandy, or wine

¼ cup slivered almonds

½ tspn. grated lemon rind and 2 Tbspn. juice

1 (10-oz.) jar red raspberry jam (or tomato preserves)

Powdered sugar, for sprinkling on top

KRAUT KRAPFEN

2 cups flour

1 tspn. salt

2 eggs

½ cup water (or slightly less)

Some sauerkraut, raw, squeezed dry

2 Tbspn. lard

Mix first 4 ingredients like a noodle dough. Roll out on a floured board and spread with sauerkraut.

Roll up like a cinnamon roll and cut in ½-inch slices.

Have ½ inch water and the lard simmering in a frying pan. Put the slices in, cut side down, and let simmer until all water has disappeared and the krapfen are browned on one side. Then turn and continue cooking until the other side is nicely browned.

Years ago, when Fridays were meatless days, this dish was a tradition in some homes.

These krapfen are delicious when served hot, but are also good cold.

MAI BOWLE

1 quart fruit (strawberries, pineapple, peaches, and so on)

1 pint brandy

1 quart May wine or Rhine wine

Essence of Woodruff

1 quart Rhine wine

1 quart charged water

1 quart champagne

Pour the first five ingredients together in a crock or jar, and let sit for at least 4 hours (up to 36 hours).

When serving add a ring of ice (molded), preferably with some cherries in it for color. Add the charged water and the champagne. This makes about forty-eight 4-oz. punch cups.

A cool and springlike drink for special gatherings, family reunions, or any other festive get-together.

A million Canadians waiting in a downpour inspired the first summer Minneapolis Aquatennial. It was Winnipeg, 1939, and some Minneapolis business leaders were attending a celebration to honor the visit of King George VI. Observing the wet throngs, the group members couldn't help but think of home. If Winnipeg and King George could attract a million people on a rainy day, what about Minneapolis in midsummer? And so was born the idea of a festival to celebrate the natural summer splendor of Minneapolis: blue skies, warm sunshine, and water everywhere.

In 1940 the first Minneapolis Aquatennial was a cooperative effort among city officials, businesses, and citizens, featuring more than 150 events. Now, many festivals later, Minneapolis has its million who turn out to celebrate summer in the Land of Lakes with parades, fishing, sporting and boating events, wacky contests on land and water, good food, and more.

MINNEAPOLIS AQUATENNIAL

MINNEAPOLIS, MINNESOTA, MID-JULY

Throughout its history Aquatennial has upheld its founding purpose: to promote the natural and cultural opportunities of Minneapolis and Minnesota, and to create a spirit of goodwill among its people.

Traditional values and civic pride are the themes of most Aquatennial events: the vigorous Family Stride is a chance for families to exercise together and benefit local food banks; the Mississippi RiverRaft awards go not only to the team with the fastest time but also to the team that collects the most litter. The Milk Carton Boat Race is a match between crafts constructed exclusively of, well, yes, milk cartons! And Senior Days include even the most experienced generations in the fun, with a senior arts and crafts bazaar, coronation of senior royalty, a senior prom, and a health fair.

The festival week features numerous parades on water and land, the king of which is the Torchlight Parade in downtown Minneapolis. There is a skateboard jam, various bike and running races, and a Queen of the Lakes coronation.

Of course Aquatennial means water activities galore! The week brings a waterski Show of Stars, the Aquatennial Sailboard Classic, the Aquatennial Sailing Regatta, and zany attractions such as the Tom Thumb Flotilla Frolic (an ensemble of showboats and floating stages that travels along the river between two city parks). The premier boating event is the Champion Spark Plug Powerboat Classic on the mighty Mississippi, a part of the International Outboard Grand Prix Circuit, with a lineup of top-notch international boats and drivers.

The traditional close of Aquatennial is the annual Fireworks Finale, a dazzling fireworks show synchronized to music. It is a fitting, exciting climax to this festival, which provides people of all backgrounds a chance to contribute to the community and enjoy a true variety of good old-fashioned family entertainment.

Aquatennial *is* summer fun in Minneapolis.

MINNESOTA SUMMER SUN

2 (3-oz.) pkg. ladyfingers

2 (14-oz.) cans sweetened condensed milk

8 eggs, separated

2 tspn. grated lemon peel

¾ cup plus 3 Tbspn. fresh lemon juice

¼ tspn. cream of tartar

Powdered sugar, for sprinkling on top

Thin lemon slice, for garnish

The light texture and refreshing taste of this dessert bring thoughts of summer and Aquatennial. We make it year round as a pleasant reminder of great things to come in July.

Preheat oven to 375° F. Grease a 9-inch springform pan; cover bottom of pan with ladyfingers. Stand remaining ladyfingers around sides of pan, cutting bottom ends so tops of ladyfingers are even with top of pan. Combine sweetened condensed milk, egg yolks, lemon peel, and lemon juice in large bowl. Combine egg whites and cream of tartar in medium bowl; beat until stiff. Fold in lemon mixture. Pour batter into prepared pan. Bake for 25 minutes or until top is lightly browned. Cool completely; cover with foil and freeze (will keep for up to 3 months in freezer). To serve, remove side of springform pan. Sprinkle top of dessert with powdered sugar. Garnish with twisted lemon slice in center. Any remaining dessert may be covered and refrozen.

SPRING THAW FRUIT CUPS

In Minnesota we make these fruit cups in November and put them in nature's freezer: the great outdoors. And whenever summer and Aquatennial seem impossibly far away, we bring one in, thaw it out, and enjoy. The cool, refreshing taste conjures up warm thoughts of July weather and festival time.

Mix thawed frozen orange juice, water, sugar, and lemon juice until sugar dissolves. Slice bananas and combine with strawberries and pineapple, including pineapple juice. Pour orange juice mixture over fruit. Pour into 6-oz. plastic cups, leaving 1 ½ inches of space at top. Freeze. Partially thaw for 20 minutes before serving. Pour 7-Up over fruit cups. Makes 18 fruit cups.

1 (12-oz.) can frozen orange juice, thawed

1½ cans water

1 cup sugar

¼ cup lemon juice

6 bananas

2 (10-oz.) pkg. frozen strawberries, thawed

2 (1 lb., 4 oz. each) cans chunky pineapple, including juice

2 (16-oz.) bottles 7-Up

Marin's "function at the junction" features live music, gourmet food, fine wines, and specialty arts and crafts on Anselmo Avenue. A celebration of the charm and elegance of this beautiful area, the festival is sponsored by the San Anselmo Chamber of Commerce, and produced by Terry Pimsleur & Company.

These recipes were created by Dennis Allison, well-known local amateur chef, and Zell Trippsmith, coast-to-coast commuter cook.

SAN ANSELMO ART AND WINE FESTIVAL

MARIN COUNTY, CALIFORNIA, MID-JULY

FRESH SALMON CAVIAR

A fresh salmon roe

Brine of about 2 Tbspn. salt dissolved in 1 quart of water

Baked potatoes

Sour cream, crème fraîche, or yogurt

Fresh salmon caviar is particularly light and flavorful. Second best but still wonderful is Japanese salmon caviar, but it is more oily and gummy than the fresh.

Choose a roe that has nicely colored eggs. Remove and wash the eggs from the roe. Fingers and a colander are useful here. The eggs are much less fragile than you'd think; force them through the holes in a colander. The idea is to remove all the membrane that holds them together. Soak the eggs in the brine for about 20 minutes. Wash the eggs and drain them. They will form a compact solid mass.

Ensure the potatoes are warm. Split each potato and place a generous spoonful of the caviar in the middle. Pass the sour cream, crème fraîche, or yogurt.

SPINACH PIE

Preheat oven to 350° F. Sauté onions in butter and mix with spinach, cottage cheese, and nutmeg. Fold into pie crust, sprinkle with Parmesan cheese. Bake for 25–30 minutes.

1 small onion, minced

2 Tbspn. butter

1 bunch fresh steamed spinach

1 cup cottage cheese

Dash nutmeg

1 baked pie crust

¼ cup Parmesan cheese

The first Gilroy Garlic Festival, in 1979, achieved worldwide headlines. It was inspired by reports of a tiny French town that drew thousands to its yearly garlic fete. Because Gilroy and adjoining agricultural areas process 90 percent of United States garlic, in addition to processing imported garlic, Gilroy proclaimed itself Garlic Capital of the World, and a legend sprouted!

A group of Gilroy residents staged the first weekend celebration of the "scented pearl" to promote a positive image of their community—which Will Rogers described as "the only town in America where you can marinate a steak by hanging it on the clothesline." The public has been enthusiastic, and attendance has grown from 20,000 to well over 150,000 in ten years.

"The ultimate in summer food fairs!" comments the *Los Angeles Herald-Examiner* about the Garlic Festival. And indeed it presents a fine blend of entertainment, activities, and food, glorious food.

Gilroy Garlic Festival entertainment is continuous from 10 A.M. to 7 P.M. on four stages scattered throughout the creekside park area. Music styles run the gamut from bluegrass

GILROY GARLIC FESTIVAL

GILROY, CALIFORNIA, LATE JULY

and country and western to jazz, big band, and rock 'n' roll. Entertainment for children includes puppets, clowns, and face painting.

Fine arts and crafts are offered in a special section of the festival. Other events include golf and tennis tournaments, the Garlic Queen pageant, the Tour de Garlique bicycle tour, the 10/5K Garlic Gallop, and the Garlic Squeeze Barn Dance.

Be sure to see the Garlic Grove exhibits and watch skilled workers top and braid garlic during the garlic topping contests. There's plenty of garlic for sale in the form of braids, buckles, necklaces, and headbands. Just the thing for those family members and friends on your gift list who appreciate the unusual!

Gourmet Alley is the heart of the festival's food showcase. There local chefs perform culinary magic over the fire pits before hungry spectators. Iron skillets the size of bicycle wheels sizzle with the famed Gilroy Garlic Festival calamari, or gently sauté bright red and green peppers to nestle with top sirloin in pepper steak sandwiches.

Wines of the Santa Clara Valley are available to complement garlic-laced delicacies ranging from pasta con pesto to mountains of garlic bread to tons of scampi swimming in a mouth-watering lobster butter sauce. Gourmet Alley's chefs create true culinary delights, and clubs and civic groups adhere to the same high standards—as well as the garlic theme—in presenting a large variety of international dishes that distinguish this great garlic extravaganza. The seventy-five food booths and Gourmet Alley use about eight tons of fresh garlic during the three-day festival.

The Great Garlic Cookoff features amateur cooks creating wonderful dishes from their original recipes, which have been submitted in advance to a jury of professional home economists. Eight finalists are selected to prepare their own dishes for the judges, who select the winner.

Information about the various festival events may be obtained from the festival office. If you want to pit your tastebuds and culinary skills against those of other amateur chefs in the cookoff, you can obtain the rules by sending a stamped, self-addressed envelope to the festival office. The admission price for the festival includes all entertainment, parking, and shuttle service.

The Gilroy Garlic Festival has produced an interesting variety of souvenirs, ranging from tote bags, aprons, potholders, and dish towels to shirts, hats, jogging suits, and charms. Best of all, however, are two wonderful cookbooks of garlic-laced recipes by local chefs, cookoff winners, and contest entrants. You may choose volume one or two, or go all out and order the deluxe edition, which includes both volumes, plus prizewinning recipes unavailable elsewhere. Write to the festival office for the souvenir brochure.

These recipes are from the finalists in the 1987 Great Garlic Cookoff; the winner is indicated. The judges must have had a difficult, albeit delicious, time making a decision!

AMBROSIAL GRAPE LEAVES

Rinse grape leaves, cut off stems, and lay flat on work surface. Sauté onion in butter or olive oil until translucent. Add lamb, crumbling as you cook, until done. Stir in garlic and season with salt and pepper. Remove from heat and add pine nuts, raisins, sugar, and cinnamon. Place 2–3 Tbspn. of the mixture in the center of each grape leaf. Fold each leaf over filling, and roll up like a cigar. Preheat oven to 350° F. Fill a baking dish with the stuffed grape leaves in a single layer and dribble melted butter over them. Bake for 20 minutes and serve hot. Makes 10 servings.

by Elaine Corrington
Finalist, Los Angeles

1 jar grape leaves

1 onion

2 Tbspn. butter or olive oil

1½ lb. ground lamb

1–2 heads fresh garlic, peeled and chopped

Salt and pepper to taste

4 (10-oz.) pkg. pine nuts (pignolias)

2 cups seedless raisins

2–3 Tbspn. sugar

6 Tbspn. cinnamon

8 Tbspn. (1 stick) butter, melted

GARLIC CHICKEN PINEAPPLE

1 head fresh garlic, peeled

1 piece (1 inch square) fresh ginger, peeled

5 Tbspn. vegetable oil

9 black peppercorns

5 cardamom pods

5 whole cloves

1 cinnamon stick

1 large onion (preferably red), chopped

1 chicken, skinned and cut up

2 potatoes, peeled and diced (optional)

1 can sliced pineapple, drained and cut in triangular pieces

In blender grind garlic and ginger to form a smooth paste; add a little water for good consistency, but not too much. Heat vegetable oil and add peppercorns, cardamom pods, cloves, and cinnamon stick, cooking until all release delectable aromas (about 3 minutes). Add onion and cook until it is light golden in color. Add garlic-ginger paste and cook about 5 minutes, stirring constantly. If this masala is sticking to the pan, add a little water and stir. Add cut-up chicken to the masala, and cook until chicken is browned. Do not worry if the masala is sticking to the pan. Reduce heat to medium. Once chicken is browned, add about 1 cup water and deglaze pan. Reduce heat to medium-low, cover pan, and let chicken cook 50 minutes or until tender. Add potatoes, if desired, after chicken has cooked 20 minutes. Just before serving, add pineapple. Makes 4 servings.

by B. K. Kermani
Finalist, San Jose

LINGUINE WITH CARAMELIZED GARLIC

3 heads fresh garlic

2 Tbspn. olive oil

1 Tbspn. chopped fresh thyme

⅓ cup chicken stock (if using canned, use regular, not double-strength)

Salt and pepper to taste

6 oz. linguine

Separate garlic cloves. Immerse in boiling water for 30 seconds and peel. Heat olive oil in large sauté pan over medium-low heat. Add garlic. Reduce heat to low and very slowly sauté garlic until golden brown. Stir frequently. Be careful not to burn garlic. It will take approximately 20 minutes for the garlic to reach the golden brown state. Stir in fresh thyme. Cook 2 minutes longer. Add chicken stock and salt and pepper. Simmer 5 minutes. Meanwhile, cook linguine according to package directions. Drain. Toss linguine with eggs. Add to sauté pan and toss with Parmesan cheese. Adjust seasonings. Serve immediately. Makes 3–4 servings.

by Kimra Foster
Finalist, San Jose

2 eggs, beaten

3 oz. freshly grated Parmesan cheese

GARLIC ONION BAKE

Preheat oven to 350° F. Place soda and Ritz crackers in a bowl and pour all but 2 tablespoons butter over. Mix well. Press half the cracker mixture into bottom of 9-inch-by-11-inch baking dish. Slice onions thin and sauté with garlic in remaining butter until translucent but not brown. Place in baking dish and spread over crackers. Grate cheese and sprinkle over garlic-onion mixture. Beat eggs and reserve. Scald milk, let cool a little, and then incorporate into eggs. Pour this mixture over cheese and sprinkle remaining crackers on top. Bake for 30 minutes. Makes 8–10 servings.

by Ira J. Jacobson
Finalist, Oakland

3 oz. soda crackers (about 35 crackers) rolled fine

3 oz. Ritz crackers (about 35 crackers) rolled fine

10 Tbspn. (1¼ sticks) unsalted butter, melted

3 large red onions

1 cup chopped fresh garlic

8 oz. sharp white Cheddar cheese (no dyes)

2 eggs

1½ cups milk

HEALTHY, HOT, AND GARLICKY WINGS

2 lb. chicken wings (approximately 15 wings)

3 heads fresh garlic

1 cup plus 1 Tbspn. olive oil

10–15 drops Tabasco

1 cup grated Parmesan cheese

1 cup Italian-style bread crumbs

1 tspn. black pepper

Preheat oven to 375° F. Disjoint chicken wings, discarding tips, rinse, and pat dry. Separate garlic cloves and peel. Place garlic, olive oil, and Tabasco in blender or food processor and puree. Combine Parmesan, bread crumbs, and pepper in a plastic bag. Dip wings in the garlic puree and roll in bread crumb mixture, 1 at a time, coating thoroughly. Coat a shallow nonstick baking pan with oil, and add wings in a single layer. Drizzle with remaining garlic puree and sprinkle with any remaining bread crumb mixture. Bake for 45–60 minutes until brown and crisp.

by Winifred Harano
Winner, Los Angeles

GARLIC-PUMPED CHICKEN

3 heads fresh garlic, whole and unpeeled

1 chicken (3½–4 lb.)

¾ lb. fresh mushrooms

8 Tbspn. unsalted butter

Salt and freshly ground pepper to taste

A little butter, to rub on outside of chicken

Freshly ground black pepper, to sprinkle on outside of chicken

Juices from cavity of roasted chicken

¼ cup Marsala (or port or red wine)

¼ cup heavy cream

Wrap garlic in foil and roast in preheated 400° F oven about 30 minutes or until garlic is cooked and soft. Cool and then squeeze out pulp of cloves and set aside. Rinse chicken and pat dry. With breast side up, beginning at the neck end, separate the skin from the flesh, loosening as far into the legs and wings as possible without tearing the skin. This creates a pocket for the stuffing. Set chicken aside. Clean mushrooms and finely chop (a food processor works best). Sauté in 2 Tbspn. of the butter over high heat until all moisture has evaporated, stirring and taking care not to burn. Cool. Combine ⅔ garlic pulp, mushrooms, and remaining 6 Tbspn. butter. Mix thoroughly; add salt and pepper.

To stuff chicken, fill a pastry bag (use a

medium tip) with garlic mixture. Insert point under skin and pump filling into pocket, spreading it evenly, using your fingers. Rub outside of chicken with a little butter and sprinkle with freshly ground pepper. Place chicken, breast side up, in a roasting pan with a rack, and roast at 400° F for approximately 1½ hours until juices in thigh run clear. Reserve juices from cavity; carefully cut up chicken into serving pieces (shears work best) and keep warm. Prepare sauce by combining remaining ⅓ of garlic pulp, reserved juices, wine, and cream in a small saucepan over high heat. Stir until thickened. Serve with chicken. Makes 4 servings.

by Joseph Bonello
Finalist, San Francisco

PATRICIAN ESCARGOTS

Peel garlic and chop fine. Place olive oil and butter in a frying pan over medium heat. When butter is melted add garlic, onion, rosemary, and thyme. Then add nutmeg and salt and pepper. Reduce heat to low and add snails and parsley; simmer for 30 minutes. While snails are simmering clean and remove stems from mushrooms. Arrange mushroom caps upside down in a 2-inch-deep baking dish, and place 1 snail into each mushroom cap. Pour garlic mixture over snails, cover with foil, and bake at 350° F for 30 minutes. While snails are baking cut the crusts off bread slices and cut each slice into 4 squares. Toast bread. Serve with escargots. Makes 4 servings.

by Pat Trinchero
Finalist, Gilroy

4 heads fresh garlic

½ cup olive oil

½ cup butter

1 onion, finely chopped

1 tspn. finely chopped fresh or dried rosemary

¼ tspn. ground thyme

2 dashes nutmeg

Salt and pepper to taste

24 large canned snails

½ cup chopped parsley

24 medium to large fresh mushrooms

12 pieces thinly sliced white bread

NANCY'S GLORIOUS GARLIC TART

PASTRY CRUST:

1½ cups all-purpose flour

1 tspn. sugar

1 tspn. salt

1 stick (¼ lb.) frozen butter, cut into 6 pieces

¼ cup ice water

FILLING:

3 heads fresh garlic, cloves separated and peeled

2 tspn. Dijon-style mustard

1 cup grated Gruyère cheese

1 egg

¼ cup heavy cream

1 tspn. nutmeg

¼ tspn. pepper

Pastry crust: Preheat oven to 350° F. In food processor combine flour, sugar, salt, and butter until mixture looks crumbly. With motor running, slowly add ice water. Mixture will gather into a ball. Wrap dough in plastic wrap and refrigerate for at least ½ hour. Butter and flour a 9-inch tart pan with removable bottom. Roll out dough to fit into pan. Trim edges. Line dough with foil and fill center with pie weights or dried beans. Bake for 20 minutes. Remove foil and weights. Continue baking crust for additional 10 minutes, until crust begins to brown.

Filling: Half fill a large saucepan with water. Add garlic cloves and bring to a boil. Drain garlic and repeat process with fresh water. Drain and reserve garlic. With back of spoon smear Dijon-style mustard across bottom of pastry crust, which can be hot from oven or at room temperature. Distribute Gruyère evenly in crust. In a food processor puree reserved garlic with egg, cream, nutmeg, and pepper for 30 seconds. Pour garlic mixture over cheese. Bake tart at 350° F for 25 minutes, until filling is firm. Serve hot or at room temperature. Makes 8 servings.

by Nancy Ash
Finalist, San Francisco

The Pro Football Hall of Fame Festival is a six-day tribute to the great all-American game of football and those men who've become great playing it. The occasion is the annual election of new enshrinees into the Pro Football Hall of Fame, which is also located in Canton.

The festival celebrated its twenty-fifth anniversary in 1988, and traditionally it offers much more than football. First, a festival queen and court are selected at the queen pageant. Kickoff Sunday starts with a five-mile race, a parade, and a marching band concert. In the following days visitors can enjoy a succulent Ribs Burnoff, a drum corps show by some of the top drum corps in the nation, a concert by the Air Force band, and a rousing fireworks display, as well as Ohio's largest and most spectacular fashion show—an afternoon of high fashion, glamour, and celebrities. In the final days of the celebration, the Balloon Classic fills the sky with the dazzling color and graceful beauty of dozens of hot air balloons.

PRO FOOTBALL HALL OF FAME FESTIVAL

CANTON, OHIO, LATE JULY/EARLY AUGUST

No doubt about it, though, football is the cause célèbre here. The first big event of interest to fans is the mayor's breakfast on Friday morning, when the enshrinees are introduced to the public for the first time. On Friday night more than 3500 people, including team owners, sports stars, and celebrities, mingle during a social hour and dinner with the enshrinees and their presenters.

The actual enshrinement occurs on Saturday morning, on the steps of the Pro Football Hall of Fame, in a happy, emotional ceremony that is open to the public. Afterward the newest Hall of Famers are honored at the festival parade. This nationally televised spectacle proceeds through downtown Canton, featuring floats, bands, and sports stars past and present. A pro game follows the parade, capping off the day's activities. The teams differ each year, but the game is always a hard-hitting, action-packed finale at which the enshrinees take their final bows.

The Pro Football Hall of Fame is open every day of the festival and is a must-see for all football fans. The complex includes exhibitions, a research library, memorabilia and video displays, a football action theater, a museum store, and the two enshrinement halls, where the heroes of pro football are permanently honored.

The Pro Football Hall of Fame Festival celebrates America's favorite sport and some of its greatest players. Together with the Hall of Fame complex, it offers football, fireworks, fashion, food, and fun for all.

The festival is currently putting together its own cookbook; following are two favorite drink recipes.

QUICK KICK
The Official Drink
of the NFL Hall of Fame

Enough ice to half-fill 15-oz. glass

1½ oz. light rum

1 oz. liqueur

¼ oz. sloe gin

Squeeze of lime wedge

Orange juice to fill glass

Cherry, for garnish

Lime and orange slices, for garnish

Fill 15-oz. glass half-full of ice. Add the next 5 ingredients. Garnish with cherry and lime and orange slices. Makes 1 serving.

FESTIVAL SUNBURST
(Nonalcoholic)

4 cups cranberry juice, chilled

1 cup ginger ale, chilled

3 Tbspn. lemon juice

8 ice cubes

½ pint orange sherbet

Combine first 3 ingredients in a pitcher. Put a cube of ice in eight 6-oz. glasses. Pour beverage into glasses and top each with a scoop of sherbet. Makes 8 servings.

From the earliest days of this country, people from all over the world have been coming to settle in Texas, bringing with them bits and pieces of their own heritage. Throughout the years their varied cultures, honored customs, and rich folklore have been woven into the fabric of the state's history to create an intricate and multicolored tapestry of Texas traditions.

Once a year the many people of Texas gather together in a celebration to preserve the folkways of their ancestors and honor the glorious variety that is Texas. Whether you're a native, a newcomer, or a visitor just passing through, you won't want to miss the Texas Folklife Festival.

This four-day event is presented by the Institute of Texan Cultures of the University of Texas at San Antonio, as an extension of the educational programs offered throughout the year by the statewide research, education, and communication center.

TEXAS
FOLKLIFE
FESTIVAL
SAN ANTONIO, TEXAS, EARLY AUGUST

Nearly 6000 representatives of the more than 30 ethnic groups who settled and developed Texas share their traditions, crafts, music, dance, and food in a blend of education and entertainment for the whole family. Many of them return each year to work as technicians, stuff sausage, deliver ice, and do the dozens of tasks necessary to make this a very special event. (The present director, Jo Ann Andera, started out as a tour guide at the first festival in 1972.)

Like a kaleidoscope of history and culture, folk dancers and musicians from across the state color the festival's ten stages with the lively sights and sounds of Texas. There's a sort of grouping of styles which makes it easier to find your favorite music, but there's no easy way to make a choice when faced with such variety. There's country, folk, and jazz, and then subgroupings of country rock, blues, bluegrass, and soul. There's one stage for gospel music, which sounds pretty simple until you discover that this covers everything from music from the 1830s to modern gospel with musical instruments, from old-time spirituals and Southern gospel to jazz-influenced gospel.

There's German and Tex-Mex polka music and music from the Caribbean and South America, folkloric groups and flamenco troupes, and Lebanese belly dancers. Fiddlers and string bands, pipers and drummers, and Japanese folk musicians vie with Cajun bands and Irish musicians. There's an incredible variety of dancers and one stage devoted to folk singers and storytellers.

Once you've realized that you can't possibly hear it all, you are confronted with another problem: you can't see it all, either. Spinning cotton, relaxing at the fishin' hole, and splitting shingles are just a few of the experiences from pioneer Texas that you can share in the festival's "Back 40" area. The gifted people who work here encourage questions and active participation from kids and grandparents alike.

There are folk games taught and played, stirring up memories and creating new ones. There are demonstrations of a variety of crafts and pioneer skills, such as basketmaking, spinning and weaving, log construction, breadmaking, whittling, and chair caning. You can watch the United States Cavalry shoeing horses or a woman making lye soap in a big black kettle, while over there a woman makes piñatas and other women have a quilting bee. Other activities include joining the soldiers at the fort, practicing handwriting in the one-room schoolhouse, and learning about the lives of Indian Texans at the Tipi.

No one can possibly spend hours each day doing all these things, without food and drink. Not to worry. The food served at this festival is as superb as it is diverse. The vendors who prepare this amazing variety of dishes are members of various churches, clubs, and organizations throughout the state, carefully selected to represent their various ethnic groups.

A local journalist, Jim Beal, Jr., says "The only food I call weird is food I taste and don't like, so I would naturally recommend eating one of everything . . . and two or three of most." More than 30 ethnic and cultural groups, including American Indians, offer a taste of Texas tradition and make it very hard to resist Beal's advice. A partial list includes Alsatian, Belgian, British, Dutch, Greek, German, Italian, Korean, Japanese, Lebanese, Norwegian, Hungarian, and Mexican. Had enough? No? Try Czech, Filipino, Cajun, Jewish, Ukrainian, Irish and Wendish. (No, not fast food: Wends are descendants of a group of Slavic tribes from central Europe.) There are Italian, Scottish, Vietnamese, Spanish, Chinese, Indian-Asian, Khmer, Welsh, Trinidadian, and Polish foods, as well as soul food, those two All-American favorites, chili and peanuts, and chicken-fried steak, sometimes referred to as "the national food of Texas." If you have room for dessert, many of these cultures have their own specialties, or you can end it all with some of the delicacies made from Texas-grown strawberries or pies from East Texas–grown yams.

Iced tea and beer seem to be the two favorite drinks at the festival. Iced tea comes in a variety of flavors, beer in a variety of brands. There are beer booths with the usual brands on tap, while imports, canned or on tap, are available at various ethnic booths. Of course, soft drinks are everywhere, and fruit juices, wine, sangria, and margaritas are sold. Davis Mountain water, cool, clear, and refreshing, is free!

INDIAN FRY BREAD

Mix ingredients with tap water to make a stiff dough. Place in covered bowl and let set 4–5 hours. Then pinch off small balls of dough and work out into circles about 5 inches wide. Deep fry in hot fat until golden brown. Serve while hot with butter, syrup, jelly, or with vegetables or meats.

by Alabama-Coushatta Pow Wow Committee
Alabama-Coushatta Indian Reservation
Livingston, Texas

3 cups sifted flour
4 tspn. baking powder
½ tspn. salt
Fat for frying

CACTUS CAFÉ CHICKEN FRIED STEAK
(Texan)

Tenderize round steak cut in 1-inch strips. Coat with flour seasoned with salt and pepper. Dip in mixture of egg beaten with milk. Recoat with flour mixture. Deep fry in Crisco until golden brown.

Cream Gravy: Heat drippings and add flour, salt, and pepper. Add milk, stirring constantly until gravy begins to thicken.

by All Saints Episcopal Church
Colorado City, Texas

1 round steak
Flour
Salt to taste
Pepper to taste
1 egg
2 cups milk
Crisco, for frying

CREAM GRAVY:

4 Tbspn. drippings
2 Tbspn. flour
Salt to taste
Pepper to taste
2 cups milk

ALSATIAN SAUSAGE

35 lb. pork

15 lb. venison or beef

8 oz. salt

1 oz. pepper

1 oz. coriander

½ oz. allspice

½ oz. cloves

Garlic to your taste

Pork casings (enough for 50 lb. of meat)

Mix all ingredients together. Stuff into pork casings and hang in smokehouse. (Makes 50 lb.)

(Editor's note: This recipe requires scrupulous cleanliness. Use your own grinder, scalded, if possible. Keep refrigerated. Discard unused portions.)

St. Louis Parish of Castroville
Castroville, Texas

CASTROVILLE PARISA
(Alsatian)

1 lb. lean ground sirloin

½ lb. diced or grated American cheese

½ lb. finely chopped onion

Salt and pepper to taste

Juice of ½ lemon

Mix ground sirloin, cheese, onion, salt, and pepper together. Squeeze juice of ½ lemon over mixture. Cover and refrigerate for 2 hours. Serve on crackers. Makes 1½ pounds.

(Editor's note: This recipe requires scrupulous cleanliness. Use your own grinder, scalded, if possible. Keep refrigerated. Discard unused portions.)

YAKITORI

Cut meat and vegetables into ½-inch chunks. Put meat, vegetables, and pineapple chunks onto skewers. Make yakitori sauce by combining soy sauce, sugar, wine, cornstarch, and ginger. Brush over skewered ingredients. Cook skewered meat, vegetables, and pineapple over barbecue grill, turning several times during cooking. Brush with yakitori sauce each time you turn it. Makes 10 skewers.

Japan America Society of San Antonio
San Antonio, Texas

1 lb. meat
1 bell pepper
1 onion
1 small can pineapple chunks
10 bamboo skewers
4 Tbspn. soy sauce
4 Tbspn. sugar
4 Tbspn. wine
2 Tbspn. cornstarch
¼ teaspoon ground ginger

HONEY CAKE

Preheat oven to 350° F. Beat eggs till light. Add sugar and honey. Beat very well. Sift flour, baking soda, cinnamon, and ginger. Mix oil, vanilla, and chopped walnuts or pecans. Add oil mixture and flour mixture alternately to egg mixture.

Grease and line with wax paper a 9-inch-by-13-inch cake pan. Pour in batter. Rap pan on table or counter to remove all air bubbles. Bake for 45–50 minutes, or till done.

Note: For a heavier textured, moister cake, *don't* sift flour before adding to batter.

This cake needs no glaze or frosting.

Jewish Community Center
San Antonio, Texas

4 eggs
1 cup sugar
¾ cup honey
2 cups flour
½ tspn. baking soda
½ tspn. cinnamon
½ tspn. ginger
1 cup oil
1 tspn. vanilla
½ cup chopped walnuts or pecans

NOM PANG CHEAN (Shrimp Toast)

1 lb. peeled shrimp

2 cups diced water chestnuts

1 cup green onion (bottom part)

2 tspn. freshly ground ginger

4 eggs

2 tspn. salt

½ tspn. MSG (Accent), optional

2 tspn. sugar

½ tspn. white pepper

½ cup sesame oil

1 loaf white bread

Blend together shrimp, water chestnuts, green onion, and ginger in food processor. Mix together well by hand eggs, salt, MSG, sugar, white pepper, and sesame oil. Add the shrimp mixture and mix by hand again.

Trim edges of bread. Cut each slice in half. Spread 2 Tbspn. of the shrimp mixture on one side of each slice of bread.

Fry at 360° F, first with shrimp side down and then the reverse. Drain on paper towels. Makes about 30 pieces.

Khmer Society of San Antonio
San Antonio, Texas

BREAD PUDDING

4 eggs

1 cup sugar

4 cups milk

1 tspn. vanilla

1½ loaves bread, cubed

3 oz. raisins

½ cup brown sugar

BUTTER SAUCE:
¾ cup sugar

3 beaten egg yolks

3 Tbspn. melted butter

2 Tbspn. cornstarch dissolved in ¼ cup water

1½ cups boiling water

2 tspn. vanilla

⅛ tspn. salt

Preheat oven to 350° F. In bowl beat eggs and sugar. Add milk and vanilla and beat. Add bread and raisins. Mix well. Put in two 9-inch-by-9-inch-by-2-inch loaf pans. Sprinkle each pan with ¼ cup brown sugar. Bake for 30 minutes or until pudding has risen to top of pan. Serve warm, topped with Butter Sauce.

Butter Sauce: In double boiler cream sugar, egg yolks, and butter. Add cornstarch mixture. Then add boiling water slowly. Cook in double boiler until thickened, stirring constantly. Add vanilla and salt.

New Braunfels Wurstfest Association
New Braunfels, Texas

SALTED NUTS OR
CHILI NUTS

Into roaster or oven set at 350° F, put the nuts and oil. Stir often. Cook until nuts are almond colored. Or else deep fry 2-cup portions of raw nuts at a time until nuts are almond colored. Drain on paper towels. Salt to taste for Salted Nuts.

For Chili Nuts add the red pepper, the 4 Tbspn. salt, and rest of spices.

Makes 8 cups Salted Nuts or Chili Nuts.

Pearsall Women's Civic Club
Pearsall, Texas

8 cups shelled peanuts

¼ cup peanut oil

Salt to taste

1 tspn. red pepper

4 Tbspn. salt

2 Tbspn. chili powder

1 tspn. garlic powder

2 tspn. onion powder

PLACKI
(Potato Pancakes)

Grate potatoes and let drain. Mix eggs, salt, and pepper with onions and combine well. Add potatoes and flour. Mix thoroughly.

Drop by rounded spoonfuls into hot oil that is not too deep. Fry until golden brown—turn only once.

Makes approximately 7 servings (14–15 patties).

Polish Arts & Culture Foundation
San Antonio, Texas

4 cups potatoes

2 whole eggs, beaten

1 tspn. salt

⅛ tspn. black pepper

Scant ⅓ cup onions, finely chopped

2 rounded Tbspn. flour

FLOUR TORTILLAS

2 cups all-purpose flour

1 tspn. salt

1 tspn. baking powder

1 Tbspn. lard or shortening

½–¾ cup warm water

In mixing bowl stir together flour, salt, and baking powder. Cut in lard or shortening till mixture resembles corn-meal. Add ½ cup warm water and mix till dough can be gathered into a ball (if needed, add more water, 1 Tbspn. at a time). Let dough stand 15 minutes. Divide dough into 12 portions; shape into balls. On a lightly floured surface, roll each ball into a 7-inch round. Cook in ungreased skillet over medium heat about 1½ minutes per side, till lightly browned. Makes 12 tortillas.

St. Alphonsus Church
San Antonio, Texas

SCOTCH EGGS

Owens country sausage

Raw egg

Cornflake crumbs

Hardboiled eggs, peeled

Fat for deep frying

The amounts of ingredients vary, depending on how many hard-boiled eggs you want and how thick the sausage is.

Take sausage meat and mix with raw egg and part of the cornflake crumbs so that it has a meatloaflike consistency.

Make sure that the hardboiled, peeled eggs are dry. Take enough of the sausage meat mixture to cover each egg about 1 inch. Roll in the rest of the cornflake crumbs and deep fry in hot fat until sausage is cooked, approximately 7 minutes. Scotch Eggs are served cut through the middle.

Scottish Society of San Antonio
San Antonio, Texas

BOUDIN

Cut pork roast in about 2-inch squares. Boil pork, liver, white onions, and parsley with just enough water to cover ingredients. Cook until meat is tender. Remove meat from broth and reserve broth. Grind meat with course blade of grinder. Mix meat, rice, green onions, salt and pepper to taste, and enough broth to make a slightly moist dressing. Stuff dressing in casing with sausage stuffer to make about 6-inch-long to 10-inch-long sausages. Cook in simmering water about 10 minutes.

Texas Cajun Club, Inc.
Port Arthur, Texas

6-lb. Boston butt pork roast

3-lb. pork liver

3 medium white onions

2 bunches parsley

12–15 cups cooked rice

3 bunches green onions

Salt and pepper to taste

Sausage casing soaked in water

ROUX

Mix oil and flour in iron skillet over medium heat. Cook until dark brown, about 45 minutes to 1 hour, stirring constantly.

1 cup oil

2 cups flour

UKRAINIAN SPICED TEA

Boil together for 10 minutes: 8 cups of the water, sugar, orange and lemon juice and rinds, and cloves and allspice tied in a bag of cheesecloth. Boil the remaining 2 cups of water and pour over the tea; let stand 5 minutes, and then add to the first mixture. Strain through a thin cloth. If too strong, a little more water may be added. Serve very hot or very cold. Serves about 15.

10 cups water

2 cups sugar

Juice and rind of 2 oranges

Juice and rind of 2 lemons

10 whole cloves

10 whole allspice

4 tspn. tea leaves

There's something fishy going on in Gloucester, and you'll certainly want to take your taste buds to investigate. It's the good old-fashioned Yankee fish fry that has been the highlight of the Gloucester Waterfront Festival since 1980: a weekend of arts and crafts, schooner cruises, whale watches, a colonial militia battle reenactment, a two-mile harbor swim race, live entertainment, and special children's events.

Gloucester claims to be America's oldest seaport, known for its fishing fleet, wonderful sailing opportunities, and delectable seafood. The annual Waterfront Festival is a celebration of all this and more.

Several hundred artists and craftspersons are selected by jury to display and sell their wares along Stacey Boulevard on Saturday and Sunday. They are joined by vendors of ethnic, exotic, and traditional foods and a veritable circus of entertainers—everything from story-tellers to skydiving teams to popular country and western bands.

To experience a bit of what Gloucester is famous for, climb aboard

WATERFRONT FESTIVAL

GLOUCESTER, MASSACHUSETTS, MID-AUGUST

one of the big sloops or schooners that offer cruises on the harbor loop. Or review a thrilling chapter of Gloucester's—and America's—history. Each year a local company reenacts the famous Falcon Battle of the Revolutionary War, in which a handful of Gloucester residents foiled an attempted British invasion of Gloucester Harbor. For hardy souls there is the harbor swim competition. (The harbor water is so cold, even in August, that competitors must meet strict health requirements, but nevertheless this race has become so popular that festival officials must limit entries.)

And for hearty appetites, of course, there is the Yankee fish fry. While popular bands play to the big Sunday afternoon crowd, the best deal in town goes down: fried fish, French fries, coleslaw, yogurt, and beer or soda, with change back from your $5 bill!

Tens of thousands attend the Waterfront Festival each year. Admission to the festival is free, but some activities (such as the harbor swim and schooner charters) should be arranged for in advance. The festival is produced by Waterfront Festivals, Ltd.; contact it for further information.

EASY GLOUCESTER HADDOCK

You can cook 1 piece or 25, as many as needed.

Set oven at 550° F (or its hottest setting), or you can use a toaster oven. Cut fillet of haddock into serving pieces. Dip in salted milk. Roll in bread crumbs. Put on piece of foil on baking sheet. Bake 10 minutes. Serve with melted butter.

1 lb. fillet of haddock

1 cup milk to which 1 Tbspn. salt is added (this is correct; it is not too much salt)

½ cup soft bread crumbs

Melted butter or margarine

LOBSTER STEW GLOUCESTER

In heavy fry pan sauté diced lobster in butter until butter has a good lobster color. Add 1 Tbspn. of the sherry while sautéing. Add cream slowly to lobster and simmer until hot. Add milk a little at a time. Transfer to large pot and continue to add milk. Keep warm but do not allow to boil. Can be set aside at this point. When ready to serve, heat until hot and add sherry to taste; sprinkle individual servings with paprika. Yields 4 servings.

1 lb. lobster meat (frozen, canned, or fresh), diced

¼ lb. butter

Sherry to taste

½ pint cream

1 quart milk, more or less

2 tspn. paprika

Wine tasting and dancing in the streets on University Avenue, gateway to Stanford University, are highlights of the Palo Alto Celebrates the Arts Festival. Exciting entertainment includes award-winning artists, a swing dance contest, and tea dances. Gourmet foods and plenty of sunshine make the two days complete. Sponsored by the Downtown Palo Alto Arts Fair Committee, the festival is produced by Terry Pimsleur & Company.

The Good Earth Restaurant, 185 University Avenue, Palo Alto, California, 94306, contributes this recipe.

PALO ALTO CELEBRATES THE ARTS FESTIVAL

PALO ALTO, CALIFORNIA, LATE AUGUST

YOGURT CREME PIE

PIE CRUST:

½ cup ground almonds

Graham crackers

FILLING:

10 oz. cream cheese

½ lb. ricotta cheese

½ cup fructose

¼ cup powdered milk

½ cup plain yogurt

2 tspn. grated lemon rind

4 tspn. lemon juice

2 tspn. vanilla

P*ie Crust:* Preheat oven to 400° F. Mix almonds and graham crackers together and press into pie tin. Bake for 10 minutes or until brown.

Filling: Bring cream cheese to room temperature. Beat until lumps are gone. Add ricotta cheese and beat until smooth. In a separate bowl mix fructose, powdered milk, and yogurt. Mix until fructose is dissolved. Add to cream cheese–ricotta mixture. Add lemon rind, lemon juice, and vanilla and mix until smooth. Put into pie crust (the filling should be slightly rounded and mounded) and refrigerate. Makes 1 pie.

For lovers of live music played in fascinating, beautiful surroundings, there's no better place than Bethlehem, Pennsylvania, during the nine days of Musikfest. From noon to 11 P.M. each day, a stroll around historic Bethlehem will bring music to your ears.

At Main and Spring streets, twirl to polka; at the landmark Sun Inn Courtyard, clap and tap to barbershop quartets, show music, and bluegrass; at City Center Plaza, dance and reminisce to the sounds of big band, folk, jazz, and brass bands.

In all, at least eight locations, or platz, offer a smorgasbord of music, art, food, traditional crafts (such as soap making and metalsmithing), and ethnic dancing. At Kinderplatz children can experiment with art activities and sidewalk chalk drawings in the company of clowns, jugglers, and storytellers. At Muralplatz local artists paint freestanding murals, and guests are encouraged to relax and enjoy watching the works in progress. Street performers and musicians wander from platz to platz, delighting all

MUSIKFEST

BETHLEHEM, PENNSYLVANIA, LATE AUGUST

in transit. There are also historic displays and demonstrations that honor the city of Bethlehem and the state of Pennsylvania.

All platz performances are outdoors and free to the public. In addition, several ticketed indoor concert series are available each evening for those who enjoy chamber, instrumental, jazz, or classical music.

Since 1984, the festival's first year, Musikfest has earned the respect and participation of many big-name performers. Ray Charles, Joan Baez, Dizzy Gillespie, the Spinners, the Clancy Brothers, the Air Force Band of the East, the Glenn Miller Orchestra, and many other versatile performers have appeared as part of the festival.

Musikfest is a celebration of beauty and diversity in food, costume, art, and, of course, music. During the nine days more than two hundred performers give hundreds of free performances—all within walking distance of each other!

Each spring Musikfest organizers publish a complete schedule of all performances and other essential festival information. These program books can be obtained from the festival office.

Audrey L. Szabo of Maison Suisse, at the Americus Centre, Allentown, Pennsylvania, says the following two desserts are among its biggest sellers. She has included both family and quantity recipes.

ROYAL VIENNESE WALNUT TORTE

YIELDS ONE 9-INCH TORTE TO SERVE 14:

Butter
___
Fine, dry bread crumbs
___
¼ cup strained unsweetened cocoa
___
1 lb. (4½ cups) walnuts, finely ground
___
12 eggs, separated
___
2 cups sugar
___
¼ tspn. salt

"8 x" RECIPE–YIELDS EIGHT 9-INCH TORTES:

Butter
___
Fine, dry bread crumbs
___
2 cups strained unsweetened cocoa
___
8 lb. (36 cups) walnuts, finely ground
___
96 eggs (8 dozen), separated
___
16 cups sugar
___
2 tspn. salt

COFFEE BUTTERCREAM:

Crème de cacao
___
6 egg yolks
___
½ cup sugar
___
3 Tbspn. instant coffee
___
½ cup boiling water
___
1 lb. (2 cups) butter
___
1 tspn. vanilla extract
___
3 Tbspn. dark rum or cognac
___
Chocolate coffee bean, for decoration

Torte: The layers for this torte should not be baked too high or too low in the oven or they will *burn*. Preheat oven to 350° F (325° F convection). Line the bottoms of the cake pans with paper. Butter the paper. Dust all over lightly with bread crumbs.

Add the cocoa to the walnuts and, with a fork, stir to mix. Set aside. Beat the egg yolks with an electric mixer at high speed about 3 minutes, until thick and pale lemon colored. Reduce the speed and gradually add the sugar. Increase the speed to high again, and continue to beat for 5 minutes more, until *very* thick.

Beat the egg whites and the salt until stiff but not dry. Remove from mixer. Fold ½ of the nut mixture into the yolks, and then, in the following order, fold in ⅓ of the whites, the remaining ½ of the nut mixture, ½ of the remaining whites, and then the balance of the whites.

Divide the batter among the prepared pans. Spread tops level. Bake 30–40 minutes or until tops spring back (layers come slightly away from the sides of the pans).

Coffee Buttercream: Brush torte layers with crème de cacao.

Place yolks in top of double boiler (not over heat). Beat a little, just to blend. Stir in the sugar. Dissolve instant coffee in boiling water. Gradually whisk the coffee into the yolk mixture. Place over hot water on moderate heat. *Water must not touch top of double boiler and it must not boil,* or the mixture will curdle. Cook for about 10–15 minutes until mixture thickens to a soft custard consistency, about 170° F–175° F on a candy thermometer. Remove from heat.

Place the custard mixture over ice water. Stir occasionally until mixture is *cool*.

Beat butter in small bowl of electric mixer to cream it slightly. Very gradually add the custard mixture, the vanilla, and the rum or cognac, and beat until smooth. (If necessary, refrigerate mixture to firm it, and then beat again at high speed to increase volume.) Decorate top of each torte with a chocolate coffee bean.

"8 x " RECIPE:
Crème de cacao

48 egg yolks (4 dozen)

4 cups sugar

24 Tbspn. (or 12 oz.) instant coffee

4 cups boiling water

8 lb. butter

8 tspn. vanilla extract

24 Tbspn. (or 12 oz.) dark rum or cognac

8 chocolate coffee beans, for decoration

WHITIES

Preheat oven to 325° F. Melt chocolate and butter. Whisk together eggs, sugar, and vanilla. Add chocolate and butter to egg mixture. Mix flour and salt into the chocolate-egg mixture. Pour batter into a 9-inch-by-9-inch pan. Melt white chocolate and drizzle on top, and then sprinkle slivered almonds on top. Bake for 20–30 minutes.

YIELDS 12:
9 oz. white chocolate (or ½ dark, ½ white)

1 stick (¼ lb.) butter

4 eggs

2 cups sugar

1½ tspn. vanilla

1 cup flour

½ tspn. salt

⅔ cup slivered almonds

"8 x" RECIPE YIELDS 96:
4½ lb. white chocolate (or ½ dark, ½ white)

2 lb. butter

32 eggs

16 cups sugar

4 Tbspn. vanilla

8 cups flour

1 Tbspn. plus 1 tspn. salt

5⅓ cups slivered almonds

WURST (SAUSAGE) KABABS

Bratwurst

Knackwurst

Polish kielbasa

Smoked bratwurst

Bauernwurst

Double-smoked bacon

Cooked ham

Green peppers

Boiling onions

Button mushrooms

Cherry tomatoes

Cut meats and peppers into 2-inch lengths. Blanch all vegetables except tomatoes. Place ingredients on skewers. Preheat grill or broiler and brown for 6–10 minutes on each side.

from Karl Ehmer
Quality Meats
Allentown, PA

Inn of the Falcon was established in 1809 on the land that was formerly a grant from England to William Penn. It is being restored by Al and Shirlee Newmeyer, who share two unusual recipes:

PAVLOVA

2 egg whites, room temperature

1 tspn. white vinegar

1 tspn. vanilla

3 Tbspn. boiling water

¾ lb. (1½ cups) superfine sugar

2 cups whipping cream

Kiwi fruit slices, as garnish

Pavlova, one of New Zealand's favorite desserts, is made of egg white and sugar. It is said to have been invented as a tribute to Anna Pavlova, who came to the island nation to dance as lightly as the fluffy dessert. The dessert is embellished with kiwi fruit, the native succulent that is brown on the outside, green on the inside, and named for New Zealand's curious flightless bird.

Preheat oven to 250° F. Generously grease and flour 9-inch flan pan with removable bottom, shaking off excess flour, or line baking sheet with parchment or waxed paper and draw 9-inch circle.

Using electric mixer on low speed, beat egg whites until soft peaks form. Add white vinegar and vanilla and continue beating on high until stiff. With mixer still on high, add boiling water in a slow, steady stream and beat well. Reduce mixer to low and gradually add superfine sugar, beating constantly until it is thoroughly incorporated.

Turn meringue into prepared pan or onto paper circle, spreading evenly. Bake 1 hour. Remove from pan or paper and let dry on rack in draft-free area.

Whip cream until stiff. Spread evenly over meringue, swirling or making design as desired. Decorate with kiwi slices. (Although the kiwi fruit makes it authentic, any type of berry can be substituted for the garnish.) Makes 6 servings.

INN OF THE FALCON PUMPKIN SOUP

In a stockpot sauté onions in butter until translucent; then add chicken stock and bread and bring to a boil. Meanwhile, puree parsley, garlic, coarse salt, and Tabasco in a blender or food processor. When stock has begun to boil, add puree and stir until blended. Reduce heat to simmer, add pumpkin or squash, and cook thoroughly until pumpkin is soft. Serves 4–6.

2 medium onions, peeled and sliced

2–4 Tbspn. butter

4 cups chicken stock

4 slices white bread

¼ cup chopped fresh parsley

1 clove garlic

1 Tbspn. coarse salt

Dash of Tabasco

2 cups cubed and peeled pumpkin or squash (canned pumpkin can be substituted; the flavor is heartier)

Three days of festivities in 1936 planted the seed for the Alaska State Fair, Inc., which now produces the biggest annual extravaganza in the state from its 220-acre site in south central Alaska. Wondering what a trip to this fair might have to offer?

Entertainment: Tap your feet to the music, marvel at the feats of jugglers, behold the world through a mime's eye. The fair's two major entertainment stages are supplemented by performers throughout the grounds—every day of the fair!

Exhibits: A fifty-five-pound cabbage just doesn't make the grade here: the winner usually weighs in at around seventy-five pounds. The giant vegetables are renowned, but they're only the beginning. Exotic mushrooms, beautiful handwork, furry rabbits, colorful flowers, breathtaking photographs, and doe-eyed calves are all here: Alaska's bounty on display.

Concessions: The fairgrounds host an array of vendors offering tempting foods, authentic Alaskan crafts, the latest innovations in industry, and everything in between.

Parade: The first Saturday morning is quiet on the fairgrounds; everyone is in downtown Palmer watching the parade. The valley's

ALASKA STATE FAIR, INC.

PALMER, ALASKA, LATE AUGUST/EARLY SEPTEMBER

oldest and largest parade features military bands, floats, horses, antique cars, and youth groups—more than seventy-five entries in all.

Carnival: Hours of entertainment await you on Alaska's largest midway. The rides are thrilling, and the games of skill and chance can make you a big winner.

Horse show: Western or English riding—whichever you prefer—you'll find it during the Labor Day weekend at the France Equestrian Center. The symmetry of equitation classes and the excitement of the gymkhana classes bring the state's best riders to the grounds for the last major show of the season.

Rodeo: Stakes are high, thrills and excitement abound, and competition is keen for cash prizes at the rodeo arena. Each Saturday and Sunday contestants ride wild bulls, team up to rope calves, and race around barrels. Midway through the action children converge on the arena for the calf scramble, gamely attempting to pluck a ribbon from the calf's tail. The calf works just as hard to keep the prize.

Sports events: You can run up Lazy Mountain in the marathon or sprint around the Springer road system. Wrestle in Alaska's only summer wrestling tournament, enter your baby in the Diaper Derby, or stake your claim to a seat and watch them all.

Colony village: Historic colony era buildings grace the southern end of the fairgrounds. The present Valley Performing Arts Center was once a church. A log structure and a historic building, transported from Anchorage, house the fair's offices. Postcards and letters can be mailed on the fairgrounds during the fair from another historic building. A small segment of Alaska is preserved here.

Special events: From parachutes floating downward on sunny afternoons over captivated crowds to the crackles and exploding lights of fireworks filling the night skies, special attractions are devised for the delight of fairgoers every year.

As the recipes that follow suggest, when you come to this fair you should leave your calorie conscience at home and take a culinary cruise around the world. More than fifty vendors offer an endless array of tempting treats of all descriptions. It's true, Scarlett: at this fair you'll never be hungry again. And if your waistline isn't quite the seventeen inches it used to be, why, frankly, my dear, you won't give a damn.

The culinary competitions at the fair are the source for *The Alaska State Fair Fiftieth Anniversary Cookbook*, a nicely balanced collection of main dishes, salads and vegetables, breads, pastries and desserts, and cookies and candies. There are also two sections of special interest: canning and Alaskan favorites. Recipes are clearly written, some with the kind of note your sister or best friend might tack on. Prizewinners are identified. The cookbook is available from Alaska State Fair, Inc.

BREAKFAST CASSEROLE

Melt butter or margarine in 9-inch-by-13-inch pan. Layer half of bread, ham, and cheese. Repeat with other half. Beat eggs, milk, mustard, spices, and salt; pour over top. Let stand overnight in refrigerator. Bake uncovered at 350° F for 45 minutes. Serves 2–8.

Excellent for a company breakfast; only fruit or juice is needed to complete the meal.

by Candie Graham

1 stick (¼ lb.) butter or margarine

12 slices bread, cubed

1 cup cubed ham

1 lb. shredded cheese, any kind

6 eggs

3 cups milk

1 tspn. prepared mustard

½ tspn. onion powder

Dash of pepper

½ tspn. salt

HALIBUT ALYESKA

Salt to taste

Pepper to taste

Halibut or flaky white fish

1 cup sour cream

1 cup mayonnaise

½ cup finely chopped onion

Tillamook or similar cheese

Preheat oven to 350° F. Salt and pepper enough halibut or flaky white fish for your family. Mix sour cream and mayonnaise. Place in pan slightly bigger and deeper than fish. Place fish in pan. Sprinkle onion on top. Sprinkle cheese on top of mixture. Bake for 35 minutes or until fish is done.
by Gloria Garrett

CHIRIKOF BEANS

4 cups dried pinto beans

1 tspn. garlic powder

1 tspn. onion powder

1 tspn. crushed red pepper

½ tspn. onion or garlic salt

½ tspn. chili powder

1 large pork hock, cut into medium-sized chunks

½ large onion, chopped

2 cloves garlic

Pick over and wash beans thoroughly. Start beans in cold water. Bring to simmer with garlic powder, onion powder, crushed red pepper, onion or garlic salt, and chili powder. Boil until beans are still fairly firm. Put in pork hock (cured or fresh—fresh will require a bit more salt at end of cooking), chopped onion, and garlic cloves. Cover with boiling water and continue to cook very slowly until beans are done and meat falls off the bone. (Total cooking time is 6–8 hours.) Side dishes of fresh corn bread and grated Cheddar cheese are great. Split your corn bread in half on your plate, cover with beans, and top with grated cheese. Enjoy. Serves a crew of 6.
by Island Chef

RABBIT SOUP

About 4–5 lb. rabbit (1 very large rabbit or 2 small ones), in pieces

6 cups water

Use enough rabbit to make 2 lb. of meat when boned. Put water, rabbit (with bones in), celery, carrot, and onion in pot. Heat to boiling, reduce

to simmer, and cover pot. Simmer for 2
hours. Add salt and pepper and simmer
another ½ hour. Strain broth, bring
to boil, add rice, and cook for 20 minutes.
Remove meat from bone, chop small,
and add to broth with balance of strained
vegetables. Add parsley and serve immediately. Serves 5–6.

by Mary Longenecker

½ cup celery, diced
1 carrot, diced
1 small onion, chopped
Salt and pepper to taste
¼ cup uncooked rice
2 Tbspn. parsley

GRANOLA

Preheat oven to 325° F. Cook oil and
honey over low heat until blended.
Combine dry ingredients in flat pan.
Remove blended oil and honey from
heat and mix in vanilla. Pour over dry
ingredients in 10-inch-by-15-inch pan,
and mix until dry ingredients are coated.
Bake until browned to your preference
(about 45 minutes), stirring every
10–15 minutes. Optional raisins or dried
apricots may be added while cooling.
Keeps for weeks in sealed container.
Makes about 13 cups.

by Diane K. S. Owens

½ cup oil
½ cup honey
8 cups uncooked oatmeal
1 cup slivered almonds
1 cup wheat germ
½ cup dried coconut
1 cup sunflower seeds
½ cup sesame seeds
½ cup bran
1 tspn. vanilla
1 cup raisins or diced dried apricots (optional)

SIX-WEEK RAISIN BRAN MUFFINS

Mix raisin bran cereal, sugar, flour,
baking soda, and salt together
in a large bowl. Add beaten eggs, shortening, and buttermilk. Mix well and
store in refrigerator until needed. Bake
in muffin pan at 400° F for 15–20 minutes. This batter will keep for up to 6

1 (15-oz.) box raisin bran cereal
3 cups sugar
5 cups flour
5 tspn. baking soda
2 tspn. salt

4 eggs, beaten

1 cup melted shortening

1 quart buttermilk

weeks, refrigerated in an airtight container.

by Carol Muncy
First-Place Blue Ribbon Winner

ALMOND CHEESECAKE WITH CHOCOLATE WEDGE GARNISH

1½ cups finely crushed vanilla wafers

1¼ cups sugar

½ cup chopped pecans

½ tspn. lemon rind

¼ cup margarine, melted

3 (8-oz.) pkg. cream cheese, softened

3 eggs

¾ tspn. almond extract

1 cup sour cream

CHOCOLATE WEDGES (OPTIONAL DECORATION):

3 squares semisweet chocolate

1 tspn. shortening

6 large strawberries, halved

Preheat oven to 375° F. Combine crushed wafers, 2 Tbspn. of the sugar, pecans, lemon rind, and margarine. Press into bottom of greased 8-inch springform pan. Chill. Cream the cream cheese and 1 cup of the sugar till light and fluffy. Add eggs one at a time, beating well after each. Blend in ½ tspn. of the almond extract. Pour into chilled crust. Be sure that oven is actually at 375° F and bake for 45 minutes exactly. Remove from oven and cool 30 minutes. Meanwhile, blend sour cream, the remaining 2 Tbspn. sugar, and the remaining ¼ tspn. almond extract. Spread over cooled filling. Bake for another 10 minutes. Cool. Refrigerate overnight before serving. Serves 12–16.

Chocolate Wedges: In saucepan over low heat, melt chocolate and shortening. On a 9-inch waxed paper circle spread chocolate; refrigerate till just set. Cut chocolate into 12 wedges. Chill until serving time. To decorate: Leaving green tops attached, slice strawberries in half. Carefully break apart chocolate wedges. Using strawberry halves as supports, place wedges on cake top so that 1 long end is resting on cake and the rest is up at an angle.

by Joan Paal-Fridley
Grand Champion, 1985

WINE CAKE

reheat oven to 350° F. Mix all Wine Cake ingredients together, blend well. Pour in greased and floured angel food cake pan. Bake for 35–40 minutes. When cooled mix the Cake Drizzle ingredients until well blended and drizzle over cake. Also nice with blueberries or raspberries on top.

by Pamela Knight
First-Place Blue Ribbon Winner, 1985

WINE CAKE:

1 pkg. yellow cake mix

1 (3-oz.) pkg. vanilla pudding

4 eggs

¾ cup cream sherry

¾ cup salad oil

CAKE DRIZZLE:

1 cup sifted confectioners sugar

5 tspn. milk or orange juice

1 to 2 drops vanilla

MOM'S BEST

ream together first 6 ingredients until light and smooth. Sift together next 4 ingredients, and add to creamed mixture. Stir. Add the oats, chocolate chips, and butterscotch chips. Stir. Put ⅓ dough in center of each of 3 sheets of wax paper and shape into rolls 2 inches in diameter. Twist ends of paper and refrigerate dough until firm. Preheat oven to 325° F. Cut ¾-inch slices and place 2 inches apart on cookie sheet. Bake for 15 minutes.

Dough can be frozen if properly sealed. To enhance flavor use the hands of little helpers to stir and sift.

by Mrs. Mary C. Bailey
First-Place Blue Ribbon Winner

½ cup soft butter

½ cup Crisco

1 cup white sugar

1 cup brown sugar

2 eggs

1½ tspn. vanilla extract

2 cups flour

2 tspn. baking powder

¼ tspn. salt

½ tspn. baking soda

2 cups old-fashioned oats

6 oz. semisweet chocolate chips

3 oz. butterscotch chips

PEANUT BUTTER RICE KRISPIES COOKIES

1 (6-oz.) pkg. butterscotch morsels

½ cup peanut butter

4 cups Rice Krispies

1 (6-oz.) pkg. chocolate chips

½ cup powdered sugar

2 Tbspn. butter or margarine

1 Tbspn. water

Melt butterscotch morsels with peanut butter in heavy saucepan over low heat, stirring constantly till well blended. Remove from heat. Add Rice Krispies, stirring till well coated with butterscotch mixture. Press half of mixture into buttered 8-inch-by-8-inch-by-2-inch pan. Refrigerate. Set remaining mixture aside. Combine chocolate chips, powdered sugar, butter or margarine, and water in the top of a double boiler. Stir over hot water until chocolate melts and mixture is well blended. Spread over chilled mixture. Spread remaining cereal evenly over top. Press in gently. Chill. Remove from refrigerator about 10 minutes before cutting.

by Robbie Johnson
Grand Champion, Governor's Cookie Jar

SANTA'S WHISKERS

1 cup lightly salted butter or margarine, softened

1 cup sugar

2 Tbspn. milk

1 tspn. vanilla

2½ cups flour (sift before measuring)

¾ cup finely chopped red and green candied cherries

½ cup chopped pecans

¾ cup shredded or flaked coconut

In large bowl mix butter or margarine and sugar. When creamy beat in milk and vanilla. Stir in flour, ¼ at a time, mixing well each time. Mix in candied cherries and pecans. Divide dough in half and shape each half into a cylinder 10 inches long and about 2 inches in diameter. Roll each in coconut; then wrap in wax paper and chill till firm, 2 or more hours. Heat oven to 375° F. Slice dough into ¼-inch rounds and place 1 inch apart on ungreased baking sheets. Bake 10–12 minutes or till edges are lightly browned. Cool.

Grand Champion, Governor's Cookie Jar

People seem to agree that summer—warm, relaxed, and usually all too short—deserves one heckuva sendoff come Labor Day weekend. The Yankee folks of Newburyport are no exception. Their annual Newburyport Waterfront Fest celebrates summer in grand fashion, filling three days with the best of a New England summer by the sea: a lobster fest and New England clambake, a seafood festival and beer garden along the Merrimack River, biplane and helicopter tours of the coast, and boats upon boats upon boats.

Newburyport is a restored Yankee seaport, billed as the Birthplace of the American Coast Guard. It is no surprise, then, that the Newburyport Waterfront Festival provides a unique and exciting blend of boating activities and more traditional festival events.

From Saturday through Labor Day, the Plum Island Fairgrounds (a mile from the restored downtown district) hosts an arts and crafts show with more than one hundred exhibitors, live entertainment, and a wide array of international foods and seafood specialties (a three-day lobster fest and clambake!).

NEWBURYPORT WATERFRONT FESTIVAL

NEWBURYPORT, MASSACHUSETTS, LABOR DAY WEEKEND

Children (and adults) can enjoy a number of special events: a child-sized puppet performance, a magic show, the annual downtown Diaper Derby, and the one-ring Pandemonium Circus. On Labor Day the Continental Navy of Newburyport adds a touch of history as, dressed in replicas of the uniforms of the day, they recreate the spirit of Revolutionary and post-Revolutionary War days.

Throughout the three-day festival, a thrilling selection of aerial activities is available: open cockpit biplane and ultralight rides, as well as more conventional helicopter and airplane tours of the coast. Downtown, meanwhile, restaurants overlooking the harbor offer cold brews and their finest culinary temptations at the "A Taste of Newburyport" seafood festival.

The boating activities begin on Sunday, and the Newburyport Yanks seem to define "boat" as just about anything that floats. The Mighty Merrimack Rowing Race is the annual dory rowing race down the Merrimack. Colorful sailboards run triangle and slalom courses in the Newburyport Sailboard Race. The Grand Prix of Newburyport provides the thrill of high-performance speedboat racing in the open ocean, paralleling Plum Island's beaches. Finishing up the racing circuit, kayakers and canoeists paddle down the Merrimack to the first buoy at the mouth of the river, in the annual Race to the Sea.

Appropriately, the Newburyport Waterfront Fest's organizers have recently adopted the motto: "Bigger . . . Better . . . Boatier . . ." Their unique combination of many and varied boating events with more traditional festival activities has created an exciting, sporty celebration that could only happen "on the waterfront."

The Newburyport Waterfront Festival is produced by Waterfront Festivals, Ltd., and it may be contacted for further information.

Following are a few samples of the delights you might find at the Newburyport Waterfront Festival.

THE BEST OF NEWBURYPORT
CHICKEN BRIE

4 chicken fingers

Flour in which to dredge chicken

2 Tbspn. butter

Splash dry vermouth

2 oz. Brie cheese (without rind)

¼ cup heavy cream

Salt, pepper, nutmeg to taste

Dredge chicken in flour, preheat skillet, add butter, and sauté chicken, but do not brown. Deglaze pan with vermouth; add Brie cheese and cream, reduce until sauce thickens. Season with salt, pepper, and nutmeg to taste. Serve with rice. This quantity serves 1; multiply accordingly.

by E. Stephen Farrell
Ten Center Street Restaurant

THE BEST OF NEWBURYPORT
SHRIMP IN PROSCIUTTO
AL FORMAGGIO

1 lb. shrimp (U/12)

½ lb. prosciutto, sliced thin

½ lb. butter

4 cloves fresh garlic, chopped

4 fresh shallots, chopped

2 tspn. flour

2 cups dry white wine

Juice of 1 fresh lemon

Peel and devein shrimp. Cut prosciutto in half lengthwise, wrap each shrimp and set aside.

Preheat oven to 375° F.

In large sauté pan melt butter; add garlic, shallots, and flour and cook at low heat for 2 minutes; add wine, lemon juice, and basil and cook until reduced by ⅓.

In separate pan boil water, cook sun-dried tomatoes 3 minutes; add to wine sauce.

Bake shrimp in prosciutto 30 minutes; add cheeses on top and bake until melted.

Top with sauce and serve. Serves 4.

by Michael Cardarelli
Ferlita's Restaurant

2 sprigs fresh basil, chopped
4 oz. sun-dried tomatoes
8 oz. mozzarella cheese, grated
4 oz. freshly grated Parmesan and Romano cheese (mixed)

THE BEST OF NEWBURYPORT CHILI

ook all ingredients except kidney beans and tomatoes in large covered roasting pan until vegetables are done. Remove to a large pot and then mix in kidney beans and tomatoes.

Heat to simmering. Be careful not to allow it to burn on the bottom. Stir well, but not violently. Makes 10 gallons.

by The Grog Restaurant

15 lb. hamburger
5 quarts onions, diced
5 quarts peppers, diced
12 serving spoons chili powder
4 serving spoons granulated garlic
4 serving spoons cumin
1 serving spoon coriander
2 serving spoons sugar
2 serving spoons black pepper
2 serving spoons salt
6 #10 cans kidney beans
3 #10 cans diced tomatoes
1 #10 can crushed, concentrated tomatoes

An "umbrella" for the arts. An umbrella for Seattle's weather. Combine the concepts and you get an old-fashioned word— *bumbershoot*—for a very up-to-date festival that is being hailed as the major arts event in the Northwest United States.

Nearly four million people have attended Bumbershoot since the city of Seattle created this celebration of the arts in 1971. It is situated on the beautifully landscaped grounds of the seventy-four-acre Seattle Center, site of the 1962 World's Fair.

Bumbershoot is dedicated to creativity, artistic excellence, and fun. More than 2000 artists from every discipline—music, dance, theater, performance art, visual and literary arts, film, video, and the crafts—assemble for Labor Day weekend to present the largest cultural hors d'oeuvres tray in the country.

The unique setting of Bumbershoot blends open park space with excellent entertainment facilities, including the Coliseum, Opera House, Center House, Play-

BUMBERSHOOT

THE SEATTLE ARTS FESTIVAL, SEATTLE, WASHINGTON

LABOR DAY WEEKEND (NOW INCLUDES PRE-EVENTS)

house, and Bagley Wright Theatre, plus outdoor stages. There's the Winegarten, the Café, and a minifestival, the Taste of Seattle, which features the best restaurants in the city.

Each year Bumbershoot invites hundreds of top regional performing groups to play, as well as legendary national headliners. There are nonstop performances in theater, dance, comedy, and the literary, visual, and culinary arts. One entire area, the For Kids' Sake Pavilion, is just for families with children.

International entertainers are an integral part of the festival. Special projects include dozens of street performers, unusual on-grounds artworks, an internationally recognized film festival, and the most extensive book fair on the West Coast.

This is a must-see festival for anyone within traveling range and a great destination for a family vacation. There is much thought and effort given to welcoming everyone: all readings and writers forums are signed for the hearing impaired, disabled visitors are admitted free, and there are various discounts for juniors (twelve and younger) and seniors (sixty-five and older). The single admission charge covers all Bumbershoot events for the day. Concert seating is on a first-come, first-served basis. No matter how you experience it, you can bet that your visit will be full of the unexpected and memorable.

Several Bumbershooters created recipes especially for us, to show off the fun and flavor of their festival.

BUMBER CALICO BEANS

Preheat oven to 350° F. Brown bacon, ground beef, and chopped onion. Drain off fat. Add all 3 cans of beans. Mix the rest of ingredients in bowl and add to bean-meat mixture. Cover and bake 40 minutes.

by Ken Kurata

½ lb. bacon

½ lb. ground beef

1 cup chopped onion

1 can kidney beans, drained

1 can butter beans, drained

1 can pork and beans

½ cup catsup

2 Tbspn. vinegar

1 tspn. powdered mustard, such as Coleman's

1 tspn. prepared mustard, such as French's

⅛ cup white sugar

¼ cup brown sugar

BUMBERSHOOTING ZUCCHINI PIE

Preheat oven to 375° F. Sauté onion, garlic, and zucchini in margarine until tender. (Use a nonhydrogenated margarine for better health.) Mix rest of ingredients in bowl. Add sautéed mixture to ingredients mixed in bowl, and pour into your favorite pie crust. (A simple crust idea to try: press a premade crescent roll dough into a pie dish. Due to the lard content of the dough, however, vegetarians should avoid this.) Bake 20–30 minutes.

by Bobbi Massari

1 cup chopped onion

3 cloves garlic, pressed

4 cups sliced zucchini

¼ cup melted margarine

2 eggs, beaten

1½ tspn. basil

½ tspn. oregano

½ tspn. tamari (or ¼ tspn. salt)

½ tspn. pepper

8 oz. shredded mozzarella cheese

APPLE ALMOND CAKE FOR BUMBERSHOOTERS

¾ cup flour

¾ cup whole wheat flour

1½ tspn. baking powder

¼ cup white sugar

3 Tbspn. butter, at room temperature

1 egg, beaten

1 tspn. almond extract

Enough milk to bring mixture to ¾ cup

6 cups sliced tart baking apples

Raisins and almonds

½ cup white sugar

½ cup brown sugar

2 tspn. cinnamon

3 Tbspn. melted butter

Preheat oven to 425° F. Combine flours, baking powder, and the ¼ cup sugar in mixing bowl. Blend in butter. Mix egg, almond extract, and milk separately in 1-cup measure. Add to flour-butter mixture. Spread in shallow greased pan. Arrange apples in overlapping rows on mixture in pan. Sprinkle with raisins and almonds. Mix the ½ cup white sugar, brown sugar, cinnamon, and melted butter. Sprinkle over apples. Bake 25 minutes.

by Kathleen McLaughlin

POTATO SAUSAGE SKILLET COMBINATION

¼ cup vegetable oil

1 lb. kielbasa or Polish sausage, diagonally sliced ½ inch thick

3 medium potatoes, pared, thinly sliced

½ cup sliced onion

1 tspn. caraway seeds

1 apple, cored and chopped

Dash pepper

2 Tbspn. minced fresh parsley

1 Tbspn. chopped fresh chives

Heat oil. Brown sausage. Remove and reserve. Mix together potatoes, onion, and caraway seeds and toss lightly to coat with the heated oil. Cover and cook over medium heat for 15 minutes. Uncover and add rest of ingredients. Cook 10 minutes, turning mixture carefully.

by Julie Peterson

FESTIVE FRUIT COMPOTE

Preheat oven to 350° F. Layer apples and pears in 1-quart casserole dish. Combine 1½ Tbspn. of the reserved pear syrup with rest of ingredients. Spoon over fruit. Bake uncovered for 9 minutes or until apples are tender. Serve warm with whipped cream.

by Julie Peterson

2 medium apples, peeled, cut in eighths

1 (16-oz.) can pears, drained (reserve syrup)

⅓ cup whole cranberry sauce

¼ tspn. cinnamon

¼ tspn. allspice

¼ tspn. cloves

Whipped cream

Todos Santos Park is the site for the Concord Fall Fest. For those who really enjoy personal participation in events involving food, there are grape stomps and chili cookoffs. For those who prefer to be entertained, there's an exceptional arts and crafts exhibition, a variety of music, and special treats for children. The festival is sponsored by the Concord Chamber of Commerce and produced by Terry Pimsleur & Company.

These recipes are the work of Dennis Allison, a well-known amateur chef who lives in San Francisco.

CONCORD FALL FEST

CONCORD, CALIFORNIA, LABOR DAY WEEKEND

QUAIL EGGS EN COCOTTE

3 medium to large mushrooms per person

Olive oil

Small quantities of savory fillings (see suggestions below)

3 quail eggs per person

Cream

Paprika or cayenne

Mushroom caps are filled with a savory mixture, capped with quail eggs, coated with cream in the manner of shirred eggs, baked briefly, and served just warmed through, with the yolks still liquid.

Preheat oven to 375° F. Clean and stem the mushrooms. Reserve the stems for another purpose (see savory stuffings that follow). Brush the caps with olive oil, place in a shallow pan, and bake for 10 minutes, basting every 3–4 minutes with oil, until they are just barely done.

Stuff the mushrooms with savory fillings according to directions below. Remember that the total quantity of filling for each mushroom cap is about ½–1 tspn., so a small quantity of ingredients goes a long way. Also remember that everything must be precooked, as the final preparation time is very short.

Place the mushroom caps in the oven until the fillings are heated through. Remove from the oven. Carefully break a quail egg into each mushroom cap.

Cover each quail egg with a thin layer of cream, sprinkle a dusting of paprika or cayenne if you wish, and return to the oven just long enough for the egg whites to set. Serve immediately.

Spinach and Cheese Filling: Steam spinach until barely done. Squeeze it in the corner of a kitchen towel to remove as much water as possible. Chop, mix with Parmesan cheese, salt, and pepper. Fill mushroom caps and add ½ tspn. of cream.

Italian Sausage, Mushroom, and Onion Filling: Take 1 small Italian sausage (some prefer the hot variety, but you may want to use the mild or the sweet). Prick the sausage, cover with water, and boil for 10 minutes or until done. Remove and chop a small quantity into fine dice. Dice the reserved mushroom stems, salt them lightly, and let them sit for 5 minutes. Squeeze them in the corner of a tea towel to remove as much moisture as possible, then sauté them over high heat with a little oil until dry. Sauté a small onion or shallots in olive oil. When golden add the reserved sausage and the mushroom duxelles and sauté for a few moments more. Drain off any excess fat. Place the mixture in the mushroom caps.

Salmon and Fennel Filling: Take a small piece of fennel and dice it fine. Take a small piece of onion, shallot, or the white of green onion and likewise dice it. In a small sauté pan, sauté the vegetables briefly and then add a small piece of salmon. Cook the salmon on one side until it's barely warm on the top. Remove from stove, dice the salmon, mix with the sautéed vegetables. Season with salt and pepper and place in mushroom caps.

Shrimp, Crab, or Scallop and Pea Pod Filling: String and steam a small number of pea pods until just tender. Cut into rough julienne and line the bottom of the mushroom caps with them. Cover with small quantity of diced cooked shrimp, crab, or scallops, and pea pods. If desired a small strip of nori or a tiny sliver of scallion might be used to complete the filling.

Asparagus and Cheese Filling: This is suitable only for the thinnest spear; wild asparagus is ideal. Steam the asparagus until just barely done. Reserve the tips and chop the remaining stalks very fine. Fill the mushroom caps with the asparagus dice, then ¼ tspn. Parmesan cheese and ½ tspn. of cream.

Although this recipe may seem to require a lot of last-minute preparation, it's possible to prepare the stuffed caps ahead of time, refrigerate them, and then reheat and stuff them. A microwave would work just as well if not better for the reheating process. The egg has to be cooked in an oven because a dry heat is needed.

These are rich and need something to cut the flavors. Present them on triangles of plain white bread toast (homemade style) and accompany them with a slice or two of bread buttered and coated with caraway or fennel seeds and then toasted in the oven. On the plate put a slice or two of melon, peeled oranges, or other fruit.

CHILI GLAZE CHICKEN WITH TWO BEAN PUREES

BLACK BEAN PUREE:
½ cup black beans

½ onion

1 ham hock

Olive oil

Salt

This dish is a study in contrasts. The centerpiece is grilled chicken, breast or thigh, glazed with a complex chili-flavored sweet and sour glaze, which adds a hot, richly spicy flavor to the basic flavor of the chicken.

Two separate bean purees, each the essence of simplicity, offset the complexity of the spiced chicken. The black bean puree is smooth and rich. The white bean puree is deliberately bland for contrast. Each accents the chicken's spicy flavor and offers an interesting texture and color contrast.

For the bean purees, wash and pick over the beans. If possible let them soak overnight. Put the black beans in a saucepan, add onion and ham hock, and cover with water. Do the same with the white beans and onion. Bring each to a boil and boil for 2–3 minutes, and then allow to cool for ½ hour. Add water as necessary. Repeat the process. Then simmer until the beans are tender.

Remove ham hock from the black beans. Puree black and white beans separately in a blender or food processor. Begin with only part of the cooking liquid and thin as necessary. The purees should be thin but not runny. Cut the meat from the ham hock, dice it finely, and add it to the black bean puree. Cover each puree with a thin layer of olive oil, cover with plastic wrap, and refrigerate until ready to use.

The day before serving, prick the skin of the chicken through the subcutaneous fat everywhere. This will allow the chicken to pick up the flavor of the marinade and also allow the fat to escape when it is cooked. Alternatively, remove the skin. Mix the paprika, red chili pepper flakes, black pepper, oregano, basil, and salt together. Dry the chicken, rub it with the cut side of limes or lemons, and then work the spice mixture into the chicken using the heel of your hand. In a covered glass or stainless steel bowl just large enough to hold the chicken, mix the mirin, olive oil, soy sauce, ginger, and pressed garlic together with the juice of the lemons or limes. Put the chicken into the marinade; the pieces should be covered by the liquid. Cover the chicken and refrigerate ovenight. Stir occasionally.

Black pepper

WHITE BEAN PUREE:
½ cup white beans

½ onion

Olive oil

Salt

White pepper

CHICKEN:
8 chicken thighs or breasts, preferably from free-range chicken

4 tspn. butter

2 Tbspn. olive oil

Fresh cilantro or basil, for garnish

CHICKEN MARINADE:
Paprika to taste

Red chili pepper flakes to taste

Black pepper to taste

½ tspn. oregano

½ tspn. basil

Salt to taste

2 limes or lemons

¼ cup Japanese mirin wine

¼ cup olive oil

¼ cup soy sauce (dark Chinese preferred)

1 tspn. ground ginger

2 cloves garlic, pressed

2 tspn. arrowroot

To prepare chicken, drain off the marinade. Heat butter and olive oil in a sauté pan or large frying pan on medium-high heat until the butter foams. Be careful not to let it brown. Brown the chicken quickly (2–3 minutes), turn down heat, cover, and simmer slowly. Every 10–15 minutes turn the chicken and spoon on a bit of the marinade. When the chicken is done, place the pieces in a broiler pan and turn on the broiler. Mix the pan juices and any remaining marinade, wet the chicken, and place it in the broiler for 2 minutes. Repeat the process until a thick and shiny glaze is formed.

To serve, use a warmed deep dinner plate. Reheat the two bean purees over low heat or use a microwave. Season each puree to taste with salt and pepper. Place the white bean puree on one side of the plate and the black bean puree on the other to form a yin-yang shape. Place the chicken in the center. Place a small quantity of aromatic fresh herbs (cilantro or basil) on the chicken for color.

Accompany the chicken and beans with a dark leafy green vegetable (kale, chard, or spinach), steamed, drained, and dressed with a squeeze of lemon juice, served on a separate plate with tortillas (flour, corn, or blue corn).

VALLEJO WATERFRONT FESTIVAL

VALLEJO, CALIFORNIA, EARLY SEPTEMBER

The beautiful marina park on the bay is the setting for the Vallejo Waterfront Festival, which includes an arts and crafts exhibition, entertainment of many kinds, and delicious food and wine. Saturday night features a *Great Gatsby* theme party, with guests in period dress or black tie. Sponsored by the Vallejo Chamber of Commerce, the festival is produced by Terry Pimsleur & Company.

GRILLED GREEN BEANS

This dish is simplicity itself. The grilling process gives a slightly smokey taste.

Blanch the green beans briefly in boiling water; they should be very crisp. Cool them quickly in cold water to stop their cooking.

Slice the garlic thinly, place it in the olive oil, and heat gently until the garlic colors. Remove from heat and let the oil cool.

Clean the red pepper and cut 8 thin, uniform slices.

Use a grill pan, that is, a cast-iron pan with a ridged bottom. Heat over high heat. Brush the green beans with the garlic-flavored oil and grill, turning once. Season with salt and pepper to taste. Using the same technique, grill the red pepper. The red pepper should be cooked until limp, the green beans should be crisp.

To serve, divide the beans between 4 white plates and garnish each serving with 2 slices of the red pepper. Dress with lemon juice. Serve warm, not hot. Serves 4.

by Dennis Allison
San Francisco

2 lb. green beans

2 cloves of garlic

2 Tbspn. olive oil

1 red bell pepper

Salt and pepper to taste

Lemon juice

MOCK OYSTER CASSEROLE

1 medium eggplant

8 oz. fresh or canned minced clams

Cream to make 1 cup (in combination with the clam juice)

1 Tbspn. butter

1 minced onion

1 Tbspn. flour

1 Tbspn. chopped parsley

Buttered bread crumbs

Grated Cheddar cheese, for garnish

Pimientos, for garnish

Preheat oven to 350° F. Peel eggplant and cut into good-sized chunks. Boil for 10 minutes in salted water. Drain clams, reserving the juice, and add cream to clam juice to make 1 cup. Melt butter and sauté onion till transparent. Add flour and clam juice with cream, stirring until mixture thickens. Fold in eggplant and parsley. Place in buttered baking dish and top with bread crumbs. Bake for 30 minutes. Garnish with grated Cheddar cheese and pimientos.

by Zell Trippsmith

"Take a Grape Escape." The Michigan Wine and Harvest Festival and the Michigan Grape and Wine Industry Council proudly welcome you to a celebration of tastes. Michigan is capturing growing national recognition as a leading grape grower and produces some of the country's finest foods and beverages.

Southwest Michigan wineries use a mixture of native American and French American hybrid grapes to produce their special blends of wines and juices. The festival showcases Michigan's wine industry, with area wineries offering various tours and tastings and local service organizations producing a number of events. All profits go into helping worthy programs.

The festival has grown enormously since its inception as the Grape Festival in 1968, drawing more than 250,000 people for the four-day event. And no wonder! There's something for everyone, from original events and live entertainment to carnival rides to the real roots of the festival: the taste sensations found in the wine tents, juice tents, and ethnic food booths.

MICHIGAN WINE AND HARVEST FESTIVAL

KALAMAZOO/PAW PAW, MICHIGAN, EARLY SEPTEMBER

In addition to carnival midways in both Kalamazoo and Paw Paw, there are KLS&C train rides in Paw Paw and steamboat rides on Maple Lake. Both towns have lots going on, from a Turtle Derby to square dancing, and each town has an arts and crafts fair and various kinds of live entertainment.

The highlight on Saturday is a big parade in downtown Kalamazoo, with marching bands, cartoon characters, and beautifully decorated floats. Saturday evening offers a choice between a street dance and a Las Vegas Night, but don't stay up too late. Sunday in Paw Paw starts early, with registration at 7 A.M. for the Vineyard Classic Bike Tour, which gives cycling enthusiasts a chance to tour the area vineyards while enjoying the softly rolling hills and peaceful farmlands.

The Grape Stomp takes place in Paw Paw from noon to 5 P.M. on Saturday, and the Grape Stomp-Off, ending with the Champagne Race, closes out the festivities on Sunday afternoon. What a wonderful way to escape the dog-days of summer.

The following recipes were created for the St. Julian Wine Company of Paw Paw, Michigan, producers of fine wines and champagnes. The creator, Eva Braganini, is a well-known local chef, as well as the wife of the festival's vice-president.

CHAMPAGNE LEMONADE PUNCH

1 (6-oz.) can lemonade concentrate, thawed

2 fifths St. Julian champagne, chilled

2 pkg. frozen strawberry halves (or 2 cups fresh strawberries)

1 bottle sparkling water

Reconstitute lemonade concentrate as directed on can. Pour into ice cube tray or mold and freeze. Mix together other 3 ingredients. Add frozen lemonade to punch.

SOLERA CREAM CAVIAR

1 pkg. unflavored gelatin

¼ cup cold water

1 medium onion, finely chopped

6 hardboiled eggs, finely chopped

1 (3-oz.) jar caviar, drained on paper towels

1¼ cups mayonnaise

1 Tbspn. Worcestershire sauce

½ cup heavy cream, whipped into soft peaks

½ cup St. Julian Solera cream sherry

This is a delightful dip or spread. Soften gelatin in cold water, and then warm in pan over low heat (do not boil). Cool. Mix onion, eggs, caviar, mayonnaise, and Worcestershire sauce. Add cooled gelatin. Fold in whipped cream. Add Solera cream sherry. Pour into serving dish. Chill at least 6 hours. Serve with melba toast rounds or crackers.

WINE MUSHROOM CAPS

2 cloves of garlic, pressed

3 Tbspn. butter

½ cup Asiago or Parmesan cheese, grated

½ cup seasoned bread crumbs

½ cup St. Julian Village White wine

16 large mushroom caps, washed and stems removed

Preheat broiler. Sauté garlic in butter in saucepan. Add the grated cheese, bread crumbs, and wine. Mix well. Fill mushroom caps with mixture. Place under broiler until golden brown. Makes 16 hors d'oeuvres.

Fall is in the air, the trees burst with color. Of all the events planned across North America to delight local residents and their visitors alike, the Jackson County Apple Festival is what a scriptwriter would describe to set up a warm family atmosphere.

Back in the spring of 1937, some members of the Jackson Chamber of Commerce, wishing to do something that would have significance for all the county residents, decided to promote one of the county's leading industries, apple growing. More than forty farmers were producing apples commercially. The chamber members wanted some occasion to bring together people of the rural areas and the cities in a cooperative way. They also hoped that this would give former residents of the area a special time each year to come back home and visit family and friends. On the second day of that first festival, a severe storm blew off most of the roofing that covered the booths, but the crowds came anyway, everyone had a good time, and the festival was on its way.

JACKSON COUNTY APPLE FESTIVAL

JACKSON, OHIO, LATE SEPTEMBER

From Tuesday night through Saturday night, the whole town celebrates with a variety of activities. There's the really big machine event: a tractor pull. Visit the Appalachian Old Car Show, watch a demonstration of remote control cars, or marvel at the radio control air show. Rather ride than watch? Hire one of the horse-drawn carriages available each day. Or, if you're really serious about rides, head to the midway, where there are rides for both young and adult thrill-seekers.

Daily, there are exhibits of quilts, colonial needle art, and apple butter making. Also, each day the activities are geared toward special age groups.

On Kids Day there's a school parade, with Little Queen contestants, and contests in apple bobbing and apple peeling are held. The Grand Opening Parade leads up to the crowning of the Jackson County Apple Festival queen, who reigns over the weekend of festivities. And the men aren't left out in Jackson: there's the Men's Leg Contest (open to all men eighteen years and older, entry fee $3).

Thursday is Preschoolers Day, and their activities include a coin hunt, a baby crawling contest, a preschoolers parade, and a stuffed animal competition. For adults there's an apple pie baking contest. The Little Baton Corps competition is open to groups from eight counties. And the dogs have their day with a Beagle Bench Show.

Friday is Senior Citizens Day, with a craft show and sale. That night everyone brings lawn chairs to the outdoor stage to enjoy the featured entertainers.

Saturday has competitions in volleyball and cheerleading, as well as continuous entertainment on stage. At 5 P.M., when all the display apples go up for sale, "Your chance to buy some of the finest apples in Ohio comes." Then it's time for the Grand Finale Parade. The participants in this parade are present by invitation only, so the crowd is certain to see a fine spectacle, worthy of its billing as Ohio's Largest Lighted Parade.

The tempting recipes that follow were featured in the 1987 festival program, which was titled Wonderful World of Apples.

APPLE STREUSEL PIE

3 cups sliced apples

3 Tbspn. tapioca

1 cup sugar

1 tspn. cinnamon

½ cup water

¼ tspn. salt

9-inch pie shell, baked

1 cup flour

½ cup brown sugar

½ tspn. cinnamon

1 tspn. orange juice

4 Tbspn. butter

Preheat oven to 350° F. Combine first 6 ingredients in saucepan and cook over low heat until apples are tender. Pour into pie shell. To make streusel, combine flour, brown sugar, cinnamon, and orange juice. Spread streusel over apple mixture, and dot with butter. Bake for 35–40 minutes.

APPLE CUSTARD PIE

2 cups sliced apples

9-inch pie shell, unbaked

1 cup sugar

1 cup flour

1 tspn. cinnamon

Preheat oven to 375° F. Arrange ½ the apples in bottom of pie shell. Mix sugar and flour and spread ½ the mixture evenly over apples. Place the rest of apples on top and spread remaining sugar and flour over them. Sprinkle with cinnamon and nutmeg and dot with butter. Pour milk mixed with egg, vanilla, and salt over entire mixture. Bake for about 50 minutes.

Dash of nutmeg

2 Tbspn. butter

1½ cups milk

1 egg, beaten

1 tspn. vanilla

¼ tspn. salt

PINEAPPLE-APPLE BLUSH PIE

Preheat oven to 375° F. Combine first 8 ingredients in order given and pour into pie shell. Dot top with butter and make a lattice top crust. Bake for 50–60 minutes or until crust is golden brown and apples tender.

2 cups sliced apples

1 small can pineapple chunks

½ cup brown sugar

½ cup red hots (cinnamon candy bits)

¼ tspn. salt

2 Tbspn. cornstarch

½ tspn. nutmeg

1 Tbspn. lemon juice

9-inch pie shell, unbaked, and dough for lattice crust

1 Tbspn. butter

WALDORF SALAD

In large bowl mix first 6 ingredients. Thin mayonnaise with cream. Add salt. Add mayonnaise mixture to other ingredients and toss together. Chill before serving.

2 cups chopped apples

2 Tbspn. lemon juice

2 cups chopped celery

2 cups seedless grapes, halved

1 cup chopped dates

1 cup chopped walnuts

1 cup mayonnaise

2 Tbspn. thick cream

½ tspn. salt

APPLE BUTTER COOKIES

¼ cup sugar

½ cup butter

1 cup apple butter

1 tspn. baking soda

2 cups flour

½ tspn. salt

1 tspn. baking powder

½ cup buttermilk

½ tspn. vanilla

½ cup raisins

½ cup nuts

Preheat oven to 350° F. Cream sugar and butter. Mix apple butter and baking soda, and add to creamed mixture. Sift together flour, salt, and baking powder, and add alternately with buttermilk and vanilla to first mixture, mixing thoroughly. Stir in raisins and nuts. Bake for 10–12 minutes on greased cookie sheet.

APPLE CARROT SALAD

SALAD:

2 cups diced apples

1 cup grated carrots

1 cup diced celery

½ cup nuts

½ cup raisins

DRESSING:

1 egg, beaten

⅔ cup cream

⅓ cup vinegar

Mix Salad ingredients. Combine Dressing ingredients and cook until slightly thickened. Mix Salad and Dressing.

⅔ cup brown sugar

½ cup granulated sugar

1 tspn. salt

APPLE BREAD PUDDING

Preheat oven to 350° F. Sauté bread cubes in butter, and spread over bottom of greased casserole dish. Pour applesauce over bread cubes. Sprinkle lemon juice, brown sugar, cinnamon, and salt over applesauce. Pour maple syrup over top of all. Bake for 30–35 minutes. Serve warm with cream.

2 cups bread cubes

3 Tbspn. butter

2 cups applesauce

½ tspn. lemon juice

½ cup brown sugar

1 tspn. cinnamon

Pinch of salt

⅓ cup maple syrup

Cream, for topping

COOL, CREAMY APPLE SOUP

Combine grated apple, wine, lemon juice, sugar, ginger, and salt. Cook in saucepan over low heat for about 1 hour, stirring occasionally. Cool. Blend in cream. Garnish with nutmeg.

2 cups grated apple

1 cup red wine

1 tspn. lemon juice

1 cup sugar

1 tspn. ginger

¼ tspn. salt

1 cup thick cream

Dash nutmeg

The Pacific Coast Fog Festival, a tongue-in-cheek event, promises history, humor, and sunny skies on the Pacific coastline. There is a parade, there are oyster shucking contests, there are kayak races. For history buffs there are treks to the discovery site of San Francisco Bay. Arts and crafts are on exhibit, and there are outdoor cafés for every taste. On Sunday emphasis is placed on a special Family Fest. Sponsored by the city of Pacifica, the festival is produced by Terry Pimsleur & Company.

PACIFIC COAST FOG FESTIVAL

PACIFICA, CALIFORNIA, LATE SEPTEMBER

FOG CUTTER

1½ jiggers Puerto Rican rum

⅔ jigger brandy

⅓ jigger gin

⅔ jigger orange juice

1 jigger lemon juice

⅓ jigger Orgeat syrup

Sherry

Shake ingredients, except the sherry, with cracked ice, and pour into a 14-oz. glass. Float sherry on top. Serves 1.
by Tom Schaaf

FILLET OF SOLE WITH CILANTRO SAUCE

Spinach leaves, washed and stemmed, to make about 1 cup, packed

Cilantro to taste

1½ lb. fillet of sole

Fish stock, unsalted clam juice, or water and white wine

This is a simple dish with a distinctive sauce colored bright green.
Steam the spinach until it is just barely tender, plunge it into cold water, and then drain on towels. Squeeze the spinach in the corner of a tea towel to remove as much moisture as possible, and coarsely chop it. You should have a

scant ¼ cup. Put it into the container of a blender or food processor.

Wash the cilantro, stem it, and place the leaves in the blender with the spinach.

Poach the sole slowly over very low heat in fish stock or unsalted clam juice to cover. If neither is available, use water mixed with a small amount of white wine (⅔ water, ⅓ wine or less). When the fish is still slightly underdone, remove from the poaching liquid to a platter and keep it warm.

Reduce the poaching liquid over high heat until there is about ½ cup. Put the liquid into the blender container, and blend at high speed until the sauce is smooth and uniform.

Return the sauce to the sauté pan, pouring through strainer to catch any big fibers from the vegetables. The result should be a bright green sauce with a distinct flavor. Ideally, it should have the consistency of cream and coat a spoon. If it is too thin, stir in ¼ tspn. of arrowroot; if too thick, add a small quantity of water. Season to taste with salt and pepper. Raise the heat under the sauce, quickly whisk in the butter, dress the fish, and serve immediately. Makes 4 servings.

Serve the fillets, flat or rolled, on individual plates. Rolling it, 2 to 3 part-fillets per person, makes for a neater presentation. Arrange the fish in the center of the plate with a slosh of green sauce cutting across it and white unsauced fish on either side. Accompany it with a boiled potato or two and a small fresh tomato, peeled, seeded, chopped, and dressed with a mild aromatic vinegar (rice, berry, or sherry). Some onion and hot chilies could also be included for contrast to the blandness of the fish.

by Dennis Allison

Arrowroot

Salt and pepper to taste

A small piece of butter

So, you want to experience the world! Would you pack up your travel bag and head for . . . the Midwest? You would if Ohio's Middfest International were your destination.

This three-day festival in Middletown, Ohio, is an opportunity to experience languages, traditions, dance, art, music, and (of course) food from around the world. And each year the history and culture of a selected featured country are given special focus. Since Middfest International's first year in 1980, the featured countries have included Mexico, Luxembourg, Egypt, Brazil, Japan, Switzerland, Canada, and Italy.

Many activities vary from year to year, depending on what country is featured. In 1985, for example, when the featured country was Japan, there were sushi tastings, Japanese kite exhibitions, traditional tea ceremonies, concerts by the elegant Mizuki dancers, calligraphy demonstrations, and a chance to examine the important U.S.–Japan trade relationship and meet the Japanese ambassador to America.

The festival receives impressive cooperation from foreign consulates and cultural groups. A big, delightful Middfest International souvenir

book offers fascinating and thoughtful pieces on both ordinary and extraordinary aspects of the year's featured country.

Each year there are sporting events (such as darts and chess tournaments, bike tours, and running races), essay and photography contests, and an endless variety of fine, free entertainment: ethnic and international music, dance, and drama.

Youth Park, constructed around themes from the featured country, educates and entertains juvenile visitors. At the World Bazaar tent, vendors offer jewelry, games, arts and crafts, and travel information from around the globe. Next door, at an American handcrafts tent, the same variety of works, handcrafted in America, is seen. An international gift shop offers a wide selection of items and displays exclusively from the featured country.

Of course all adventures at Middfest International must lead to that great cultural common denominator: food! Extraordinary care is taken by Middfest International organizers to ensure that the food is both varied and authentic. Each year they select twenty to twenty-five menus of international taste treats that festival vendors may serve—from mango ice cream to curried lamb. There are also opportunities at the Global Deli or the International Café or the Wine and Cheese Garden for closet gourmets to sample some of the tastiest vices from around the world!

Although the festival originated as a showcase for Middletown's worldwide business and industry connections, it quickly developed a higher purpose: by stimulating curiosity and fostering understanding of other peoples, each year the festival moves a different country off the map and into our realm of experience. It's also a lot of fun. And when Middfest International has featured every country on the globe, we can only hope they do the wise thing: start all over again!

The following recipes and introductions are from two collections of *Middfest Annual Cooking Contest Prize Winners*.

MIDDFEST INTER- NATIONAL 1983, FEATURED COUNTRY: EGYPT

The first thing visitors [to Egypt] will notice is that the local restaurants are highly specialized and usually serve only one kind of food. The Haty serves kabab and kofta (a recipe for which [kofta] follows). The Musmut serves the heads and knuckles of veal and beef. The Koshary restaurant serves a mixture of rice, macaroni, lentils and fried onion, with a tomato sauce made with vinegar. The fish restaurants serve only fish and shrimp, and finally—the favorite of all Egyptians—the bean restaurants which serve fava beans and falafel.

Egyptian cooking, in general, is very simple, as might be seen from the following recipes.

FALAFEL

Soak shelled fava beans for 24 hours. Put in a food processor with metal blade and add parsley, spring onions, onion, bread, and garlic. Process until you get a smooth green paste. Add salt and pepper.

Just before serving heat oil in a deep pan, and then add baking soda to the paste. Wet your hands and make small round patties about the size of silver dollars and twice as thick. Put into the hot oil one by one, and fry until dark brown. Remove and drain on a paper towel. Keep warm until ready to serve. Serve with salad and tahini (Tahini Dip recipe follows) or make into sandwiches with pita bread.

1 lb. shelled fava beans
1 bunch parsley
6 spring onions
1 medium onion, diced
2 bread slices soaked in water and squeezed dry
8 cloves garlic
Salt and pepper to taste
2 tspn. cumin
Oil for deep frying
½ tspn. baking soda

TAHINI DIP

2 cups tahini

3 cloves garlic

1 tspn. cumin

Juice of 1 lemon

Salt and pepper to taste

Water

Put the tahini, garlic, cumin, lemon juice, and salt and pepper in a food processor. Process for a minute, then start adding water slowly until you get a creamy consistency. Chill and serve as a dip, or add to other recipes as suggested.

KOFTA

2 lb. ground lamb meat

1 large onion, cut in chunks

Salt and pepper

½ bunch parsley

3 cloves garlic

Put meat in a bowl and set aside. Process all the other ingredients for 2 minutes in a food processor with a metal blade. Add to meat and mix very well; let stand for 3 hours. Shape the meat into long fingers ½-inch thick; run a skewer through the fingers and barbecue. Serve like kabob, or with it.

WARA EINAB
(Stuffed Vine Leaves)

½ kilo vine leaves (about 1 lb. 2 oz.)

1 cup rice

1 ½ b. ground beef

1 large onion, chopped

6 Tbspn. tomato puree

2¼ tspn. salt

Mint to taste

Tomatoes, sliced

A few cloves garlic

Soften vine leaves by plunging into boiling water, a few at a time, for about 1 minute or until limp. Wash and drain rice. Mix rice with meat, onion, tomato puree, salt, and mint. Cut stems off vine leaves. Place on plate right side up and fill with small amount of meat mixture. Fold over stem end, then sides, and roll like a cigar. Line bottom of saucepan with tomato slices or leftover vine leaves. Pack the stuffed leaves in tight layers on top, pushing the odd piece of garlic here and there between them. Sprinkle with lime juice and add water. Simmer, covered, over low heat for about 1 hour, adding more water if necessary.

Serve hot or cold by turning pan upside down over serving dish. It should turn out like a mold. (Note: It will take about 2 hours to do the rolling.)

Juice of 1 lime

1¼ cups water

EL BELEHAT

Mix the ground beef with 2 of the eggs, chopped garlic, cumin, and salt and pepper. Form the mixture into small sausage shapes. Dip each sausage into the third beaten egg, and then roll in the bread crumbs. Pour olive oil into a frying pan and heat on medium-high. Brown the meat in the hot oil. Cover with tomato sauce. Lower heat, cover, and cook slowly for ½ hour. Serves 6.

1 lb. ground beef

3 eggs, beaten

2 cloves garlic, chopped

½ tspn. cumin

Salt and pepper to taste

Bread crumbs

Olive oil

Rich tomato sauce

FOOL

Fool consists of black beans that have been cooked the previous night. Its popularity and price make it the Egyptian equivalent of the hot dog.

The night before serving cook the beans slowly until they are reddish brown and soft. The day of serving mash the beans with a fork. Add vegetables, oil, salt, pepper, and lemon or vinegar. Tahini may also be added. Serve on pita bread or on a bun.

Cooked black beans

Freshly chopped tomato to taste

Chopped cucumber to taste

Chopped onion to taste

Corn or olive oil to taste

Salt and pepper to taste

Lemon or vinegar to taste

B razilian cuisine is most unusual! It is flavored by its historical ties to Portugal and Africa. In northeastern Brazil, the African influence is strong and one will find seafood, and dishes made with sauces combining hot peppers, coconut, and coconut milk. In the southerly areas, the cuisine relies more on beef and pork dishes—many with spicy sauces including garlic, onion, tomato, and fresh coriander.

The one dish found in all parts of Brazil is the Feijoada—the national dish. It is a festive dish of smoked and fresh meats (sometimes even including the pig's ears and pig's feet), black beans, rice, and trimmings—orange slices, shredded kale, or collard greens. This is most often eaten on Saturday—after eating it no one has the energy to do anything else.

These Brazilian recipes will treat you to a gastronomical adventure unlike any you will find anywhere else. ENJOY!

FEIJOADA

1 lb. slightly salted shoulder of pork

1 lb. slightly salted spare ribs

1 lb. pig's tail, slightly salted

2¼ lb. slightly salted trotters

1 lb. smoked shoulder of pork

¾ lb. smoked breast of pork

1 lb. smoked sausage

2¼ lb. carne seca (Brazilian dried beef) (optional)

4½ lb. small Brazilian black beans

2 onions, chopped

1 head garlic, cloves separated, peeled, and crushed

1 stalk celery, finely chopped

3 bay leaves

1 bouquet garni

1 tspn. freshly milled black pepper

T his is the most famous dish in Brazil. It is a party dish. There are as many recipes for it as there are Brazilian families.

The evening before serving, rinse the slightly salted meats, and leave to soak all night under a thin trickle of water.

The next day put all the meat, beans, onions, crushed garlic, celery, bay leaves, bouquet garni, and pepper in a large, heavy pot. Fill with water. Bring slowly to boiling point and leave to simmer 2 hours. Remove each piece of meat from the pot as soon as it is cooked. Cook the beans for another hour. (The liquid should become thick and creamy.) Pour the beans into a cast-iron pot. Cut the meat into cubes and add to the beans. Bring to a boil, simmer for 10 minutes, and serve. Makes 10 large servings.

Serve with white rice Brazilian style, green cabbage cut in strips, pepper sauce, ground cassava meal, and orange slices, all mixed together.

CAMARAO PIRIPIRI
(Deep-Fried Shrimp with
Spicy Spinach)

Clean the spinach, removing stems, and steam for several minutes until limp. Set aside.

In a frying pan sauté the onion and tomatoes in the palm oil for 5 minutes over medium heat, and then add the spinach. Season with salt and cook for 3 minutes. Add 2 Tbspn. of Piripiri Hot Sauce. Reserve remaining Piripiri Hot Sauce for other uses.

Heat vegetable oil to 375° F in a deep pot and fry the shrimp until they are golden brown, 1–2 minutes. Drain on paper towels. To serve, place some of the spinach mixture on each plate and top with 4 shrimp. Serves 4.

Piripiri Hot Sauce: Place all ingredients in a blender and puree until liquid.

12 oz. fresh spinach
1 large onion, sliced
2 tomatoes, peeled and sliced
½ cup palm oil
Salt to taste
Vegetable oil for deep frying
16 jumbo shrimp

PIRIPIRI HOT SAUCE:

3 jalapeño peppers, stems removed, chopped
⅓ cup Tabasco sauce
2 tspn. olive oil
1 Tbspn. lemon juice

PALMITO GRATINADO
(Gratinéed Hearts of Palm)

In a saucepan over medium-low heat, melt the butter and then add the flour, whisking constantly for about 5 minutes.

Slowly whisk in the wine and the liquid from the hearts of palm; then add the cream. Continue cooking and whisking until the mixture thickens, about 10 minutes.

Remove the palm hearts from the can and cut them into pieces. If any of the tough outer husk remains attached to the palm hearts, trim it off. Place the

⅓ stick butter
5 Tbspn. all-purpose flour
¾ cup dry white wine
¾ cup liquid from hearts of palm
8 oz. heavy cream
1 (20-oz.) can hearts of palm
¼ tspn. white pepper, or to taste
6 Tbspn. grated Parmesan cheese

palm hearts in the white sauce. Stir well
over low heat and add pepper.

Place the mixture in a shallow baking
dish and sprinkle with the cheese.
Place under a broiler until the cheese is
golden brown and crisp. Serves 6.

BRAZILIAN PASTEIS

4 cups flour

1 Tbspn. butter, melted

1 Tbspn. Crisco, melted

1 egg

½ cup rum

1 tspn. salt

Fillings (see suggestions following
directions)

Oil, for frying

Sift flour onto board or work table.
Make a hole in the center and put
butter, Crisco, egg, rum, and salt in it.

Carefully mix into a smooth dough. If
necessary, add more rum.

Knead the dough, roll it, cover it with
plastic, and let it sit for an hour.

Lightly flour the board or table. Roll
out the dough until it is very thin.
Cut the pasteis in the shapes and sizes
you prefer. Fill them (see suggestions
below), fold over, and seal cut edges by
pressing with the tines of a fork so that
the filling does not come out when
frying.

Fry them in very hot oil.

Fillings: Well-seasoned chopped meat,
shrimp, hearts of palm, and shredded
cheese are some of the traditional
fillings, sometimes mixed with chopped
hardboiled eggs. You can, in addition,
put an olive in each pasteis.

BATIDAS AND CAIPIRINHA

 t is a new custom in Brazil to drink cocktails with a base of cachaça (local rum) and fruit juices. The batida, a punchlike drink, has always been found in the cafés, but recently it has been adopted by the *gentle fina* and has now become a widespread national custom, particularly on Saturdays, when the feijoada is normally eaten.

Batida de Limão and Maracuja: Combine all ingredients and process in a blender until smooth. Serve immediately.

Batida de Coco: Combine all ingredients; shake and serve.

Caipirinha: Mull lime, lemon, and sugar. Add cachaça and crushed (not fine) ice. (Cachaça can be replaced by vodka or very good white rum. In this case, the drink is called Caipirissima.) Stir and serve.

BATIDA DE LIMÃO AND MARACUJA:
1 jigger freshly squeezed fruit juice

1 tspn. castor sugar

1 jigger white rum

1 ice cube

BATIDA DE COCO:
1 jigger coconut milk

1 tspn. sweetened condensed milk

1 jigger white rum

1 ice cube

CAIPIRINHA:
½ medium lime, cut into 6 pieces

⅓ medium lemon, skin removed, cut into 4–6 pieces

2 tspn. sugar

1½ oz. cachaça

When the Great Pumpkin comes, he just has to make his first appearance at the Circleville Pumpkin Show, which is billed as The Greatest Free Show on Earth. One of the major festivals in the United States, this four-day event draws about 500,000 people from the United States, Canada, and many other countries, to Pickaway County, Ohio.

When the leaves are beginning to fall and there's a nip of frost in the air, the efforts of hundreds of people in Circleville focus on pumpkins and pleasure.

The Circleville Pumpkin Show (like so many festivals) began in a small way, as a display of Mother Nature's bounty and beauty. In 1903 Mayor George R. Haswell, a merchant, built a display using corn and pumpkins in front of his business. The idea caught on and his neighboring merchants joined him the next year. There were no rides or carnival games, just displays of produce. The next year they added a merry-go-round. For years the show was regarded by the state

as a county fair. In 1946 a group of citizens, led by the late Robert Colville, formed the present Pumpkin Show, Inc. Because of his tireless efforts, the title of Mr. Pumpkin Show is Colville's for eternity. The current general chair, Ned Harden, is a wonderful friend to festival people all over the world, as he spreads the word about the show and bestows his pumpkin stickers on everyone.

During the four-day festival there are seven parades, featuring Little Miss Pumpkins, Miss Pumpkins, babies, bands and youth organizations, pets, lodge and civic and fraternal organizations, and, on Saturday night, the queens from the various groups that are members of the Ohio Festival and Events Association.

In between parades, from Wednesday through Saturday, there are contests in hog calling, egg tossing, pie eating, and the selection of Miss Pumpkin and Little Miss Pumpkin. Displays include home arts and crafts, fruits and vegetables, flowers, art, baked goods, and, of course, carved pumpkins. There is the traditional display of pumpkins, which, in 1988, weighed in at a total of more than 100,000 pounds. And there is the world's largest pumpkin pie: 350 pounds and 5 feet in diameter.

There are three entertainment stages at the show, with both amateur and professional acts. Clowns visit throughout the day, along with jugglers, magicians, and ventriloquists. There are also rides for children and adults.

Another attraction is the Ted Lewis Museum. Entertainer Ted Lewis and his wife, Adah, returned to his hometown of Circleville whenever his schedule allowed. He mentioned Circleville—"the capital of the world"—in his every performance. He rose in the entertainment world to achieve lasting fame with his battered top hat, cane, and clarinet, his "Shadow" song, and his familiar call, "Is everybody happy?" On his visits he rode in the parades, mingled with the home folk, and enjoyed the festivities. After his death in 1971, the Ted Lewis Museum was opened, so he is still, in spirit, a part of the show.

Festival food, served up by vendors and local restaurants, is readily available during the entire time. The Senior Center, in conjunction with the Community United Methodist Church, provides a hospitality house for senior citizen groups; this has become a popular part of the Pumpkin Show, with senior citizen groups from all over Ohio and neighboring states making arrangements months in advance for visits. Write or call for information.

The following recipes are excerpted, with kind permission, from a delightful book called *Pumpkin Recipes*, compiled by The Crusader Sunday School Class of Calvary United Methodist Church, P.O. Box 8, Circleville, Ohio 43113. Write to it for price and shipping information. A nice addition to any collection of specialty recipe books, it contains many prizewinners from past years, plus recipes for using pumpkin in everything from soup to burgers, a page on nutrients and weights and measures, and instructions for freezing pumpkins.

PRIDE O'PUMPKIN CAKE

From the provider of this recipe: "This recipe was Champion and Grand Champion for several years at the Pumpkin Show. . . . I baked it when I was sixteen years old and won a blue ribbon. I baked it every year after and won more blue ribbons, also placing as Champion and Grand Champion. It is a very good cake."

Preheat oven to 350° F. Measure flour, add baking powder, salt, baking soda, and spices. Sift together 3 times.

Cream butter, add sugars gradually, and cream well. Add egg and egg yolks one at a time, beating until light. Add flour mixture alternately with buttermilk,

2¼ cups sifted cake flour

3 tspn. baking powder

½ tspn. salt

¼ tspn. baking soda

1½ tspn. cinnamon

½ tspn. ginger

½ tspn. allspice

½ cup butter

1 cup firmly packed brown sugar

½ cup granulated sugar

1 egg

2 egg yolks (unbeaten)

¾ cup buttermilk

¾ cup canned pumpkin

½ cup chopped nuts

in small amounts, beating after each addition until smooth. Fold in pumpkin and nuts. Bake in two round 8-inch layer pans for 30–35 minutes.

Cool. Frost with your favorite frosting.

ROASTED PUMPKIN SEEDS

2 cups pumpkin seeds

1½ Tbspn. melted butter

1¼ tspn. salt

Preheat oven to 250° F.
Combine pumpkin seeds, butter, and salt. Mix well. Spread in shallow pan. Roast in oven for 30–40 minutes, or until browned and crisp, stirring often to brown evenly. Serve for snacks instead of nuts. Makes 2 cups.

PUMPKIN PRESERVES

5 lb. raw pumpkin

4 lb. sugar

3 lemons, thinly sliced

1 orange, thinly sliced

Few grains of salt

Remove pumpkin peel; cut pumpkin in slices ¼ inch thick and about 1 inch long. Place in large crock or enamel kettle. Add sugar and let stand overnight. Drain liquid from pumpkin. Boil liquid until it spins a thin thread, about 245° F on a candy thermometer. Add pumpkin pieces, lemon and orange slices, and salt. Continue cooking until thick and clear. Remove from heat and ladle immediately into hot jelly or canning jars. Fill to within ⅛ inch of top; screw cap on evenly and tightly. Invert for a few seconds and stand jars upright to cool. Makes about eight (8-oz.) jars.

PUMPKIN PUFF PANCAKES

Sift together flour, sugar, baking powder, salt, and cinnamon. Combine milk, pumpkin, egg yolks, and butter or margarine. Add to dry ingredients, stirring just till flour is moistened. Fold in egg whites. Using about ⅓ cup batter for each pancake, cook, turning once, on hot griddle. Serve with Hot Cider Sauce (recipe follows). Makes 8 pancakes.

1 cup sifted all-purpose flour

1 Tbspn. sugar

2 tspn. baking powder

½ tspn. salt

½ tspn. cinnamon

1 cup milk

½ cup canned pumpkin

2 slightly beaten egg yolks

2 Tbspn. butter or margarine, melted

2 stiffly beaten egg whites

HOT CIDER SAUCE

In saucepan combine all ingredients and bring to boiling; simmer about 15 minutes. Makes 1¼ cups sauce.

¾ cup apple juice or cider

½ cup brown sugar

½ cup light corn syrup

2 Tbspn. butter or margarine

½ tspn. lemon juice

⅛ tspn. cinnamon

⅛ tspn. nutmeg

hat spooky season of goblins and ghosts is celebrated with all manner of Halloween events at the Great Halloween and Pumpkin Festival. There are pumpkin-carving demonstrations and an urban pumpkin patch. Contests, hayrides, and trick-or-treating in local stores add to the fun. There are arts and crafts, music, and, best of all, a costume parade featuring the Great Pumpkin. And even pumpkin wine! The Greater Clement Street Merchants Association sponsors this event, which is produced by Terry Pimsleur & Company.

The two recipes that follow come from Mary Bettencourt of Half Moon Bay, California, who is a well-known local cook and recipe developer.

THE GREAT HALLOWEEN AND PUMPKIN FESTIVAL

SAN FRANCISCO, CALIFORNIA, LATE OCTOBER

PUMPKIN SOUP

2 Tbspn. butter

2 green onions, chopped

½ cup chopped celery

1 Tbspn. tomato paste

1 bay leaf

2 cups cooked pumpkin or canned pumpkin

2 cups beef or chicken broth

¾ cup light cream

½ tspn. salt

Dash pepper

Nutmeg

Chopped parsley

Melt butter in a large pan, add onion and celery, sauté until soft but not brown. Add tomato paste, bay leaf, pumpkin, and broth, and simmer for 30 minutes. Press through a wire strainer. Add cream, salt, and pepper to strained soup, and heat to the boiling point, but do not boil. Simmer 5 minutes. Serve hot with a dash of nutmeg; sprinkle with parsley. Makes 4–6 servings.

PUMPKIN CHEESECAKE

For Crust, preheat oven to 375° F. Combine graham cracker crumbs, sugar, and melted butter. Mix well. Press firmly on bottom of 9-inch springform pan. Bake for 8 minutes or until edges are browned. Cool.

For filling, lower oven temperature to 300° F. Beat cream cheese and brown sugar until well blended. Beat in pumpkin and spices. Add eggs one at a time and beat well after each. Pour into the crust. Bake for about 1 hour or until cheesecake is set.

Meanwhile, combine sour cream, vanilla, and granulated sugar. When cake is set remove from oven and spread sour cream mixture over the filling. Return to oven and bake 8 minutes. Cool cake on wire rack. Before serving remove sides of pan, and garnish with a border of sliced almonds if desired. Serves 12.

CRUST:

1¼ cups fine graham cracker crumbs

¼ cup sugar

6 Tbspn. melted butter

FILLING:

16 oz. cream cheese, softened

¾ cup packed brown sugar

1½ cups cooked mashed pumpkin or canned pumpkin

1 tspn. cinnamon

½ tspn. ground ginger

2 eggs

2 cups sour cream

1 tspn. vanilla

¼ cup granulated sugar

Sliced, toasted almonds (optional)

The International Institute of Wisconsin is a nonprofit agency that helps immigrants and refugees adapt to the American culture, while helping ethnic groups to preserve and celebrate their rich and diverse heritage. To this end it has created a spectacular event for people of all ages.

The Holiday Folk Fair is a learning experience, a culinary delight, and an opportunity for all ethnic groups to come together under one roof, sharing their customs and traditions with pride. Started by a small group of volunteers in 1943, the fair has grown to become the largest indoor ethnic festival in the United States.

Each year one ethnic group is chosen as the special honored guest and featured in various ways. (Also, a performing group from that country is invited to appear at the festival.) Fifty ethnic groups from southeastern Wisconsin participate in this festive preliminary to the Thanksgiving season.

Numerous cultural exhibits explore the customs, traditions, and arts of different cultures

and examine what makes each one unique. Demonstration workshops offer chances to observe or participate in music, dancing, language lessons, and various crafts.

The Folk Spectacle has six main stage performances, with international performing groups and festive dancing from forty ethnic groups.

At the World Mart visitors can go on an international shopping spree from the bazaars of Old Delhi to the boutiques of Paris. More than thirty booths of imported handcrafted gifts provide ample opportunity to take care of Christmas shopping.

Although dancing, crafts, and exhibits from all corners of the world are represented, the real star of this show is food.

The Sidewalk Café boasts mouth-watering homemade ethnic specialities. Appetizers, entrées, and desserts from more than three dozen nationalities are served, created from traditional recipes handed down from generation to generation. At the Coffeehouse you can relax over international desserts and beverages, while watching a variety of entertainers. And at Old Pabst Park continuous entertainment is offered in a beer garden setting.

The Holiday Folk Fair Cookbook contains recipes from forty-four ethnic groups. A number of the recipes are not available elsewhere in print. The editor, Aenone M. Rosari, writes in the introduction: "[The book] is a reminder that we are all immigrants, and that by taking pride in the traditions, customs, beliefs and values from our homelands, we preserve and pass on to future generations those characteristics that make us unique." For further information write to Virginia Topitzes, Coordinator, Holiday Folk Fair, International Institute of Wisconsin, 2810 West Highland Boulevard, Milwaukee, Wisconsin 53208.

GREEK—TIROPETA
(Cheese Pita)

Mix cheese, eggs, cottage cheese, and a little melted butter. Preheat oven to 350° F. Place 4 or 5 layers of phyllo on bottom of 11-inch-by-15-inch buttered pan, spreading each layer with melted butter. Add mixture. Top with 4 or 5 layers of phyllo, remembering to butter each layer. For large pita add an additional 1 lb. cottage cheese, ½ cup milk, and 2 more eggs. Bake for an hour or more, until top is golden brown. Cut into diamond-shaped pieces and serve warm.

by Ms. Dora Lambron
SS. Constantine and Helen Church Philoptochos

1 lb. feta cheese, crumbled

3 eggs, beaten

1½ pints small curd cottage cheese

½ lb. melted butter

Phyllo dough, in sheets

IRISH—CAMOGA LE BEACAIN

Place the scallops in boiling water for 2 minutes. Cool and set aside. Heat the oil and fry the onion until soft, and then add the mushrooms and scallops. Cook until mushrooms are soft, turning occasionally. Add the lemon juice, salt and pepper, and parsley. Serves 4.

by Mrs. Betty Mikush
Shamrock Club of Wisconsin

1 lb. scallops

3 Tbspn. olive oil

1 large onion, sliced

2 oz. button mushrooms, sliced

Juice of 1 lemon

Salt and pepper to taste

1 Tbspn. chopped parsley

ISRAELI–CHOPPED LIVER

1 medium Bermuda onion, sliced

1 stick (¼ lb.) margarine (for frying)

1 lb. calves' liver or chicken liver

5 hardboiled eggs, peeled and cooled

Salt and pepper to taste

2–4 Tbspn. rendered chicken fat or canned undiluted chicken soup or melted margarine, for binding, as needed

3 mashed hardboiled eggs, for decoration (optional)

Prepare ingredients ½ hour before grinding so all will be cool. Sauté onion in margarine on low heat till transparent. If using calves' liver, broil 4 or 5 inches from heat on rack of broiler pan (so juices will drain). Do not let the edges burn or liver will be bitter and gritty. If chicken liver is used, sauté in margarine until juices stop running. Slice liver in long pieces for easier grinder feeding.

Put onion, liver, and hardboiled eggs through electric or hand food chopper using small-hole wheel. Do not use a food processor; the consistency will be pasty and stringy. Toss chopped ingredients in bowl with salt and pepper to taste. (Tasting is easier before adding binder.) If chicken soup is to be used as a binder, do not salt.

Put mixture through grinder a second time for smoother consistency. Add desired binder and mash with large cooking fork. Transfer to serving bowl. For extra taste add crisply fried, thinly sliced onions and little pieces of chicken skin (cracklings). Decorate with mashed hardboiled eggs if desired.

Serve as cracker spread or as hors d'oeuvres mounted on lettuce leaves.

by Mrs. Miriam Orenstein
Milwaukee County Council of Pioneer Women

PERSIAN–ABDUGH KHIYAR (Cold Yogurt and Cucumber Soup)

2 cups yogurt

3 cups cold water

½ tspn. salt

In mixing bowl beat yogurt until it is smooth. Add water and salt, and stir well to completely dissolve yogurt and salt in the water.

Add all remaining ingredients except raisins and mix well. Sprinkle raisins over the mixture just before serving.

Serve with dry crackers, such as melba toast, broken into bite-sized pieces and dropped in the soup.

by Mrs. Kathy Moosavi
Persian Cultural Organization of Wisconsin

2 grated cucumbers
1 small onion, grated (optional)
2 tspn. chopped fresh mint, or 1 tspn. dried
¼ tspn. pepper
¼ cup chopped walnuts
¼ cup raisins

THAI–SPICY BEEF WITH MINT LEAVES

Brown ground beef, without oil. Place in a mixing bowl; let cool for 5 minutes. Wrap the chopped red onion and garlic in aluminum foil. Put the packet on the heat and cook until it is almost burned. Unwrap it and add onion and garlic to the beef. Season the beef with nampla, salt, lemon or lime juice, coriander, rice powder, chili powder, and green onion. Pour the mixture into a serving dish. Top with mint leaves. Serve with vegetables.

Note: Nampla is a fish sauce available at Asian grocery stores.

by Mr. Joseph E. Ryan
Thai-Am Association

1½ cups ground beef
1 Tbspn. chopped red onion
3 cloves garlic, chopped
1 Tbspn. nampla (see Note)
1 tspn. salt
2 Tbspn. lemon or lime juice
1 tspn. coriander seeds, powdered
1 Tbspn. rice powder, browned
1 tspn. chili powder
3 small green onions, chopped
10 mint leaves, for garnish
Some lettuce, long green beans, celery stalks

UKRAINIAN–BORSCH SOUP

Cover the meat with the 10–12 cups cold water and add salt. Bring it slowly to the boiling point and then skim. Cover and simmer for 1½ hours, and then add the onion and beets; cook for 10–15 minutes or until the beets are

1½ lb. soup meat with bone
10–12 cups cold water
1 tspn. salt
1 medium onion, chopped

2 medium beets, cut in strips

1 medium potato, diced

½ cup celery, thinly sliced

½ cup diced string beans or cooked white beans

2–3 cups shredded cabbage

¾ cup strained tomatoes or tomato juice

½ clove garlic, crushed

1 Tbspn. flour

3 tablespoons cold water

Fermented beet juice or fermented lemon juice

Salt and pepper to taste

Chopped dill to taste

½ cup sour cream or rich sweet cream

almost done. (If young beets are used, cook them together with the other vegetables.) Add the carrot, potato, celery, and string beans, if using (cooked white beans should be added after cabbage is cooked, to retain their white color). Continue cooking for about 10 minutes. Finally, put in the cabbage and cook until tender. Do not overcook. Stir in tomatoes or tomato juice and crushed garlic, and blend the flour with the 3 Tbspn. cold water. Spoon into it some soup liquid and then the flour. Add a small quantity of the fermented beet juice or fermented lemon juice, taking care not to use too much. (A good borsch should be pleasantly tart but not sour.) Season with salt and pepper and bring to a boil. Flavor it with chopped dill, and, when ready to serve, add sour cream or rich sweet cream. Some prefer to put cream in each serving, which is the custom in the central Ukraine. When the borsch is reheated, do not add more cream. Additional water may be added if too much liquid has boiled away.

by Ivanna Richardson
Ukrainian Congress Committee of America,
Milwaukee Branch

WELSH–LEEK SOUP

1¼ cups sliced leeks

3 Tbspn. butter

4 cups water

1 bay leaf

2 Tbspn. chili sauce or catsup

2 medium potatoes, diced

½ small onion, chopped

¼ cup chopped celery

In soup kettle over medium heat, sauté leeks in butter until soft.

Add water, bay leaf, and chili sauce or catsup. Stir. Cover and simmer 20 minutes, reducing heat to low if necessary.

Add potatoes, onion, celery, carrots, and parsley. Cook, stirring occasionally, until vegetables are tender, about 12–15 minutes, covering kettle during last 5 minutes of cooking time.

Season with salt and pepper. Stir in

milk. Heat through and serve. Makes 4–6 servings.
by Mrs. Gwen Howell
Welsh Women's Club

½ cup chopped carrots

2 Tbspn. chopped fresh parsley

Salt and pepper to taste

1 cup milk

CHINESE–KUNG-BAU CHICKEN WITH PEANUTS

Cut chicken lengthwise into ½-inch strips. Then cut the strips crosswise to make ½-inch squares. Mix together all ingredients for Chicken Marinade and marinate chicken pieces for 15 minutes.

Heat the 2 cups corn oil in wok over medium-high heat. Stir up chicken and marinade thoroughly and then blanch chicken in the hot oil. Stir the chicken until it separates or until most of the chicken has changed color but is not yet completely cooked. Remove chicken with strainer and set aside.

Mix all ingredients for the Seasoning Sauce and put aside. Remove all oil from the wok except for 2 Tbspn. Brown the chili peppers until they turn dark red. Then add scallions and chicken and stir fry for 1 minute. Stir the Seasoning Sauce well, and add it to the chicken over high heat, stirring until it thickens and coats the chicken. Add the peanuts and mix well. Serve hot.

by Mrs. Susan Ho
Chinese-American Civic Club of Milwaukee

2 whole chicken breasts, boned and skinned

2 cups corn oil

4–8 whole red chili peppers

4 scallions, finely chopped

½ cup skinless roasted peanuts

CHICKEN MARINADE:

1 Tbspn. medium soy sauce

1 tspn. cornstarch

1 Tbspn. sherry

1 Tbspn. corn oil

2 Tbspn. broth

SEASONING SAUCE:

1 Tbspn. dark soy sauce

1 Tbspn. oyster sauce

1 Tbspn. sherry

1 Tbspn. red wine vinegar

½ tspn. salt

1 tspn. sugar

1 tspn. sesame oil

1 tspn. cornstarch mixed with 2 Tbspn. water

CROATIAN– BOSANSKI LONAC (Bosnian Casserole)

2 lb. mixed meat (beef, pork, lamb)

4 oz. slab bacon

1 medium onion

½ lb. soup vegetables (carrots, celery, parsnips, parsley)

1½ lb. potatoes

2 Tbspn. vinegar

2 cups white wine

Water

Garlic to taste

Salt and pepper to taste

Cut mixed meat into 1½-inch cubes and brown with finely chopped bacon. Cut onion and vegetables into fine slices. Dice potatoes.

Preheat oven to 300° F. Arrange the meat, onion, vegetables, and potatoes in layers in a deep earthenware pot. Pour in vinegar and wine and enough water to cover layers. Add garlic and salt and pepper. Cover the pot with greaseproof paper and tie tightly. Let simmer 3–4 hours in oven.

by Ms. Sue Khatchadourian
Plavi Jadran

ENGLISH–STEAK AND KIDNEY PUDDING

SUET CRUST PASTRY:
¾ lb. self-rising flour

½ tspn. salt

4½ oz. shredded suet

Cold water to mix (about ½ cup)

FILLING:
1½ lb. stewing steak

½ lb. ox kidney

1 tspn. salt

½ tspn. pepper

1½ Tbspn. flour

2 medium onions, sliced

Water

For pastry, sift flour and salt; stir in suet. Grease a 1½-quart casserole and a piece of paper for covering the top. Roll out ⅔ of the pastry into a round and line the casserole evenly, leaving about ½ inch of pastry above the rim.

For filling, cut meats into pieces about ¾ inch square. Mix seasonings and flour and roll the meats in it. Put meats and onions into casserole and half fill with water. Roll out the remaining pastry into a round for the top. Dampen edges and put in position, pressing the edges firmly together. Cover with greased paper and steam for 3 hours. You can also put sliced carrots and potatoes in with the meat.

by Janice Bould
The English Club

SCOTTISH–
CHICKEN STOVIES

Peel and slice potatoes into ¼-inch slices. Peel and slice onions thinly. Arrange alternate layers of chicken, potatoes, and onions in a heavy frying pan. Dot each layer with butter, and sprinkle with salt and pepper. Add water or chicken stock. Cover tightly, bring to a boil, and simmer very gently for about an hour. Serves 4.

by Mrs. Meribeth Waldrop
Caledonian Highland Dancers

4 large potatoes

2 large onions

1 frying chicken, cut up

⅓ cup butter

2 tspn. salt

¼ tspn. pepper

1 cup water or chicken stock

THAI–CHICKEN CURRY
(Green)

In a saucepan heat oil over medium heat. Stir fry green curry paste for 1 minute. Add chicken and nampla. Stir fry until chicken is done. Add coconut milk or light cream and bring to a boil. Add peas and green chilies. Stir a few times. Remove from heat.

Note: Nampla is a fish sauce available at Asian grocery stores.

by Mr. Joseph E. Ryan
Thai-Am Association

2 Tbspn. vegetable oil

2 Tbspn. green curry paste

1 cup sliced chicken breasts

2 Tbspn. nampla (see Note)

2 cups coconut milk or light cream

1 cup sweet peas (frozen)

2 green chilies, cut lengthwise

DONAUSCHWABEN
(Poppy Seed Roll)

PASTRY:

½ cup margarine

⅔ cup sugar

1 oz. cake yeast

1 cup warm milk

1 tspn. sugar

4 eggs, beaten

4½ cups flour

½ tspn. salt

¼ cup butter, melted

FILLING:

8 cups ground poppy seeds

2 cups sugar

12–16 tspn. milk

Powdered sugar

Water

Pastry: Keep ingredients at room temperature. Cream the margarine and the ⅔ cup sugar. Dissolve the yeast in the warm milk; add the 1 tspn. sugar. Add this to the margarine and sugar mixture. Add the eggs, flour, and salt. Mix well; do not knead. Refrigerate dough 8 hours or overnight. Divide the dough into 4 pieces. Roll out and brush with melted butter.

Filling: Mix poppy seeds, sugar, and milk. Spread ¼ of the filling evenly on each of the 4 rolls and roll like a jelly roll. Place on ungreased cookie sheet; cover with a cloth and let stand for 1 hour. Preheat oven to 350° F and bake rolls about 30 minutes or until golden brown. Remove from oven and brush with a mixture of powdered sugar and water. Or you may use a nut filling: for each roll mix 2½ cups ground walnuts and ½ cup sugar; add 2–3 tspn. milk. Fill roll as with poppy seeds.

by Milwaukee Donauschwaben
Frauengruppe

Atradition in Detroit since 1926, this wonderful parade has been a part of the holiday season for several generations of Michigan residents. Early on Thanksgiving Day morning, old and young alike begin staking out their places on the parade route. Some families have been occupying the same spot for more years than they've lived in their current homes! When the route had to be changed in 1987, some people went out scouting for a new location days in advance; others, not quite as prepared, went to their old spots, only to see the parade passing a block away.

By now, everyone has had a chance to relocate, and nearly one million people turn out to watch the marching bands and floats, the equine units and the clowns, and the huge balloons, all of which make this parade a spellbinder.

MICHIGAN THANKSGIVING PARADE

DETROIT, MICHIGAN, THANKSGIVING DAY

Thousands of spectators bundled in blankets and sleeping bags, perched atop ladders and motor homes, and seated in chairs and on curbs, begin cheering at the first sighting of the Detroit Mounted Police horses who lead the parade. Santa makes his first appearance here, on his own magnificent float, and is duly welcomed by the mayor and given a key to the city in front of the grandstand at the parade's end.

Between these two events, there's all the usual parade activity, plus some special attractions. One of these is the inclusion of more than one hundred giant papier-mâché heads of notable historic and artistic persons; the antique heads have been created in Italy over several generations by a family famed for its artistry. Contemporary figures are added each year.

Another special part of this event is the huge contingent of clowns who make up the Distinguished Clown Corps. Business and community leaders raise $1,000 each to be allowed to dress up in customized clown suits and take part in the antics at the parade. It must be fun; there are nearly a hundred of them each year. And there is a contingent of loyal members of the Friends of the Parade Association, who participate by taking care of some of the zillion things that make an event work. Like cleaning up after the horses. One philosophical gentleman says it is easier cleaning up after the Clydesdales than the drill horses, because the Clydesdales walk in a straight line. Why does he keep on doing it? He says he gets more applause from the kids than the clowns do!

The involvement of the community in parade activities is also evident in the success of the Mr. Turkey Trot, a 10K (6.2-mile) race run along the parade route prior to the parade. Although begun just a few years ago, the run attracts over 5,000 runners and has the world's largest 10K audience.

A recent addition to the schedule is the Thanksgiving Parade band competition for high school bands, held on Wednesday night at the Cobo Arena.

The Michigan Thanksgiving Parade Foundation was founded in 1983 to produce the annual parade in Detroit when Hudson's and Detroit Renaissance could no longer sustain the expense of the growing event. The foundation has a board of directors of nearly seventy-five members, who raise the funds that are required to keep the parade on the street. The foundation's wholly-owned subsidiary, the Parade Company, actually produces the event.

Grant L. Brown is the gracious and talented chef at the London Chop House in Detroit. This menu, with the recipes that follow, was created by him especially for the Michigan Thanksgiving Parade Committee's contribution to this book.

THANKSGIVING AT THE LONDON CHOP HOUSE
A Celebration of American Game

APERITIFS
Passion Fruit and Champagne Cocktails
Tom and Jerrys

HORS D'OEUVRES
(*to be passed with Aperitifs*)
Duck, Pheasant, and Rabbit Rillettes
Game Bird Liver Sauté on Bruschetta
Scallop Seviche with Chilled Shrimp, Fruit, and Avocado
Bluefish Gravlox

APPETIZER
Poached Oysters with Vouvray, Thyme, and Spinach, served with
Chilled Fresh Foie Gras Terrine and Sherry Vinaigrette

SOUP
Game Double Consommé with Fresh Black Truffles and Rabbit Loin

SALAD
Sautéed Squab and Duck Breast Salad
with Blue Cheese Terrine and Walnut Vinaigrette

ENTRÉES

Sautéed Pheasant Breast with Cognac and Black Truffle Sauce
Roast Venison Loin with Tangerine Brandy, Green Peppercorns, and Roasted
Chestnuts

ACCOMPANIMENTS

Puree of Celery Root and Granny Smith Apples
Potato Pie with Caramelized Onions and Black Truffles
Warm Vinegared Beets
Cranberry, Orange, and Almond Relish

DESSERT

Warm Pumpkin Soufflé Flavored with Bourbon and Maple Syrup,
served with Fresh Whipped Cream

COFFEE/TEA

DUCK, PHEASANT, AND RABBIT RILLETTES

Sauté onion in butter to a golden color. Add garlic and sauté for 1 minute more. Add wine and reduce liquid by ½ its volume. Add all other ingredients except salt and pepper and bring to a simmer. Cook very slowly for 3 hours, adding the extra chicken stock as needed to keep mixture moist. Let meats cool in stock. Strain liquid from meats, saving all liquid and fat. Shred all meats, being careful to pick out all bones. This may take 2 or 3 rounds of shredding. Whip a small quantity of stock and fat into shredded meat to produce a spreadable mixture. Season with salt and pepper. Place in a ceramic container and cover with ½ inch of fat. Rillettes will stay good for weeks

1 medium onion, sliced
2 oz. butter
4 cloves garlic, minced
½ bottle dry white wine
Front and hind legs of 2 rabbits
4 pheasant legs
4 squab legs
2 duck legs
½ lb. pork shoulder
½ lb. fresh pork fat
2 bay leaves
1 sprig thyme

½ gallon chicken stock, plus 1 quart extra to keep mixture moist

½ bunch basil

Fat from the duck carcass

Salt and pepper to taste

when refrigerated and covered with fat. To serve place in a ramekin and serve at room temperature with French bread.

GAME BIRD LIVER SAUTÉ ON BRUSCHETTA

Liver from 2 squabs, 1 duck, 2 rabbits, and 2 pheasants

½ lb. fresh chicken livers

½ medium onion, chopped

2 cloves garlic, minced

2 oz. port wine

2 oz. cognac

1 crumbled bay leaf

2 fresh sage leaves, plus extra leaves for garnish

1 pinch ground ginger

1 pinch ground allspice

1 pinch ground cinnamon

2 oz. clarified butter

¼ lb. unsalted butter

Leaves from 1 sprig fresh thyme

Salt and pepper to taste

ITALIAN BRUSCHETTA:

1 loaf Tuscan bread sliced into 4-inch-by-2½-inch-by-½-inch rectangles

Small amount of virgin olive oil (preferably green fruity oil)

Marinate livers overnight in all other ingredients except butters, thyme, and salt and pepper. Next day, sauté livers in the clarified butter very quickly over high heat until livers are just cooked (medium rare). Remove livers from pan and strain juices into a container. Take all strained cooking juices and reduce over high heat until 2 Tbspn. are left. In a food processor (with steel blade), process livers, reduced cooking liquid, and the ¼ lb. of unsalted butter until the butter is incorporated into the mixture. Add fresh thyme. Season with salt and pepper. Chill mixture until firm. This mixture should have the consistency of a pâté.

Italian Bruschetta: Preheat oven to 350° F. Brush slices of bread with olive oil. Place in oven on a baking sheet. Bake 5 minutes on each side or until golden brown and crisp. Do not refrigerate.

To serve Game Bird Liver Sauté, spread on Bruschetta and garnish with fresh sage leaves.

SCALLOP SEVICHE WITH CHILLED SHRIMP, FRUIT, AND AVOCADO

To make vinaigrette, combine onion, sushi vinegar, sugar, and lime juice. Whisk in sesame oil. Add all other ingredients except salt and pepper, lettuce, and radicchio, and refrigerate for 2 hours. Drain to remove any remaining marinade. Taste for seasoning, adding salt and pepper.

To assemble, place mixture in limestone lettuce leaves and radicchio leaves. Serve immediately.

1 Tbspn. red onion, minced

2 oz. sushi vinegar

1 Tbspn. sugar

Juice from ½ lime

1 oz. dark sesame oil

8 oz. very fresh scallops, chopped

¼ lb. medium-sized shrimp, steamed, chilled, and sliced

¼ avocado, chopped into slivers

¼ mango, chopped into slivers

⅛ ripe cantaloupe melon, chopped into slivers

1 tspn. fresh dill, chopped

Salt and pepper to taste

4 or 5 very small limestone lettuce leaves

4 or 5 very small radicchio leaves

BLUEFISH GRAVLOX

Place 1 fillet of bluefish in a non-aluminum container that comfortably holds the fillet. Combine all seasoning ingredients and sprinkle on fillet. Cover with the remaining bluefish fillet and then cover the container with plastic wrap. Place in refrigerator. Flip the fillet "sandwich" over each day for 3 days.

To serve remove fillets from brine and pat dry. Slice each fillet into thin slices and serve on croutons with mustard mayonnaise.

2 (½-inch) fillets of bluefish

1 Tbspn. kosher salt

1 Tbspn. sugar

2 tspn. cracked black peppercorns

2 tspn. ground allspice

1 sprig fresh thyme

5 sprigs fresh rosemary

POACHED OYSTERS WITH VOUVRAY, THYME, AND SPINACH, SERVED WITH CHILLED FRESH FOIE GRAS TERRINE AND SHERRY VINAIGRETTE

VOUVRAY SAUCE:
16 oz. Vouvray or chenin blanc

1 clove garlic, minced

24 oz. fish fumet (fish stock)

8 oz. heavy cream

4 oz. butter

Salt and pepper to taste

Dash of lemon juice

Leaves from 1 sprig fresh thyme

SPINACH:
1 lb. fresh spinach, washed and picked

4 oz. butter (or as much as you can pump into the spinach)

4 shallots, minced

1 clove garlic, minced

Salt and pepper to taste

CHILLED FRESH FOIE GRAS TERRINE:
1 fresh foie gras

1 oz. port wine

1 oz. cognac

Salt and pepper

1 inch fresh ginger

Vouvray Sauce: Reduce wine with shallots and garlic. Add fish fumet. Reduce liquid by ½. Add cream. Reduce liquid to sauce consistency. Whisk in butter, salt and pepper, and lemon juice. Add fresh thyme.

Spinach: Sauté spinach in butter with shallots and garlic. Sauté until all the butter is incorporated into the spinach. Season with salt and pepper.

Chilled Fresh Foie Gras Terrine: Marinate liver in all ingredients overnight. Preheat oven to 200° F. Press liver into a ceramic terrine lined with plastic wrap. Place terrine in a hot water bath and bake until the internal temperature of the liver reaches 118° F. Remove from oven and let cool to room temperature. Press terrine down by fitting foil-covered cardboard onto the foie gras, and weight it down with soup cans. To remove pâté from terrine, turn terrine upside down and run under hot water. Give terrine a sharp rap, and pâté should slide out easily.

Sherry Vinaigrette: Blend sherry vinegar, raisins, dried cherries, dried aprocots, and sugar together. Whisk in olive oil.

To assemble this dish, place a small amount of Spinach in each oyster shell. Place an oyster on top of each. Coat each oyster with Vouvray Sauce. Place 3 oysters and a thick slice of Chilled Fresh

220

Foie Gras Terrine on each plate. Drizzle the Chilled Fresh Foie Gras Terrine with Sherry Vinaigrette. Serve immediately. Serves 4.

| 1 pinch allspice |
| 1 pinch cinnamon |

SHERRY VINAIGRETTE:

| ¼ cup sherry vinegar |
| 2 oz. raisins, chopped |
| 2 oz. dried cherries, chopped |
| 2 oz. dried apricots, chopped |
| 1 Tbspn. sugar |
| ½ cup olive oil |

OYSTERS:

| 12 oysters, shucked (reserve shells) |

GAME DOUBLE CONSOMMÉ WITH FRESH BLACK TRUFFLES AND RABBIT LOIN

Game Consommé: Preheat oven to 350° F. Brown venison bones, carcasses, and meat scraps in a roasting pan (in the oven) until golden. Sauté Mirepoix in clarified butter in a 20-quart pot until wilted. Add garlic, peppercorns, thyme, and bay leaves. Sauté 3 minutes longer. Add wine and reduce liquid to ½ its volume. Add browned bones and cover with cold water to 3 inches above the level of the bones. Bring to a very slow simmer. Skim often. Cook for 8 hours over a very low flame. Strain the juices. Discard the bones and scum.

To enrich the Game Consommé: Sauté beef and veal in clarified butter until browned. Remove meats from the pan. Deglaze the pan with cognac. Pour Game Consommé back into the stockpot. Add beef, veal, and deglazing liquid. Add raw chicken to the pot. Simmer the con-

GAME CONSOMMÉ:

| Venison bones (from loin) |
| 1 duck carcass |
| 2 pheasant carcasses |
| 2 rabbit carcasses |
| 2 squab carcasses |
| Meat scraps from venison loin |
| 1 large onion |
| 1 head garlic, cloves separated and peeled |
| 2 oz. clarified butter |
| 6 peppercorns |
| 1 sprig fresh thyme |
| 2 bay leaves |
| ½ bottle dry white wine |

Cold water

MIREPOIX:

1 carrot, chopped

---

1 rib celery, chopped

---

1 leek, chopped and washed

TO ENRICH THE GAME CONSOMMÉ:

1 lb. beef stew meat

---

1 lb. veal stew meat

---

4 oz. clarified butter

---

6 oz. cognac

---

1 whole raw chicken

TO CLARIFY THE CONSOMMÉ:

16 egg whites, raw

Chopped eggshells from the eggs

½ carrot, minced

½ onion, minced

1½ ribs celery, minced

Meat scraps from venison loins, minced

½ tomato

Juice of 1 lemon

TO SERVE THE GAME CONSOMMÉ:

2 raw rabbit loins cut into ¼-inch pieces

---

1 oz. fresh black truffles, sliced

---

sommé for 2 hours. Strain. Discard meats and scum. Chill the stock. Remove the grease after it rises to the surface. You should now have 1¼ gallons of consommé.

To clarify the consommé: Place consommé in stockpot. Mix all other (clarifying) ingredients together in a separate bowl; this will be called the "raft." Warm the consommé, whisk in the raft, and bring to a slow simmer. The raft will rise to the surface, bringing with it all impurities, as stock begins to boil. Make a hole in the raft to release steam. Simmer very slowly for 45 minutes. Carefully remove the raft with a skimmer.

Strain consommé through cheesecloth. You should have a completely clear consommé by now.

To serve the Game Consommé: Heat consommé to boil. Add rabbit loins and truffles. Simmer for approximately 2 minutes. Serve immediately.

SAUTÉED SQUAB AND DUCK BREAST SALAD WITH BLUE CHEESE TERRINE AND WALNUT VINAIGRETTE

Blue Cheese Terrine: Line a terrine with plastic wrap. Whip ¼ pound of the cream cheese into Danish blue cheese and ¼ pound of the cream cheese into Maytag blue cheese. Press Maytag blue cheese mixture into the terrine. Layer walnuts on top. Press Danish blue cheese mixture on top of walnut layer. Weight overnight.

Walnut Vinaigrette: Place sushi vinegar, sugar, shallots, and walnuts in a bowl. Whisk in walnut oil and salt and pepper.

To assemble the salad: Sauté duck breast in a cold pan (no butter), skin side down, over a low heat, until fat is rendered and skin is crisp. Flip duck breast over and season with salt and pepper. Cook until medium rare. Remove from pan and let rest for 10 minutes. In the meantime sauté squab breasts in clarified butter, skin side down, for 10 minutes. Flip and season with salt and pepper. Cook 3 minutes longer. Remove from pan and let rest 5 minutes. Wash bibb lettuce and radicchio. Toss leaves in Walnut Vinaigrette. Arrange on salad plates. Remove Blue Cheese Terrine from mold and slice into ¼-inch slices. Slice bird breasts very thin. Arrange Blue Cheese Terrine, slices of duck, and slices of squab on the greens. Drizzle with Walnut Vinaigrette and serve.

BLUE CHEESE TERRINE:
½ lb. cream cheese
½ lb. Danish blue cheese
½ lb. Maytag blue cheese
¼ lb. walnuts, roasted

WALNUT VINAIGRETTE:
4 oz. sushi vinegar
1 Tbspn. sugar
2 shallots, minced
8 oz. walnuts, roasted
8 oz. walnut oil
Salt and pepper to taste

TO ASSEMBLE THE SALAD:
1 whole duck breast
Salt and pepper to taste
2 whole squab breasts
2 oz. clarified butter
1 head bibb lettuce
1 head radicchio

SAUTÉED PHEASANT BREAST WITH COGNAC AND BLACK TRUFFLE SAUCE

4 shallots, minced

2 garlic cloves, minced

3 oz. whole butter (unsalted)

4 oz. cognac

4 oz. white wine

16 oz. game or chicken stock

1 oz. freshly picked black truffles, sliced (reserve a few slices for garnish)

Salt and pepper to taste

Dash of lemon juice

2 oz. clarified butter

2 whole pheasant breasts

1 Tbspn. chervil, picked

To make sauce, sauté shallots and garlic in 1 oz. of the whole butter until wilted. Add cognac and white wine. Reduce liquid by ½ the volume. Add game or chicken stock. Reduce to about 8 oz. Add the remaining 2 oz. whole butter. Add truffles. Season with salt and pepper and lemon juice.

To cook pheasant, heat clarified butter until just starting to smoke. Sauté pheasant, skin side down, for 3 minutes. Flip the pheasant. Season with salt and pepper. Sauté until cooked through. Remove from pan and let rest for 5 minutes.

To serve, warm the sauce. Add chervil. Pour sauce on a platter. Slice the pheasant breasts thin and arrange on the sauce. Garnish with a few truffle slices.

ROAST VENISON LOIN WITH TANGERINE BRANDY, GREEN PEPPERCORNS, AND ROASTED CHESTNUTS

4 shallots, minced

6 oz. tangerine brandy

12 oz. dry champagne

6 oz. tangerine or orange juice

32 oz. chicken stock

4 oz. butter

24 green peppercorns

Dash of lemon juice

To make sauce, combine shallots, tangerine brandy, champagne, and tangerine juice in a saucepan. Reduce to a glaze. Add chicken stock. Reduce to 8 oz. Whisk in butter. Add green peppercorns and lemon juice. Season with salt and pepper.

To cook venison, preheat oven to 450° F. Wrap venison loin in bacon. Place on a roasting rack with a drip pan. Place in oven for 5 minutes. Turn oven down to 300° F and cook until an internal temperature of 120° F is reached. Let rest for 10 minutes.

To serve, slice venison loin into medallions. Arrange on a plate. Coat with sauce. Garnish with tangerine slices and roasted chestnuts.

Salt and pepper to taste
1 lb. venison loin, completely trimmed of all fat and silver skin
6 slices bacon
6 tangerine slices
12 roasted chestnuts, peeled

PUREE OF CELERY ROOT AND GRANNY SMITH APPLES

Simmer celery root in unsalted butter until almost tender. Add the two chopped apples. Drain the apples and celery root. Puree in food processor until smooth. In a sauté pan melt butter. Add puree. Gently sauté. Add heavy cream and reduce until thick. Season with salt and pepper. Add the last chopped Granny Smith apple (with skin) and warm the mixture. Serve immediately.

2 lb. celery root, peeled and chopped coarsely
4 oz. unsalted butter
2 Granny Smith apples, peeled, cored, and chopped
4 oz. heavy cream
Salt and pepper to taste
1 Granny Smith apple, cored and chopped with skin on, for garnish

POTATO PIE WITH CARAMELIZED ONIONS AND BLACK TRUFFLES

Slice onions very thin and sauté in butter and sugar very slowly with a cover on, until completely caramelized and golden brown. Drain onion to remove excess butter, season with salt and pepper. Place potatoes in salted water. Bring to a boil and cook until tender but not falling apart. Cool potatoes and then grate them.

To put together pancake, use a 10-inch sauté pan of the nonstick variety. Heat 1½ oz. of the clarified butter to

2 medium Spanish onions
¼ lb. butter
1 Tbspn. sugar
Salt and pepper to taste
3 Idaho potatoes, peeled
2 oz. clarified butter
1 oz. fresh black truffles, sliced

just below smoking temperature. Add half of the grated potatoes. Scatter half of the truffle slices over potatoes. Place drained caramelized onions in center of potatoes and spread them to within 1 inch of the edge of the potatoes. Scatter the rest of the truffles over the onions, and cover with the rest of the potatoes. Reduce heat to a low flame, and cook slowly until bottom is golden brown. Carefully flip pancake over and continue to cook until golden on both sides.

Pie can be made ahead of time and reheated in a 350° F oven for 10 minutes before served. To serve cut into wedges.

WARM VINEGARED BEETS

1 lb. beets, steamed until tender, peeled, and cut in ½-inch cubes

1 small red onion, thinly sliced

6 oz. apple cider

2 oz. red wine vinegar

1 Tbspn. sugar

Salt and pepper to taste

1 Tbspn. chopped dill

Simmer beets, onion, cider, vinegar, and sugar until all liquid is absorbed. Season with salt and pepper. Add dill just before serving. Serve warm.

CRANBERRY, ORANGE, AND ALMOND RELISH

1 lb. fresh or frozen whole cranberries

¼ cup sugar

16 oz. orange juice

2 oranges, segmented

¼ lb. almonds, slivered

4 oz. vodka

Poach cranberries in boiling water for 1 minute, until they pop open. Drain. Put cranberries back in saucepan, add all other ingredients, and simmer slowly. Reduce to a thick sauce. Taste and adjust with extra sugar. Serve warm or at room temperature.

WARM PUMPKIN SOUFFLÉ FLAVORED WITH BOURBON AND MAPLE SYRUP, SERVED WITH FRESH WHIPPED CREAM

Preheat oven to 400° F. Butter the inside of a 2-quart souffle mold and dust with sugar. In a mixer mix the egg yolks, pumpkin, sugar, vanilla, maple syrup, and bourbon at high speed until the mixture is ribboned (about 5 minutes). In another bowl whip the egg whites until they form stiff peaks. Fold egg whites into the yolk mixture. Pour into mold. Cook for 10 minutes at 400° F in the center of oven. Reduce temperature to 350° F. Cook for 15 minutes longer. Serve hot with whipped cream.

Butter to rub inside soufflé mold

Sugar to dust soufflé mold

8 eggs, separated

4 oz. pumpkin pie filling or cooked pumpkin puree

6 oz. sugar

¼ tspn. vanilla

2 oz. maple syrup

2 oz. bourbon

Whipped cream, for topping

omething special is happening in Orange County! It's the Times Orange County Holiday Parade: a special opening to the holiday season and an exciting and spectacular Southern California tradition, with the largest single-day audience of any festival in the country.

The Holiday Parade begins at 10:30 A.M. on the first Saturday in December and proceeds for a mile and a half through historic Santa Ana. Approximately 6000 people-participants, including twenty-four marching bands, six international performing groups, and fifteen equestrian groups, are interspersed with twenty floats and ten giant balloons. More than 200,000 spectators crowd the parade route, while an additional one million viewers watch at home on KHJ-9 Southern California.

Majestic high-flying character balloons—"gentle giants"—excite and delight all. The musical momentum is provided by sixteen Southern California high school marching bands, plus visiting bands from all over the United States (as well as Canada and Mexico).

Beautiful floral floats are created out of natural materials and colorful flowers by hundreds of volunteers laboring during the month before the parade. Also joining the parade are Southern California's finest equestrians, including the world renowned Long

THE TIMES
ORANGE COUNTY
HOLIDAY PARADE
& TOURNAMENT
OF CHAMPIONS

SANTA ANA, CALIFORNIA, FIRST SATURDAY IN DECEMBER

Beach Mounted Police and the American Miniature Horse Group.

The Tournament of Champions is held at Eddie West Field, with the band review beginning at 8 A.M. The field competition, involving more than 5000 participants in twenty-four bands, takes place from noon until 9 P.M. The tournament is sanctioned by the Southern California School Band and Orchestra Association, Official High School Marching Band Grand Championship Competition. For those who never get enough band music, the stadium has seating for 10,000 happy listeners.

These recipes are favorites of Nancy and Bob Viking, who are President and Vice-President, respectively, of the Times Orange County Holiday Parade.

PARMESAN AND ARTICHOKE
HEARTS HOT COCKTAIL DIP

Combine mayonnaise, cheese, onion, artichoke hearts, garlic powder, and Beau Monde; spoon into 1-quart casserole.

Preheat oven to 350° F. Bake dip until bubbly (about 20 minutes) and beginning to brown at edges. Serve with crackers or French bread rounds. Makes approximately 2½ cups.

by Bob Viking

1 cup mayonnaise

1 cup freshly grated Parmesan cheese

½ cup finely chopped green onion

14-oz. can artichoke hearts, drained and diced

Dash of garlic powder

Dash of Beau Monde seasoning

Crackers or bread rounds (French bread is great)

MELTING MOMENTS
COOKIES

Preheat oven to 300° F. Mix all ingredients together and drop by teaspoonfuls on greased cookie sheet. Bake approximately 20 minutes; cookies should be light brown on bottom.

Blend powdered sugar and butter, adding cream or milk until frosting is desired consistency. Frosting may be tinted with a few drops of food coloring, if desired. Frost cookies while still warm. Makes 2 dozen.

by Nancy Viking

½ cup powdered sugar

¾ cup cornstarch

1 cup sifted flour

1 Tbspn. vanilla

BUTTER FROSTING:
1 cup powdered sugar

2 Tbspn. melted or soft butter

Cream or milk

The Fiesta Bowl is often called the fastest-growing college bowl game festival in the United States. Since its humble beginning in 1971, when it staged ten events over a ten-day period and paid $168,000 to the two competing football teams, the festival has grown to feature more than sixty events over a period of seven months. The teams participating in the football classic will each earn in excess of $2 million. The New Year's Day game is one of the top four ball games in the country.

While football is the cornerstone of the festival, dozens of other events for both the participant and spectator make the Fiesta Bowl one of America's largest annual civic celebrations. This rapid growth has been accomplished by a combination of civic pride, enthusiastic volunteer participation, and major corporate sponsorship. The successful blending of these elements has been brought about by CEO Bruce Skinner, who set the news media on its ear by insisting that event titles carry the names of sponsors.

What this means to the people who go to festivals is more events, better production, and greater involvement of local and national celebrities. It also enables the festival

THE FIESTA BOWL

PHOENIX, ARIZONA, LATE DECEMBER

itself to involve more people who want to participate. More than 3500 individuals give their time and talents each year to make the Fiesta Bowl a civic celebration second to none. For many, the commitment exceeds four hundred hours a year, the equivalent of ten full work weeks.

New to the calendar in 1989 was the Carl's Jr. Fiesta Bowl Valley-Oop Three-on-Three Basketball Tournament. In April "Fiestaval" was introduced. This cultural celebration drew over 200,000 people to the streets of downtown Phoenix for food, entertainment, arts and crafts, and spectacular fireworks done in synchronization with a performance by the Phoenix Symphony. In May, a Spring Banquet honored fourteen Samaritan All-American college football players who filmed public service announcements for the Boys and Girls Clubs of America.

In late fall major events get under way. The Phoenix Gazette Fiesta Bowl National Pageant of Bands features ten of the nation's best high school bands. JB's Restaurants Fiesta Bowl 10K road race is considered one of the country's top twenty 10K events, and the Merrill Lynch Fiesta Bowl Mile, a match race held just prior to the parade, features many of the world's top-ranked milers. The Fiesta Bowl Festival is the only college bowl game to feature professional auto racing on its calendar. April's Autoworks 200 brings the top Indy-car drivers to the world's fastest one-mile paved oval at

Phoenix International Raceway, which is also host in November to Auto-works 500, with the biggest names in NASCAR stock car racing.

Also on the Fiesta calendar are dozens of other events, ranging from the Fry's/Great American Hot Air Balloon Classic to the United Dairymen of Arizona Half-Marathon; from the Blue Cross/Blue Shield Stride, in which hundreds of folk take an enjoyable walk through the scenic Phoenix Zoo and Desert Botanical Gardens, to the spectacular Tempe Block Party in Old Town Tempe, a night of family fun culminating in an old-fashioned pep rally and a fireworks display. There's also golf, tennis, swimming, cycling, walking, softball, wrestling, and more running and basketball events, designed to provide a taste of Fiesta Bowl fun for all sports buffs.

The Fiesta Bowl Parade, one of the top parades in the country, has recently both changed its route and shifted its emphasis to be more youth-oriented. The route has been relocated and lengthened from its original two and a half miles to four miles. It now runs through the heart of Phoenix, giving an even greater opportunity for people to view the parade.

"Superkids" make this parade different from other parades. These are twelve outstanding youngsters from all over the United States, who have achieved excellence in academics, athletics, or entertainment or who have gained notoriety for a unique accomplishment. The parade will undertake to establish its identity in future years as a tribute to the youth of America.

The two-hour parade gets under way at 11:30 A.M. on December 31. Magnificent floats, marching units, equestrian groups, and costumed partici-pants in beautifully decorated carriages are accompanied by music from some of the country's most outstanding bands. The lovely queen and her court share a truly regal float, while royalty from other festivals appear on their own individual floats. Carrying the Fiesta Bowl board of directors is the 1930 Ahrens Fox Fire Engine, originally in service in River Forest, Illinois. This entry has been a Fiesta Bowl Parade participant since its inception.

The parade is an outstanding showcase of the numerous equestrian groups from the West, and is also host to an impressive number and variety of marching units, drill teams, and military groups. It is, perhaps, *the* TV event which kicks off the New Year's Eve celebration for millions of viewers. But even better than watching it on screen is being there. Happy New Year!

The following recipes are taken from the official Sunkist Fiesta Bowl cookbook, which was produced by the Women's Committee to be used as a gift to wives of visiting team members, coaches, and other special guests. Unfortunately, it is not for sale. But the Women's Committee has another, larger book, which went on sale in late fall 1989. This features a large section of recipes with a southwestern flavor, plus recipes of a more general nature. If the first book is any indication, the second should be a good addition to any collection. Write to the festival office for information.

CHICKEN AND WILD RICE CASSEROLE

2 broiler-fryer chickens

1 cup water

1 cup pale dry sherry

½ cup celery, sliced

1 medium onion, sliced

1½ tspn. salt

1 tspn. curry powder

2 pkg. Uncle Ben's long grain wild rice with seasonings

1 lb. fresh mushrooms, quartered (save 12 whole mushrooms for garnish)

¼ cup butter

Sour cream

1 can cream of mushroom soup

Parsley, chopped, for garnish

In the first years of the Women's Committee, the committee cooked meals for the fundraising committee and parties. The committee also cooked food for many of the team functions. The Chicken and Wild Rice Casserole was a mainstay recipe for the committee.

Cook chickens with water, sherry, celery, onion, salt, and curry powder. Simmer 1 hour until done. Remove chickens and cool. Strain broth. Cook wild rice according to package directions, using strained broth and water. Sauté mushrooms in butter. Remove chicken meat from bones and cut into bite-sized pieces. Stir sour cream and cream of mushroom soup into rice. Put rice into 4-quart soufflé dish or casserole. Fold in chicken and quartered mushrooms; garnish with reserved whole mushrooms. Bake, covered, 1 hour. Sprinkle with chopped parsley. Serves 8.

by Fran Bloemker

FIESTA CORN BREAD

2 large onions, chopped

6 Tbspn. butter or margarine

2 eggs

2 Tbspn. milk

2 (17-oz.) cans cream-style corn

1 pkg. (1 lb.) cornmeal muffin mix

1 cup sour cream

2 cups grated Cheddar cheese

Preheat oven to 425° F. Butter a 9-inch-by-13-inch baking dish. In a medium skillet sauté onions in butter or margarine until golden; set aside. In a medium bowl mix eggs and milk until blended. Add corn and cornmeal muffin mix. Mix well. Spread corn bread batter into prepared baking dish. Spoon sautéed onion over top. Spread sour cream over onions. Sprinkle with cheese. Bake 35 minutes or until puffed and golden. Let stand 10 minutes before cutting into

squares. May be refrigerated or frozen and reheated. A can of chopped green chilies may be added to this for more pizzazz. This goes great with chili.
by Tucky Crutchfield

HOT CHILI SALSA

Broil chilies on cookie sheet until skins burst and then peel them. Process all ingredients in blender until vegetables are finely chopped.
by Sandra Royer

1 long green chili pepper

1 yellow chili pepper

2 jalapeño chilies

1 (28-oz.) can tomatoes

1 bunch fresh cilantro

7–8 green onions

1 tspn. garlic salt, or to taste

1 Tbspn. vinegar

HOT STUFFED AVOCADO

Cook mushrooms and onion in butter until soft. Reduce any liquid from mushrooms by raising heat. Then add the sour cream, cheese, and peppercorns, and stir until cheese has melted. Taste and add salt. Preheat oven to 300° F. Cut avocados in half and remove pits. Cut out some of flesh from cavity and add to sauce. Fill the 4 halves with sauce, place in dish, and bake for 10 minutes. Sprinkle with chopped parsley or chives before serving.
by Debbie Enabnit Digate

¼ lb. mushrooms, sliced

1 large onion, diced

1 oz. butter

2 Tbspn. sour cream

1 oz. Gruyère cheese, grated

1 Tbspn. green peppercorns

Salt to taste

2 large ripe avocados

Chopped parsley or chives, for garnish

AZTEC PUMPKIN SOUP

3-pound broiler-fryer chicken

3½ quarts water

¼ cup walnut halves

1 large onion, chopped

2 cloves garlic, minced

3 Tbspn. chicken fat or butter

3 qts. homemade chicken stock

4 cups pumpkin, peeled and diced

2 pkg. frozen corn

Jack cheese, grated, for garnish

Pine nuts, sunflower kernels, or toasted pumpkin seeds, for garnish

Fried corn tortilla strips, for garnish

Diced avocados, for garnish

Simmer chicken in water until done (about 45 minutes). Cool chicken and strip meat from bones. Strain broth. In a large stockpot sauté walnuts, onion, and garlic in chicken fat or butter. Add chicken stock, pumpkin, and chicken. Simmer until pumpkin is done, about 20 minutes. Add corn and season to taste. A large pumpkin may be cleaned out and used as a soup tureen. Have small bowls of condiments—jack cheese; pine nuts, sunflower kernels, or toasted pumpkin seeds; fried corn tortilla strips; and diced avocados—ready for all to add to their bowls of soup.

by Tucky Crutchfield

PATERNO'S ITALIAN RUM CAKE

CAKE:
6 eggs, separated

½ tspn. salt

1 cup sugar

1 Tbspn. water

1 cup sifted flour

1½ tspn. baking soda

1 tspn. lemon rind

1 Tbspn. orange liqueur

Preheat oven to 350° F. Combine egg whites and salt, and beat until peaks form; gradually beat in ¼ cup of the sugar. In another bowl beat yolks until foamy; slowly beat in the remaining sugar and the water. Sift together flour and baking soda; slowly add yolk mixture and then stir in lemon rind. Fold egg whites into egg yolk mixture until well blended. Pour into two 9-inch pans lined with lightly floured waxed paper. Bake for 25–30 minutes or until cake springs back when lightly touched with finger. Allow to cool; remove from pans and peel off waxed paper. When completely cooled cut each sponge layer in half to make 4 layers, and sprinkle 3 layers with liqueur.

Filling: Combine ricotta or cottage cheese, sugar, almond extract, chocolate chips, and candied fruits. Mix well. Spread one of liqueur-soaked layers with cheese mixture; place another layer on top. Repeat, ending with plain layer. Chill for 2 hours. Combine powdered sugar, egg white, and lemon juice, mixing until smooth. Carefully spread on top of cake. Decorate with candied cherry halves. Chill thoroughly before serving.

by Sue Paterno, wife of Joe Paterno, head football coach at Penn State University (Paterno coached the Nittany Lions at the 1977, 1980, and 1982 Fiesta Bowl games, winning all 3 of those games.)

FILLING:

2 cups ricotta or sieved creamed cottage cheese

1 cup sugar

1 tspn. almond extract

¼ cup semisweet chocolate chips

2 Tbspn. candied fruits, finely chopped

1½ cups powdered sugar

1 egg white

1 tspn. lemon juice

8 candied cherry halves

TEQUILA MOCKINGBIRD PUNCH

Squeeze limes but save rinds. Mix tequila, orange liqueur, and lime juice. Rub rims of glasses with lime rinds. Dip in salt; pour tequila mixture into pitcher or punch bowl filled with crushed ice. Garnish with lime slices. Pour into salt-lined glasses or punch cups. Yields 10 (4-oz.) servings or enough for 2 thirsty hombres.

by Judy Kittoe

6 Sunkist limes

1½ bottles tequila

1½ cups orange liqueur

Salt

6–8 cups crushed ice

1 Sunkist lime, thinly sliced

SANGRIA FOR ROMANTICOS

Pour everything except club soda, in large pitcher and chill several hours. Just before serving add club soda, mix, and pour over ice. Drink in kitchen (this

1 bottle dry red wine (nothing expensive or you'll ruin the recipe)

4–6 Tbspn. sugar

Juice of 1 Sunkist lemon and juice
of 1 Sunkist orange

Sunkist orange and lemon slices

6 oz. club soda

½ cup inexpensive brandy

6 oz. club soda

has been known to take the polish off the coffee table and dye the rug). Serves 2.

by Judy Kittoe

SALAD ITALIANO IN GRAPEFRUIT SHELLS

2 Sunkist grapefruit

2 Sunkist oranges, peeled, sectioned, drained

1 medium zucchini, thinly sliced

½ cup celery, sliced

¼ cup prepared Italian salad dressing

½ cup mayonnaise or salad dressing

Grated peel of 1 Sunkist orange

rapefruit Shells: Cut each grapefruit in half crosswise; remove any seeds. Using a curved grapefruit or paring knife, cut around segments to loosen from membrane. Remove and reserve pieces; drain. Scrape shells clean with spoon. To prevent tipping cut a thin slice from bottom of each shell; chill.

Citrus Vegetable Salad: In bowl combine reserved grapefruit pieces, orange sections, zucchini, celery, and Italian salad dressing. Chill 1 hour or longer to blend flavors.

Orange Mayonnaise Sauce: Remove 2 Tbspn. Italian salad dressing and blend with mayonnaise and orange peel.

To serve spoon Citrus Vegetable Salad into Grapefruit Shells. Serve with Orange Mayonnaise Sauce. Makes 4 servings.

by Sunkist Growers, Inc.

FRESH LEMON ICE

2 tspn. unflavored gelatin

1¼ cups water

¾ cup sugar

½ tspn. freshly grated lemon peel

*often gelatin in ¼ cup of the water. In small saucepan combine ½ cup of the sugar and the remaining 1½ cups water. Bring to boil; cook 2 minutes. Add gelatin mixture, stirring to dissolve. Add lemon peel and lemon juice. Pour into 8-

inch shallow pan. Freeze *just* until slushy (about 1½ hours), stirring occasionally. Beat egg whites until foamy. Gradually add remaining ¼ cup of the sugar, beating until soft peaks form. Fold beaten egg whites into lemon mixture. Return to freezer; stir occasionally. Freeze until firm (about 4 hours). Serve in Lemon Shells or Lemon Boats if desired (recipes follow). Makes about 3½ cups. 167 calories per serving.

Lemon Shells: Cut ⅓ off end of large lemon. Carefully ream out juice; reserve. Scrape shell clean with spoon.

Lemon Boats: Cut large lemon in half lengthwise and with shallow V-shape cut, remove white center core. Carefully ream out juice; reserve. Scrape shell clean with spoon.

(Lemon Shells or Lemon Boats may be made ahead and frozen until ready to use.)

by Sunkist Growers, Inc.

Juice of 3 Sunkist lemons

2 egg whites

PUERTO VALLARTA PIE

Combine gelatin, ½ cup of the sugar, and salt in heavy saucepan. Beat egg yolks and lime juice together until foamy. Stir into gelatin mixture. Cook about 3 minutes over low heat until gelatin is dissolved. Stir in tequila, orange liqueur, and lime peel. Cool and refrigerate until mixture is thick, but not set. Beat egg whites until foamy. Slowly add remaining ½ cup sugar, and continue beating until stiff peaks form. Fold egg whites into gelatin mixture. Turn into pie crust and chill thoroughly. Pipe or spoon whipped cream around edge of pie, and garnish with lime peel twists.

by Sharon Steele

1 envelope unflavored gelatin

1 cup sugar

1 tspn. salt

4 eggs, separated

1 cup Sunkist lime juice

⅓ cup tequila

2 Tbspn. orange liqueur (Triple Sec)

2 tspn. Sunkist lime peel, grated

1 baked 10-inch pie crust

¼ cup whipping cream, whipped and sweetened to taste, for garnish

Lime peel twists, for garnish

ris Ritchie is president of Southwest Emblem Company, a supplier of many festivals, large and small. Manufacturers of embroidered patches and emblems, they are also direct importers of cloisonné and enameled pins. They are also distributors of various kinds and formats of emblematic products.

As a festival supplier, Eris has gotten to know many of the people involved in special events all over the country. His experience with festivals and parades began with a career as a high school and college band director, during which he founded and directed a music festival in Texas. Bands that he directed have appeared at Dallas Cowboys football games, in the Macy's Thanksgiving Day Parade, and in an NBC-TV Fourth of July spectacular with Bob Hope.

SOUTHWEST EMBLEM COMPANY

CISCO, TEXAS

As the mayor of Cisco from 1981 to 1986, he was instrumental in getting a $1.2 million grant from the Hilton Foundation to rehabilitate Conrad Hilton's first hotel and create a park and community center in Cisco.

Eris wanted to contribute two recipes—for hardboiled eggs and cinnamon toast. When these were rejected, his wife Annita furnished her recipe for a cookie sheet cake: a real Texas Cookie.

TEXAS COOKIE SHEET CAKE

1 stick (¼ lb.) margarine

½ cup shortening

4 Tbspn. cocoa

1 cup water

2 cups flour

2 cups sugar

2 eggs

½ cup buttermilk or sour cream

reheat oven to 350° F. Bring margarine, shortening, cocoa, and water to boil in saucepan. Mix flour and sugar, add remaining ingredients, and blend. Pour heated mixture over blended mixture and mix well. Pour into a greased sheet cake tin with low sides. Bake approximately 20 minutes.

Icing: Make icing while cake is baking. Bring margarine, milk, and cocoa just to a boil. Pour over the sugar, adding

vanilla. Beat with mixer until smooth.
Add nuts or coconut. Put on icing as
soon as cake is removed from oven.

1 tspn. baking soda

1 tspn. vanilla

ICING:

1 stick (¼ lb.) margarine

6 Tbspn. milk

4 Tbspn. cocoa

1 box confectioners sugar

1 tspn. vanilla

1 cup nuts or coconut

om and Diane Dorwart are partners in the To-Di Trucking Company. They are in the business of designing and building parade floats. They are the sole builders of floats for the Chicago Christmas Parade, and have produced floats for many festivals all over the country, including the Fiesta Bowl and the Milwaukee City of Festivals Parade.

Tom is a graduate of the Art Institute of Chicago and trained and worked as a set designer for many years at the Goodman Theater. Diane is responsible for the business operation of the company.

Together, Tom and Diane entertain several hundred friends and customers at two events each year. Their Christmas Open House is a dressy, elaborate affair. Their Corn Fest is held on or about August 24, when the corn from their Wisconsin farm is properly ripened. Held on Chicago's Navy Pier, it is a model of superb organization by two creative people who love good food.

THE TO-DI TRUCKING COMPANY

BUILDERS OF PROFESSIONAL-QUALITY PARADE FLOATS, CHICAGO, ILLINOIS

Diane offers this advice about cooking fresh corn: "Our corn is never roasted. We think that roasting dries it out and ruins the flavor. Each ear is broken in half and dropped in boiling water very briefly. We use a rectangular pan or roaster approximately 5 or 6 inches deep—never a deep kettle! This eliminates overcooking."

Here are some of the Dorwarts' favorite recipes:

BRANDWEIN'S SALMON DIP

8 oz. cream cheese, softened

2 Tbspn. green onion

2 Tbspn. catsup

1 Tbspn. horseradish

1 (7-oz.) can salmon, drained, boned, and flaked

Mix cream cheese, green onion, catsup, and horseradish with salmon. Chill. Serve with breadsticks or spread on crackers.

DIANE'S SCALLOP CASSEROLE

Preheat oven to 375° F.
Mix garlic, green onions, and chives in a bowl; you should have about 4 Tbspn. Sauté 2 Tbspn. of the herb mixture in the 1 Tbspn. butter till onions are clear. Add lemon juice, chicken stock, sherry, water, and mustard and stir thoroughly. Simmer 5 minutes. Add cream and boil down till thickened.

In a separate bowl, thoroughly mix bread crumbs, the remaining 2 Tbspn. of the herb mixture, bacon, and the ½ Tbspn. softened butter.

Place scallops in casserole. Pour sauce over. Top with bread crumb mixture. Bake for 20 minutes, until topping is browned and bubbling.

Serve with tossed salad and chardonnay.

2 medium cloves garlic, minced

2 green onions, minced

2 Tbspn. minced fresh chives

1 Tbspn. butter

1¼ Tbspn. fresh lemon juice

½ cup chicken stock

¼ cup sherry

½ cup water

1 Tbspn. Dijon mustard

½ cup cream

1 cup soft bread crumbs

¼ cup crisply cooked, crumbled bacon

½ Tbspn. butter, softened

20 large scallops

GINGER'S BAR CHEESE

Melt cheese in double boiler. Take off of heat and add other ingredients. Beat with an electric mixer at low speed for 5 minutes. Makes about 1¼ lb. Will keep 10 months in refrigerator.

1 lb. Velveeta cheese

9 Tbspn. mayonnaise

5 dashes Tabasco

2¼ oz. horseradish

TOM'S HONEY-APPLE COOKIES

2 sticks (½ lb.) butter

¼ cup white sugar

1¾ cups brown sugar

1 cup honey

4 eggs

½ cup sour cream

4 cups all-purpose flour

2 tspn. baking soda

1 tspn. salt

2 tspn. 5-Spice (or 1 tspn. cinnamon, ½ tspn. nutmeg, ½ tspn. cloves)

3 cups finely chopped apples

1 tspn. spiced apple flavoring

Preheat oven to 350° F. Cream butter, white sugar, and brown sugar. Beat in honey. Add eggs 1 at a time, beating well after each addition. Stir in sour cream. Mix and sift flour, baking soda, salt, and 5-Spice; stir into wet ingredients and blend well. Stir in apples and spiced apple flavoring. Drop by teaspoonfuls 3 inches apart on greased baking sheets. Bake for about 15 minutes or until edges are brown. Makes about 10 dozen.

JAN MILLER'S TABBOULEH

2 cups bulgur

1½ cups chopped green onions

2 cups fresh parsley, finely chopped

¾ cup peeled, seeded, finely chopped tomatoes

1 cup lemon juice

1 cup olive oil

4 Tbspn. fresh mint leaves (or 2 Tbspn. dried)

3 tspn. salt if desired

Soak 2 cups bulgur (crushed wheat) in water to cover for 2 hours. Drain and squeeze dry. Place in bowl with rest of ingredients. Mix, then let stand. Do not cook; serve either at room temperature or chilled.

ambelli Internationale Fireworks of New Castle, Pennsylvania, is America's leading manufacturer and premier exhibitor of domestic and international fireworks displays.

For decades Zambelli Internationale has stood for excellence in pyrotechnic display. That type of legacy requires an understanding of the art of fireworks manufacturing, that is, a comprehension of the artistry needed to combine vibrant colors, brilliant bursts, and musical choreography with the latest in microchip electronic detonation. Blending the forces together into a pyrotechnic portrait spectacular, Zambelli Internationale sends its flowers of fire and thunderous echoes

ZAMBELLI INTERNATIONALE
MANUFACTURER AND EXHIBITOR OF FIREWORKS,
NEW CASTLE, PENNSYLVANIA

around the world, delighting world leaders and children alike.

Zambelli Internationale's fireworks have been seen at the Statue of Liberty centennial; the inauguration of Ronald Reagan; the christening of the world's largest cruise ship, *Sovereign of the Seas*; the Florida lottery kickoff; the opening and closing ceremonies of the North Carolina Amateur Sports, United States Olympic Festival; and the Congressional Picnic on the White House lawn.

This simple recipe is a family favorite, shared with us by "Mama" Zambelli.

ZAMBELLISTIC GRAND FINALE CAKE

Preheat oven to 350° F. Prepare yellow cake mix according to directions on box and pour into 9-inch-by-13-inch pan and set aside. In separate bowl blend well the ricotta cheese, sugar, eggs, and vanilla extract. Pour these ingredients over the prepared cake batter. Bake for 60–70 minutes. Let cake cool to room temperature and then refrigerate.

Before serving top with whipped topping and fresh strawberries and cut into squares. This will be a grand finale to any dinner!

by Connie J. Zambelli

1 Duncan Hines yellow cake mix

2 lb. ricotta cheese

1 cup sugar

4 eggs

1 tspn. vanilla extract

Whipped topping

Fresh strawberries, for garnish

Appendix A
INTERNATIONAL EVENTS GROUP

If there is a recipe for producing the best festivals and special events, then two essential ingredients are surely information and sponsorships.

The world of special events is fortunate to have these ingredients in plenty due to the perspicacity of two astute young people: a sister and brother team, Lesa and John Ukman. They have been responsible for the growth and prosperity of festivals, civic celebrations, and events by way of their publications and seminars.

International Events Group has been informing the events world for 10 years now, by way of "Special Events Report," a bi-weekly publication which carries the latest in news, sponsorship opportunities, and general information about festivals and the people involved with them.

"The Official Directory of Festivals, Sports, and Special Events," with a third edition coming out in January, 1990, is a must for everyone in the business. With a solid base of advertisers, the Ukmans are able to offer free listing for festivals, sports, and special events, for suppliers and services, and for organizations and causes. This directory is invaluable.

IEG also produces an annual conference on sponsorships which brings together everyone in the business whom you've ever dreamed of meeting. These are the people who want your event to get their product before the public. And don't think they're not interested if yours isn't a mammoth event: there's plenty of interest in small events of quality.

The IEG Guide to Sponsorship Agencies, the Event Marketing Seminar Series, and IEG Consulting are valuable tools, also.

For information:

International Events Group
213 West Institute Place, Suite 303
Chicago, Illinois 60610
312-944-1727

Appendix B
MEMBERSHIP LIST

Those printed in bold are contributors to this book.

500 Festival Associates, Inc.
P.O. Box 817
Indianapolis, IN 46206
317–636–4556

600 Festival Association, Inc.
200 S. Tryon Street, #1400
Charlotte, NC 28202
704–567–9395

Affaires at Tahoe
P.O. Box 8886
Incline Village, NV 89450
702–831–1547

Alaska State Fair, Inc.
2075 Glenn Highway
Palmer, AK 99645
907–745–4827

Albuquerque International Balloon
 Fiesta
8309 Washington Place, N.E.
Albuquerque, NM 87113
505–821–1000

Alfalfafest
P.O. Box 910
Carlsbad, NM 88220
505–887–6516

All-American Festivals
1111 Brickyard Road, #202
Salt Lake City, UT 84106
801–484–7070

Alma Highland Festival
P.O. Box 506
Alma, MI 48801
517–463–5525

Aloha Week Festivals
750 Amana Street, #111-A
Honolulu, HI 96814
808–944–8857

American Decorating Company, Inc.
P.O. Box 67
Azusa, CA 91702
818–969–9716

Anchorage Fur Rendezvous
P.O. Box 100773
Anchorage, AK 99510
907–277–8615

Arbor Day Celebration
P.O. Box 245
Nebraska City, NE 68410
402–873–6654

Argonne Productions
330 Ninth Street, N.E., #10
Atlanta, GA 30309
404–897–7385

Art Deco Weekend Festival
P.O. Box Bin L
Miami Beach, FL 33119
305–672–2014

The Arts Council, Inc.
700 Monroe Street
Huntsville, AL 35801
205–533–6565

Arts Council of Richmond, Inc.
1001 E. Clay Street
Richmond, VA 23219
804–643–4993

Ashville Fourth of July
155 East Street
Ashville, OH 43103
614–860–5986

Atlanta Dogwood Festival
34 Peachtree Street, N.W., #2430
Atlanta, GA 30303
404–525–6145

Atlanta International Wine Festival
148 International Boulevard, #625
Atlanta, GA 30303
404–577–5888

Austin Aqua Festival
811 Barton Spring Road
Austin, TX 78704–1163
512–472–5664

Austin Fireworks, Inc.
4440 Southeast Boulevard
Wichita, KS 67210
316–681–0235

Karin Bacon Events, Inc.
349 West End Avenue
New York, NY 10024
212–724–3687

Ballaaret Begonia Festival Association
P.O. Box 43
Ballaaret, Victoria 3350
Australia
053–311–991

Baltimore Office of Promotion
   and Tourism
34 Market Place, #310
Baltimore, MD 21202
301–752–8632

Bands of America, Inc.
P.O. Box 665
Arlington Heights, IL 60006
312–398–7270

Barnum Festival, Inc.
Bridgeport Hilton
Bridgeport, CT 06604
203–367–8495

Barth Brothers, Inc.
P.O. Box 29404
New Orleans, LA 70189
504–254–1794

Bayfest and Winterfest
University of Wisconsin, Green Bay
Phoenix Sports Center
Green Bay, WI 54301–7001
414–465–2145

Bent Parade Floats
835 S. Raymond Avenue
Pasadena, CA 91105
818–793–3174

Big Creek Enterprises
P.O. Box 1406
LaFollette, TN 37766
615–502–2112

Bigger Than Life
1327 Fayette Street
El Cajon, CA 92020
619–449–9988

Bismarck's Folkfest
P.O. Box 1675
Bismarck, ND 58502
701–223–5660

Black Hills Heritage Festival
P.O. Box 8186
Rapid City, SD 57709
605–343–7489

Blossomtime Festival,
   Southwestern Michigan
151 E. Napier Avenue
Benton Harbor, MI 49022
616–926–7397

Blue Water Festival, Inc.
P.O Box 61628
Port Huron, MI 48060
313–985–9623

Borderfest
P.O. Box 309
Hidalgo, TX 78557
512–843–2734

Bratwurst Festival, Inc.
P.O. Box 175
Bucyrus, OH 44820
419–562–2728

Bravo Productions
P.O. Box 91505
Pasadena, CA 91109–1505
213–436–1895

Buccaneer Days
P.O. Box 30404
Corpus Christi, TX 78404
512–882–3242

Bumbershoot, Seattle Arts Festival
P.O. Box 9750
Seattle, WA 98109
206–622–5123

California Strawberry Festival
Terry Pimsleur and Company
2155 Union Street
San Francisco, CA 94123
415–346–4446

Canadian Association of Festivals
    and Events
Box 398, Station A
Ottawa, Ontario K1N 8V4
Canada
613–239–5018

Canyon Country Frontier Days
27225 Camp Plenty Road, #8
Canyon Country, CA 91351
805–252–4131

Capital City Riverfest, Inc.
529 W. Saginaw
Lansing, MI 48933
517–483–4144

Carnavale d'Viareggio
AASP—Viareggio
55049 Viareggio, Lucca
Italy
584–48881–48882

Carnival Memphis
1060 Early Maxwell Boulevard
Memphis, TN 38104
901–278–0243

Carolinas' Carousel, Inc.
P.O. Box 34644
Charlotte, NC 28234–4644
704–372–9411

Cedar River Days
300 N. Main Street
Austin, MN 55912
507–437–4561

Channel 6 Thanksgiving Day Parade
4100 City Line Avenue
Philadelphia, PA 19131
215–581–4529

Chattanooga Riverbend Festival
P.O. Box 886
Chattanooga, TN 37401
615–756–2212

Cincinnati Downtown Council
120 W. Fifth Street
Cincinnati, OH 45202
513–241–9045

Circleville Pumpkin Show
P.O. Box 127
Circleville, OH 43113
614–474–7000

City of Festivals Parade
8707 N. Port Washington, #104
Milwaukee, WI 53217
414–351–8440

Coconut Grove Arts Festival
Coconut Grove Association
P.O. Box 330757
Coconut Grove, FL 33133–0757
305–447–0401

Colores
1405 132nd Avenue, N.E., #2
Bellevue, WA 98005
206–454–6323

Columbus Area Chamber of Commerce
37 N. High Street
Columbus, OH 43215
614–221–1321

Columbus Day Parade
1728 India Street
San Diego, CA 92110
619–234–2615

Columbus Day Parade Association
P.O. Box 235
Reno, NV 89504
702–323–2011

Concord Fall Fest
see **California Strawberry Festival**

Czech Festival
Diane Uher, President
GFWC Clarkson Woman's Club
Box 414
Clarkson, NE 68629

Custom Pin and Design
P.O. Box 1232
Lake Placid, NY 12946
518–523–2810

Daffodil Festival
P.O. Box 1824
Tacoma, WA 98401
206–627–6176

Dayton Holiday Festival
1250 Kettering Tower
Dayton, OH 45423–1250
513–224–1518

Dayton River Festival
Fifth and Main Chamber Plaza
Dayton, OH 45402
513–226–8252

De Soto Celebration, Inc.
910 Third Avenue, W.
Bradenton, FL 34205
813–755–0338

Decatur Celebration
One Central Park E.
Decatur, IL 62523
217–793–3733

Dentsu Incorporated
1114 Avenue of the Americas
New York, NY 10036
212–869–8318

Detroit Renaissance Foundation
100 Renaissance Center, #1760
Detroit, MI 48243
313–259–5400

DeVore Parade Floats
1117 Hickory Lane
Hagerstown, MD 21740
301–797–8105

Disney World International
Creative Entertainment
Lake Buena Vista, FL 32830
305–345–5750

Disney World/Magic Music Days
P.O. Box 10,000
Orlando, FL 32819
407–345–5751

Dogwood Arts Festival
203 Fort Hill Building
Knoxville, TN 37915
615–637–4561

Downtown Buffalo Festival Committee
671 Main Street
Buffalo, NY 14203–1404
716–856–3150

Dynamic Displays
5450 W. Jefferson
Detroit, MI 48209
519–254–9563

Edison Pageant of Light, Inc.
P.O. Box 1311
Fort Myers, FL 33902
813–334–2550

Edmonton Klondike Days
#1660, 10020–101A Avenue
Edmonton, Alberta T5J 3G2
Canada
403–426–4055

Entertainment Research Group
47 Paul Drive, #10
San Rafael, CA 94903
415–499–4686

The Event Company
2927 S. Floyd Street
Louisville, KY 40213
502–635–1511

Evergreen Hometown Celebration
3221 S. White Road
San Jose, CA 95148
408–778–1680

EXPOdesign
5906 S. Harding
Indianapolis, IN 46217
317–784–5610

Festival of Fish
P.O. Box 418
Vermilion, OH 44089
216–967–4477

Festival of Nations
1694 Como Avenue
St. Paul, MN 55108
612–647–0191

Festival of the Pacific
969 Kanakou Place
Honolulu, HI 96825
808–395–7063

Festival of Trees
1405 Clifton Road
Atlanta, GA 30322
404–881–0137

Festivals/Jackson CVB
1510 N. State Street
Jackson, MS 39202
601–960–1826

The Fiesta Bowl
P.O. Box 9847
Scottsdale, AZ 85252
602–941–2885

Fiesta by the Bay
P.O. Box 344012
Coral Gables, FL 33114
305–856–6653

Fiesta of Five Flags
P.O. Box 1943
Pensacola, FL 32589
904–433–6512

Fiesta San Antonio
Commission, Inc.
1145 E. Commerce, #101
San Antonio, TX 78205
512–227–5191

Floats and Things
1221 Russet Court
Green Bay, WI 54303
414–434–0800

Florida Derby Festival, Inc.
P.O. Box 705
Hallandale, FL 33009
305–454–8544

Florida Strawberry Festival
P.O. Drawer 1869
Plant City, FL 34289
813–752–9194

Folklorama
375 York Avenue/Convention Center
Winnipeg, Manitoba R3C 3J3
Canada
204–944–9793

Fond du Lac Jazz Festival
207 N. Main Street
Fond du Lac, WI 54935
414–923–6555

Foundation of European Carneval Cities
P.O. Box 6615
Amsterdam, 1005EP
Netherlands

Four Seasons Festival
6733 Bridlewood Road
Boca Raton, FL 33433
407–495–0233

Fourth of July Celebration
Seward Fourth of July Community
   Celebration
P.O. Box 1976
Seward, NE 68434
402–643–3749

Fourth of July Funfest
P.O. Box 202
Clemson, SC 29631
803–654–1200

Frankenmuth Bavarian Festival
635 S. Main Street
Frankenmuth, MI 48734
517–652–8155

Freedom Festival
208 Main Street
Evansville, IN 47708–1446
812–464–9576

Freedom Festival, Inc.
119 First Avenue, S.E.
Cedar Rapids, IA 52406–5339
319–396–2616

French Quarter Festival, Inc.
P.O. Box 53362
New Orleans, LA 70153–3362
504–522–5730

German Fest Milwaukee, Inc.
9235 W. Capitol Drive
Milwaukee, WI 53222
414–464–9444

Gillette Parade Products
1425 Boyce Memorial Drive
Ottawa, IL 61350
815–433–5305

Gilroy Garlic Festival
P.O. Box 2311
Gilroy, CA 95021–2311
408–842–1625

Gigi Goff and Company
4175 S.W. Cedar Hills Boulevard
Beaverton, OR 97005
503–646–3191

Goring Associates, Inc.
77 Mowat Avenue, #210
Toronto, Ontario M6K 3E3
Canada
416–536–3509

City of Grand Rapids
201 Market Avenue, S.W.
Grand Rapids, MI 49503
616–243–4996

Great Halloween and Pumpkin
   Festival
see **California Strawberry Festival**

Greater El Paso Civic, Convention, and
   Tourist Center
One Civic Center Plaza
El Paso, TX 79935
915–534–0603

Greater Madison Convention and
   Visitors Bureau
121 W. Doty Street
Madison, WI 53703
608–255–0701

Greater Miami Festival Association
111 N.W. First Street, #625
Miami, FL 33128
305–375–4634

The Jim Halsey Company, Inc.
17351 Sunset Boulevard
Pacific Palisades, CA 90272
213–459–6694

Hamilton-Wentworth Visitors and
   Convention Service
119 King Street W., Fifteenth Floor
Hamilton, Ontario L8N 3V9
Canada
416–526–2614

Hampton Bay Days, Inc.
22 Lincoln Street
Hampton, VA 23669
804–727–6270

Hargrove, Inc.
10101 Martin Luther King, Jr., Highway
Lanham, MD 20706
301–459–1400

Hartford Downtown Council
250 Constitution Plaza
Hartford, CT 06103
203–728–3089

Heritage Corporation of Louisville
710 W. Main Street
Louisville, KY 40202
502–583–1990

Heritage Festival
81 Court Street
Hamilton, HM12
Bermuda
809–292–1681

Heritage Festivals, Inc.
302 W. 5400 S., #108
Salt Lake City, UT 84107
801–263–3445

Heritagefest, Inc.
P.O. Box 461
New Ulm, MN 56073
507–354–8850

Hispanic Heritage Festival
4011 West Flagler Street, #503
Miami, FL 33134
305–541–5023

The Holiday Bowl
9449 Friars Road
San Diego, CA 92108
619–283–5808

Holiday Folk Fair
International Institute of Wisconsin
2810 W. Highland Boulevard
Milwaukee, WI 53208
414–933–0521

Holland Tulip Time Festival
150 W. Eighth Street
Holland, MI 49423
616–396–4221

The Houston International Festival
2 Houston Center, #890
Houston, TX 77010
713–654–8808

Hull International Cycling Festival
25 Laurier Street
Hull, Quebec J8X 3Y9
Canada
819–595–7373

ICEBREAKER
500 W. Kilbourn Avenue
Milwaukee, WI 53203–1499
414–223–0285

Independence Days
P.O. Box 581
Lawrence, KS 66044
913-843-4411

Indianapolis 500 Festival
see **500 Festival Associates, Inc.**

Insta-Plak, Inc.
4115 Monroe Street
Toledo, OH 43606
419–472–5608

International Azalea Festival
P.O. Box 327
Norfolk, VA 23501
804–622–2312

International Events Group
213 W. Institute Place, #303
Chicago, IL 60610
312–944–1727

International Festival, Inc.
P.O. Box 10532
Raleigh, NC 27605–0532
919–782–1573

International Freedom Festival
P.O. Box 391, Station A
Windsor, Ontario N9A 6L7
Canada
519–252–7264

International Theater
Kleiweg 100, 3051 GW
Rotterdam, Netherlands
010–422–5244

Irish Fest
P.O. Box 599
Milwaukee, WI 53201
414–466–6640

Jackson County Apple Festival
P.O. Box 8
Jackson, OH 45640
614–286–1339

Japanese Festival
P.O. Box 299
St. Louis, MO 63166
314–577–5117

Jazz and All That Art on Fillmore
see **California Strawberry Festival**

J.C. Productions and Entertainment
P.O. Box 06178
Portland, OR 97206
503–777–1222

The Jeffersontown Gaslight Festival
9508 Garden Drive
Jeffersontown, KY 40299
502–267–1674

Jolesch Photography
4232 University Avenue
Des Moines, IA 50311
515–274–3255

July Fourth Festival, Inc.
P.O. Box 1484
Edmond, OK 73083–1484
405–348–1935

Jumbleberry Jubilee in Santa Rosa
see **California Strawberry Festival**

Junior Orange Bowl Committee
269 Giralda Avenue, #105
Coral Gables, FL 33134
305–662–1210

Kalamazoo Banner Works
P.O. Box 3597
Kalamazoo, MI 49003–3597
616–388–4532

Kalamazoo County Convention and
    Visitors Bureau
P.O. Box 1169
Kalamazoo, MI 49005
616–381–4003

Kamer Van Koophandel Rotterdam
Postbus 30025
3001 DA Rotterdam,
Netherlands
010–414–5022

K and K Insurance Agency, Inc.
P.O. Box 2337
Fort Wayne, IN 46801
219–427–3000

Kemp Balloons
180 H Penrod Court
Glen Burnie, MD 21061
301–760–0880

Kentucky Derby Festival, Inc.
137 W. Muhammed Ali Boulevard
Louisville, KY 40202
502–584–6383

Blaine Kern Artists, Inc.
233 Newton Street
New Orleans, LA 70114
504–362–8211

Knoxville Watersports Festival
530 E. Gay Street, Suite 222
Knoxville, TN 37902
615–524–1045

La Fête des Neiges
Terre des Hommes
Montreal, Quebec H2L 4L6
Canada
514–872–6093

Lakeside Winter Celebration
Fond du Lac Festivals, Inc.
207 N. Main Street
Fond du Lac, WI 54935
414–923–6555

Latin American Fiesta Association
P.O. Box 4557
Tampa, FL 33677
813–874–3163

Lincolnfest
624 E. Adams
Springfield, IL 62701
217–789–2274

Lincolnfest, Inc.
P.O. Box 81284
Lincoln, NE 68501
402–475–0433

Lompoc Valley Festival Association
P.O. Box 505
Lompoc, CA 93438
805–735–8511

Macon Cherry Blossom Festival
Southern Trust Building, Suite 1110
682 Cherry Street
Macon, GA 31201
912–751–7429

Macy's Thanksgiving Day Parade
151 W. 34th Street, 19th Floor
New York, NY 10001
212–560–4655

M-C Industries, Inc.
P.O. Box 5502
Topeka, KS 66605
913–273–3990

Main Events Production, Inc.
245 Wagner Place, Suite 340
Memphis, TN 38103
901–521–1500

Mayfest, Inc.
1110 Penn Street
Fort Worth, TX 76102
817–332–1055

McAllen International Spring Fiesta
P.O. Box 720264
McAllen, TX 78504
512–682–6221

McDonald's Charity Christmas Parade
1711 W. Fullerton Avenue
Chicago, IL 60614
312–935–8747

The Melbourne Moomba Festival, Ltd.
G.P.O. Box 497 H
Melbourne 3001
Australia
03–654–7111

City of Miami
1145 N.W. Eleventh Street
Miami, FL 33136
305–579–6853

Michigan Thanksgiving Parade
  Foundation
9600 Mt. Elliot
Detroit, MI 48211
313–923–7400

Michigan Wine and Harvest Festival
128 N. Kalamazoo Mall
Kalamazoo, MI 49007
616–381–4003

Mid-America Festivals Corporation
3525 145th Street, W.
Shakopee, MN 55379
612–445–7361

Middfest International Foundation
One City Centre Plaza
Middletown, OH 45042
513–425–7707

The Midway Caravan, Inc.
51 Main Street
Freeville, NY 13068
607–844–8666

Milan Melon Festival
27 Church Street
Milan, OH 44846
419–499–2766

Milestone Publishing, Inc.
120 N. Aspen Avenue
Azusa, CA 91702
818–969–5855

Miller Brewing Company
3939 W. Highland Boulevard
Milwaukee, WI 53201
414–931–3354

**Minneapolis Aquatennial
    Association
702 Wayzata Boulevard
Minneapolis, MN 55403
612–377–4621**

Morrison Printing Company
1135 W. Morris Boulevard
Morristown, TN 37814
615–586–4812

**Musikfest
556 Main Street
Bethlehem, PA 18018
215–861–0678**

My Waterloo Days
P.O. Box 1587
Waterloo, IA 50704
319–233–8431

Nathaniel Rochester Days
44 Exchange Street
Rochester, NY 14692
716–546–4500

National Cherry Festival
P.O. Box 141
Traverse City, MI 49685-0141
616–947–4230

National Clay Week Festival
133 Miller Avenue
Dennison, OH 44621
614–922–1246

National Date Festival
P.O. Drawer NNNN
Indio, CA 92201
619–342–8247

National Events
2910 W. 4700 S., #200
Salt Lake City, UT 84118
801–966–0112

Neches River Festival
745 N. Eleventh Street, #200
Beaumont, TX 77702
409–892–5124

Michael Neipris Productions
P.O. Box 50066
Long Beach, CA 90815–6066
213–498–2218

New Mexico Arts and Crafts Fair
5500 San Mateo N.E., Suite 111
Albuquerque, NM 87109
505–884–9043

New Westminster Hyack Festival
204 Sixth Street
New Westminster, British Columbia
    V3L 3A1
Canada
604–522–6894

Newburyport Waterfront Festival
see **Waterfront Festival**

Newport News Parks and Recreation
2400 Washington Avenue
Newport News, VA 23607
804–247–8451

Norfolk Festevents, Ltd.
120 W. Main Street
Norfolk, VA 23510
804–627–7809

Norsk Hostfest
1205 Glacial Drive
Minot, ND 58701
701–852–2029

North Beach Fair
see **California Strawberry Festival**

North Carolina Fourth of July Festival
P.O. Box 1776
Southport, NC 28461
909–457–5460

Northwest Festivals Association
27 Lodgepole Crescent
St. Albert, Alberta T8N 2R8
Canada
403–458–3900

Northwest Folklife Festival
305 Harrison Street
Seattle, WA 98109
206–684–7300

Northwest Ohio RIB-OFF
151 N. Michigan, #200
Toledo, OH 43624
419–242–9587

Norwalk Seaport Association
92 Washington Street
South Norwalk, CT 06854
203–838–9444

Nova Scotia Department of Tourism
P.O. Box 456
Halifax, Nova Scotia B3J 2R5
Canada
902–424–5000

Office of Special Events
30 Church Street
Rochester, NY 14614
716–428–6690

Ohio Festivals and Events Association
P.O. Box 571
Bainbridge, OH 45612
614–634–2997

Oktoberfest
707 S. Houston, #202
Tulsa, OK 74127
918–582–0051

Oktoberfest, U.S.A.
P.O. Box 1716
La Crosse, WI 54603
608–785–1250

Orange Bowl Football Classic/Festival
P.O. Box 350748
Miami, FL 33135
305–642–1515

City of Ottawa
Department of Recreation and Culture
111 Sussex Drive, Room 600
Ottawa, Ontario K1N 5A1
Canada
613–564–1893

Pacific Coast Fog Festival
see **California Strawberry Festival**

Pacific Coast Judging Association
P.O. Box 20999
Castro Valley, CA 94546
415–886–2937

Paducah's Summer Festival
P.O. Box 1305
Paducah, KY 42001
502–444–8503

Pageantry Productions
11904 Long Beach Boulevard
Lynwood, CA 90262
213–537–4240

Palo Alto Celebrates the Arts Festival
see **California Strawberry Festival**

The Parade Company
9600 Mt. Elliot
Detroit, MI 48211
313–923–7400

Parade Float Builders, Inc.
6450 Shepler Church Road, S.W.
Navarre, OH 44662
216–484–3378

Parade Specialties
2625 Fairway Drive
Independence, KS 67301
316–331–6363

Pasadena Tournament of Roses
  Association
391 S. Orange Grove Boulevard
Pasadena, CA 91184
818–449–4100

Paseo Del Rio Association
213 Broadway, Suite 5
San Antonio, TX 78205
512–227–4267

Pescor Plastics, Inc.
4116 Cockrell
Fort Worth, TX 76133
817–926–5471

Philadelphia Freedom Festival Parade
519 Haws Avenue
Norristown, PA 19111
215–272–6638

City of Phoenix, Office of Special Events
1202 N. Third Street
Phoenix, AZ 85004
602–495–5490

Terry Pimsleur and Company
2155 Union Street
San Francisco, CA 94123
415–346–4446

Pittsburgh Three Rivers Regatta
450 Landmarks Building
Pittsburgh, PA 15219
412–261–7055

Port of Sioux City River-Cade Festival
P.O. Box 1318
Sioux City, IA 51102–1318
712–277–4226

Portland Rose Festival
220 N.W. Second Avenue
Portland, OR 97209
503–227–2681

Poteet Strawberry Festival
  Association
P.O. Box 227
Poteet, TX 78065
512–742–8144

Potomac Riverfest
3149 Sixteenth Street, N.W.
Washington, D.C. 20010
202–387–8292

Pro Football Hall of Fame Festival
229 Wells Avenue, N.W.
Canton, OH 44703
216–456–7253

Pyro Spectaculars
P.O. Box 910
Rialto, CA 92376
714–874–1644

Radio City Music Hall Productions
1260 Avenue of the Americas
New York, NY 10020
212–246–4600

Rainbows 'n' Sandboxes
395 N.W. First Street
Miami, FL 33128
305–347–4600

Red, White, and Boom!
c/o Mid-American Federal
Columbus, OH 43228
614–278–3300

Reliable Decorating and Parade Floats
P.O. Box 4021
Riverside, CA 92514–4021
714–683–7177

Reno International Kite Fetival
1100 Nugget Avenue
Sparks, NV 89431
702–356–3367

Reno-Sparks Convention and
  Visitors Authority
P.O. Box 837
Reno, NV 89504
702–827–7636

Richmond Area Rose Festival
303 S. A Street, #1
Richmond, IN 47375-1332
317–935–7673

Rio Grande Newart Festival
423 Central, N.W.
Albuquerque, NM 87102
505–848–1370

Riofest, Inc.
P.O. Box 1105
Harlingen, TX 78551
512–425–2705

River City Roundup, Inc.
P.O. Box 6253
Omaha, NE 68106
402–554–8855

Riverfest
P:O. Box 3232
Little Rock, AR 72203
501–376–4781

Roanoke's Festival in the Park
P.O. Box 8276
Roanoke, VA 24014
703–342–2640

Rochester Lilac Festival
126 Andrews Street
Rochester, NY 14604
716–546–3070

Rochesterfest
City Hall, Room #207
Rochester, MN 55902
507–285–8769

The Royal Tournament
Horse Guards
Whitehall, London SW1A 2AX
England
930–6009

Russian River Jazz Festival
P.O. Box 763
Guerneville, CA 95404
707–576–0716

Rutgers Camden Summer Music Festival
City Hall, Suite 405
Camden, NJ 08101
609–757–7285

Sacramento Camellia Festival
917 Seventh Street
Sacramento, CA 95814
916–442–7673

Sacramento Water Festival
1030 Fifteenth Street, #100
Sacramento, CA 95814
916–442–8370

City of St. John's Marketing and
    Promotion Division
P.O. Box 908
St. John's, Newfoundland A1C 5M2
Canada
709–576–8455

St. Patrick's Irish Festival
1321 S.E. Third Avenue
Deerfield Beach, FL 33441
305–426–0405

St. Paul Winter Carnival
600 N. Central Life Tower
St. Paul, MN 55101
612–297–6957

St. Petersburg Festival of States
P.O. Box 1731
St. Petersburg, FL 33731
813–898–3654

Salute 2 America
WSB-TV Salute 2 America Parade
1601 W. Peachtree Street, N.E.
Atlanta, GA 30309
404–897–7385

San Anselmo Art and Wine Festival
see **California Strawberry Festival**

San Diego America's Cup Task Force
P.O. Box 126546
San Diego, CA 92112
619–232–2283

Santa Ana Community Events Center
P.O. Box 1988 (M86)
San Diego, CA 92702
714–647–6561

Seattle Seafair
414 Pontius Avenue, N.
Seattle, WA 98109
206–623–7100

Seaway Trail, Inc.
State University of New York at Oswego
Oswego, NY 13126
315–341–2599

Shaw Parades
Route 1, Box 381
Westernport, MD 21562
301–359–0122

Shenandoah Apple Blossom Festival
5 N. Cameron Street
Winchester, VA 22601
703–662–3863

Smith Special Productions
323 Englewood Avenue
New Castle, PA 16105
412–658–1408

Snowfest
P.O. Box 7590
Tahoe City, CA 95730
916–583–7625

South Carolina Peach Festival, Inc.
225 S. Limestone Street
Gaffney, SC 29342
803–489–1353

South Dakota Snow Queen Festival
1400 Eighth Avenue, N.W.
Aberdeen, SD 57401
605–229–4040

Southern International Fireworks
P.O. Box 8340
Atlanta, GA 30306
404–872–0552

Southwest Arts and Crafts Festival
P.O. Box 11416
Albuquerque, NM 87192
505–262–2448

Southwest Emblem Company
P.O. Box 350
Cisco, TX 76437
817–442–2500

The Speaker's Connection
3530 Pine Valley Drive
Sarasota, FL 33579–4335
813–924–3251

Special Events
1019 S. Fifth Street
San Jose, CA 95112
408–294–5800

Special Teams, Inc.
6153 Fairmount Avenue,
  Extension #203
San Diego, CA 92120–3422
619–285–1301

Spiral Festival Association, Inc.
P.O. Box 75007
Cincinnati, OH 45272
606–371–0200

Springtime Tallahassee
P.O. Box 1465
Tallahassee, FL 32302
904–224–5012

Star City Holiday Parade
129 N. Tenth Street, Room 111
Lincoln, NE 68508
402–471–7391

Stockton Asparagus Festival
46 W. Fremont Street
Stockton, CA 95202
209–943–1987

Stoffal Seals Corporation
P.O. Box 825
Nyack, NY 10960
914–353–3800

James E. Strates Shows
P.O. Box 55
Orlando, FL 32802
305–855–4330

Studio 3, Inc.
3610 Toulouse Street
New Orleans, LA 70119
504–482–6933

Summerfest
200 N. Harbor Drive
Milwaukee, WI 53202
414–273–2680

Sun Bowl Association
P.O. Box 95
El Paso, TX 79941
915–533–4416

Sun Fun Festival
P.O. Box 2115
Myrtle Beach, SC 29577
803–626–7444

Suncoast Offshore Grand Prix Festival
P.O. Box 48985
Sarasota, FL 34237
813–955–9009

Super Derby Festival
415 Kings Highway
Shreveport, LA 71104
318–868–8474

Super Holiday Tours, Inc.
5960 Lakehurst Drive
Orlando, FL 32819
305–351–4451

Swedish Festival
Mrs. Donald Rystrom
Box 411
Stromsburg, NE 68666

Tantara
16 N. Marengo Avenue, #611
Pasadena, CA 91101
818–577–9611

Target Promotions
323 Straight Street, S.W.
Grand Rapids, MI 49504
616–458–4537

A Taste of Hartford
Civic Center Plaza
Hartford, CT 06103
203–728–6789

Telx Entertainment
9100 Keystone Crossing, #725
Indianapolis, IN 46240
317–843–0060

Texas Folklife Festival
P.O. Box 1226
San Antonio, TX 78294
512–226–7651

Catherine H. Thompson and Associates
221 W. Eighth Street
Charlotte, NC 28202
704–333–5532

Dorothy C. Thorpe, Inc.
7990 San Fernando Road
Sun Valley, CA 91352
818–768–2982

Thousand Islands International
Collins Landing, Box 400
Alexandria Bay, NY 13607
315–482–2520

Three Rivers Festival
2301 Fairfield Avenue, #107
Fort Wayne, IN 46807
219–745–5556

Dan Tierney Special Events
68 Meadowview Road
Holyoke, MA 01040
413–533–0909

The Times Orange County
Holiday Parade
P.O. Box, 1988–M86
Santa Ana, CA 92702
714–647–6565

The To-Di Trucking Company
120 W. Madison
Chicago, IL 60602
312–880–0960

Toledo Festival: Celebration of the Arts
618 N. Michigan Street
Toledo, OH 43624
419–255–8968

Tucson Festival Society
425 W. Paseo Redondo, #4
Tucson, AZ 85701
602–622–6911

Tulip Time Festival
P.O. Box 721
Belle Plaine, KS 67013–0721
316–488–3831

Tulsa International Mayfest, Inc.
201 W. Fifth, #110
Tulsa, OK 74103
918–582–6435

**Union Street Festival Arts and
Crafts Fair**
see **California Strawberry Festival**

Up With People
3103 N. Campbell Avenue
Tucson, AZ 85719
602–327–7351

Vallejo Waterfront Festival
see **California Strawberry Festival**

Valley Decorating Company
P.O. Box 9470
Fresno, CA 93792
209–275–2500

Valparaiso Popcorn Festival
1 E. Jefferson Street
Valparaiso, IN 46384–0189
219–464–8332

Vaughn's, Inc.
5050 W. 78th Street
Minneapolis, MN 55435
612–835–5050

Walleye Weekend
see **Lakeside Winter Celebration**

Washington State Apple Blossom
Festival
P.O. Box 850
Wenatcheee, WA 98801
509–662–3616

Washington's Birthday Celebration
P.O. Box 816
Laredo, TX 78042–0816
512–722–0589

The Waterfront Center
1536 Forty-fourth Street, N.W.
Washington, D.C. 20007
202–337–0356

Waterfront Festivals, Ltd.
P.O. Box 6159
Newburyport, MA 01950–6159
508–462–1333

WBNS Santa Claus Parade
P.O. Box 1010
Columbus, OH 43216
614–460–3700

City of West Palm Beach
P.O. Box 3366
West Palm Beach, FL 33402
305–659–8024

Wet Light
564 Putnam Avenue
Cambridge, MA 02139
617–876–8882

Wheeling Festival Corporation
1012 Main Street
Wheeling, WV 26003
304–233–2575

Wheels, Wings and Water Festival
P.O. Box 487
St. Cloud, MN 56302
612–251–2940

The Whole Enchilada Fiesta
P.O. Drawer 519
Las Cruces, NM 88004
505–524–1968

Wichita River Festival
347 S. Laura
Wichita, KS 67211
316–267–2817

Winterfest and Boat Parade
426 E. Las Olas Boulevard
Ft. Lauderdale, FL 33301
305–522–3983

Winterlude/Bal de Neige
161 Laurier Avenue, W.
Ottawa, Ontario K1P 6J6
Canada
613–996–1811

World of Pageantry
P.O. Box 2961
Anaheim, CA 92804
714–952–2263

Ye Mystic Krewe of Gasparilla
P.O. Box 1514
Tampa, FL 33601
305–228–7338

Ypsilanti Area Visitors and Convention
  Bureau
125 N. Huron Street
Ypsilanti, MI 48197
313–482–4920

Zambelli Internationale
299 N.W. 52nd Terrace, #118
Boca Raton, FL 33487
407–994–1588

261

Appendix C
INTERNATIONAL FESTIVALS ASSOCIATION MEMBERSHIP INFORMATION

The International Festivals Association (IFA) offers valuable information and resources. Membership in IFA arms organizers and producers with the knowledge, contacts, and expertise to establish, improve, and perpetuate civic and regional celebrations. An organization for all who want to make their events the best their communities can provide, IFA may provide what is needed to make a difference between success and failure in many important elements of planning, programming, and performance.

From the new kid on the block to the old pro, IFA members have a common goal: to expand their level of professionalism by sharing ideas, concepts, philosophies, and experiences. In their annual convention as well as in an increasing number of regional and special event seminars, members share what they have learned.

The IFA staff is there to point members in the right direction for the help they need and to find answers to their questions. (How many times have you wanted to pick up the phone and ask someone how to . . . ?) Members have access to a library of professional management articles. Members may also obtain listings of the professionals who are members, and of the suppliers who provide necessary materials.

For further information contact:

International Festivals Association
505 East Colorado Boulevard
Suite M–1
Pasadena, California 91101
818–796–2636